PRAISE .
A NOVEL B\

(also availabi

"*Cody* is the unusual story of two hig   ..ıors. Novelist Keith Hale tells their story of self-discovery with great imagination, and warmth for the frail emotional condition of two distraught, but stable and intelligent, people. This, Hale's first novel, is not the growing-up-gay kind of novel one expects to find, when so much of what is available these days is written at a fifth-grade mentality with 21-year-old smut standards. *Cody* is literate, often warm, delightfully sassy in several early chapters, and may leave you wishing you could put your arms around the characters and assure them that everything will work out. It is first rate and highly memorable."
—*Torch* (Fort Wayne, Indiana)

"What makes *Cody* different from a novel such as the brilliant, but abrasive *Less Than Zero* is that the former has characters which make a reader want to keep on turning pages. Keith Hale has given *Cody* characters you would like to know rather than avoid. He's given them tenderness, wit, and humanity ... [You] should rush to purchase this book — a remarkable novel which deserves wide readership." —*Bay Area Reporter* (San Francisco)

"*Cody* packs a powerful punch in its realistic portrayal of adolescent sexuality; it will leave you shaken in its honest examination of the evolution and death of friendship. Keith Hale is a relatively young writer, but the story he tells so deftly is one for all ages. Don't miss *Cody*." —*TLN* (Eugene, Oregon)

"A haunting vision of young friendship shattered by an outrageously cruel world. Keith Hale's novel aches with adolescent first loves. It is tender, funny, and true." —William S. Burroughs

"*Cody* is a unique piece of writing, the first novel of an intensely mental young writer. You might as well read the book now so that when the mature Hale is lecturing in Wisconsin on his contribution away from a separate gay literature, you can say 'I read *Cody* before you were a rich and famous author.'" —*OUT* (Madison)

"Hale's willingness to grapple with the large question of what it is to be young, gay, and loving is the promise of this book, which has quickly established itself as one of the best-selling books of the summer in the country's gay bookstores." —*Arkansas Times* (Little Rock)

"With this refreshing presentation Keith Hale has emerged to stand along with the current 'new wave' of gay writers. Top of the heap of gay fiction." —*Gay Community News* (Boston)

IN THE LAND OF ALEXANDER

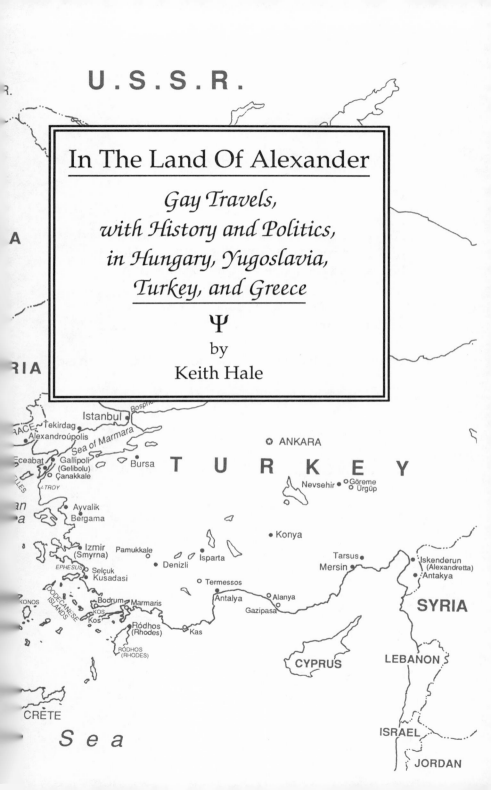

In The Land Of Alexander

*Gay Travels,
with History and Politics,
in Hungary, Yugoslavia,
Turkey, and Greece*

Ψ

by
Keith Hale

Published as a trade paperback original by
Alyson Publications, Inc., 40 Plympton St., Boston, MA 02118.
Distributed in the U.K. by
GMP Publishers, P.O. Box 247, London, N17 9QR, England.

This book has been printed on acid-free paper.

First edition, first printing: May 1990.

Library of Congress card catalog number 90-36681

ISBN 1-55583-168-0

Contents

Acknowledgments

For information and contacts, I would like to acknowledge my indebtedness to Kurt Krickler and HOSI-Wien (Eastern Europe Information Pool, Vienna), Peter Cummings (London), Jan Lány (Prague), Peter Glencross (Amsterdam), Sasha Alyson, Mark Thompson, and the International Lesbian and Gay Association.

For hospitality and other matters, I wish to thank Wout Grote, Anderson Simmons, Jasper van 't Wout, and my brother, Steve.

Thanks as well to everyone who sent a letter after reading *Cody*.

—Keith Hale

For Andy Simmons

1

Budapest

If I begin this book by saying that of the many places I visited during my fourth summer in Europe, many were difficult to leave, I do not mean that it was hard to drag myself away. Nor were communist or military officers holding me in custody. The explanation is the most unpoetic of the lot: The transportation systems of Hungary, Yugoslavia, Greece, and Turkey are not the best in Europe. Austria is generally better, but on June 20, I spent all morning trying to get out of Vienna.

I first tried to hitch my way to Budapest, but couldn't find an acceptable place to do it. I walked to the autobahn, but there were no places for cars to pull over. I took a bus out of town, but the entrance ramps in the outskirts proved no better. I took a bus back into town, bought an all-day transit pass, and went all over Vienna trying to find the correct train station from which to leave. Throughout this mess, it was raining, but I at least got to see the old Jewish cemetery and several parts of Vienna where I'm certain tourists seldom if ever go.

I had been in Europe exactly two weeks at this point, visiting friends in Holland and my brother in Germany, then spending a few days in Vienna picking up the necessary papers to journey farther east. In Vienna I had stayed at the extremely peculiar Hotel Urania at Obere Weissgerberstrasse 7. As I was walking through the lobby to go out the first evening, the desk clerk yelled after me, "If you bring a boy back to your room tonight, it is best to leave your valuables here at the desk." I'm not sure with whom I would have entrusted my valuables least, but in any case, I did not bring a boy back to my room.

I had left America in the middle of the Chinese crackdown on students at Tiananmen Square. Thankfully, Amsterdam television carried Atlanta's Cable News Network, so I had been able to follow the events in China on a same-day basis, as opposed to reading about them a day or two later in the *International Herald-Tribune* or *USA Today*. After finally arriving at the correct Vienna train station and purchasing my ticket to Budapest, I passed the time until departure by sitting in a Chinese restaurant in the company of some severely depressed Chinese.

Ψ

The Orient Express pulls into Vienna at 3:17 p.m. and sits on track eleven for a while before moving to track ten, from which it leaves at 4:22. I arrived early and claimed a window seat while it was still sitting on eleven. Even so, the train bamboozled me by changing directions once it pulled from the station, thus forcing me to watch Austria retreating into the distance, rather than coming at me, as I prefer. The train schedule they give you at the IBUSZ (Hungarian travel bureau) office in Vienna, incidentally, doesn't list the Orient Express at all. It lists only two trains, both leaving at what in Hungary would be typically inconvenient times — 7:45 a.m. and 4:04 p.m. (the latter a slow train arriving in the middle of the night).

I was joined in my compartment by a shy, nice-looking Hungarian kid who was only going as far as Hegyeshalom, the first town across the border. At the last minute, a third person joined us: Martin, a Vietnam veteran and television journalist from Orlando, Florida. Martin had not intended to go to Hungary at all, but because his Eurail Pass was good there, he decided he might as well, if only for a day — which was all his schedule would allow. There were a few other Americans traveling by Eurail Pass on the train, and I'm sure Budapest will be seeing a good many more Yankees in the coming years. But in the last summer of communist Hungary, they still were rare enough. Most tourists in Budapest were from other East European countries or from Scandinavia.

At the border, it took five Hungarian officials to do what a single official often accomplishes in other countries — check visas. This, I would soon discover, was characteristic of Hungary. I might chalk it up to communist inefficiency, which certainly exists in every communist country I've visited, but for the fact that later, in Greece, it would take three bank officials to exchange my traveler's checks.

Despite the five visa-checkers, there was no fuss. Baggage was not examined.

Just as I had six years earlier, when I traveled by train from Austria to Yugoslavia, I immediately noticed a drop in the standard of living when crossing from West to East. It stuns you, even though it is not nearly as dramatic as crossing from the United States into Mexico. Still, it was obvious that Hungary was much poorer than Austria. Around many buildings were piles of rubble for which I could not account — nothing seemed to be going up or coming down. The buildings themselves looked drab. It was not what I expected of the Hungarians.

Hungary is now about the size of Indiana. It was once much larger, which is why six hundred thousand Hungarians now live in Czechoslovakia, another six hundred thousand in Yugoslavia, and nearly two million in Romania — most in the chunk of Transylvania that once belonged to Hungary. The Hungarians account for nine percent of Romania's population, and have been the source of much conflict — but more on that later.

Victorian-style buildings line the streets of Pest, which faces the old Magyar capital of Buda across the Danube.

Hungary was a country that was lately in the news. The day after May Day, Hungarian workers had begun dismantling the section of the "Iron Curtain" — in this case an electrified double barbed-wire fence standing eight feet high and covering 160 miles — that separated Hungary from Austria. They had begun this where we sat, at Hegyeshalom, whose mayor had said residents were "pleased to see the fence going because its removal restores the unity of the landscape." After our compartment-mate had departed, and while we waited for our train to move again, Martin and I contemplated the unity of the landscape. Within three months, over forty thousand East Germans would be crossing this frontier on their way to relative freedom (before they were allowed to travel freely to the West from East Germany). Probably a full dozen of them paused to consider the unity of the landscape.

Soon after crossing the border, I got my second look at Czecho-slovakia, across the Danube. What I saw this time was heavy industry helping to make Czechoslovakia Europe's most polluted nation. What I had seen the first time, a week earlier when my brother and I climbed Mount Rachel in the German *Bayerischer Wald* National Park, was miles and miles of the Bohemian Forest. Although I had decided against going to Czechoslovakia (because getting the visa was too much of a hassle, the mandatory minimum daily currency exchange didn't fit my budget, and I had been told by a gay Austrian that the gay scene in Prague was a form of prostitution — men going to bed with foreigners in exchange for a few drinks and dinner at a nice restaurant), I can report that Czechs are friendly from a distance.

As our train pulled into Budapest, I was full of anticipation. My first impression from the train was that the city was very big and rather drab. Budapest, of course, straddles the Danube, with the old Magyar capital of Buda on the west side and the more recently constructed Pest on the east. The city sprawls over three hills, with magnificent castles and monuments sitting on the hilltops of Buda, and Victorian-style buildings lining the streets of Pest.

I had heard that the city experienced a severe shortage of hotel rooms during summer months, but I had heard that about a lot of places and had still made out all right. What I should have realized was that because conditions in Eastern Europe are always severe, for me to have actually seen the adjective applied could only mean *there were no hotel rooms to be had in Budapest*. Martin and I jumped from the train the minute the doors unlocked and trotted across the station to the IBUSZ office, where we became the first in line at the "accommodations" window. And a very good thing it was. It took half an hour for the clerk to complete the paperwork assigning us to a room in a private apartment not in Budapest, but thirty minutes from the city by Metro and bus. She also informed me that after Martin vacated his bed the next day, I would still be required to pay for it. Martin suggested that with such a room shortage, I could almost certainly find someone needing a bed, so subletting shouldn't be a problem. We left, feeling sorry for those standing at the end of the IBUSZ line. If they were able to get a room at all, it would probably be about the same time the next day at the rate the line was moving.

Trying to actually find our "B" (as in "bed," no breakfast) by bus was more than we wanted to tackle at this time of night, so we did what negotiating we could with one of the all-purpose hustlers who frequent the Budapest train stations — and, indeed, frequent all of Budapest. If my Austrian acquaintance liked Budapest, as he claimed, but felt Prague was a city of prostitutes, then I certainly don't want to visit Prague, for during the entirety of my stay in Budapest, a song you've probably never heard of — "We're All Prostitutes" by an English punk-era band called the Pop Group — kept racing through my head: "We're all prostitutes / Everybody has their price/And you too can learn to live the lie."

While negotiating for the taxi, we were approached by several shabbily dressed women offering rooms. Out of curiosity, I asked the price, and was quoted the same rate we were paying through IBUSZ — the equivalent in Hungarian forints of nine dollars a night. I suspect the rooms on the black market were closer to the center of town — although one never knows until one gets there — but I suspect, if the women took no better care of the rooms than they did of their own bodies, that they were also dirtier. In any case, going through IBUSZ took care of all the legal hassles (we were automatically registered with the police — a requirement).

We got a taxi for about four and a half dollars each, which, we would later discover, was about twice the going rate. We had to pay before the journey instead of at its conclusion, and we paid the hustler, who then took his commission and gave the driver the rest. He also short-changed us, proclaiming in English, "Business is business."

Damned capitalists.

The driver had problems finding the address, and once we arrived we couldn't see how we'd ever find it again ourselves if we ever wandered off. The apartment was one of many like apartments in one of many like buildings. We were staying at a dwelling known as the Borhidan Sandorne, at Voroskereszt u. 14. If you're ever assigned to this address in Budapest, don't go. In the parking lot was the strangest assortment of little cars I had ever seen. I suppose every country of the Eastern Bloc was represented. There were FSO 1500's, Polonezes, sad little two-cylinder Syrenas (they look like "The Little Cars That Couldn't"), and Baby Fiats from Poland; sturdy Skodas, Lada Vazes, and stupid-looking guppy-like Tatras from Czechoslovakia; three-cylinder Wartburgs, a few old IFA convertibles, and the pitiful cardboard Trabants (the older ones look like the old West German Goggomobiles, so it's no surprise they won the West Germans' hearts when they began showing up on their side of the border a few months later) from the German Democratic Republic; docile Dacias from Romania; and Volgas, Zarogets, Moskvitches (remember Ramblers?), and old Pobiedas from the Soviet Union.

As we had feared, our hosts spoke no English. Our hosts were a large man whom we saw exactly once (wearing a very dirty undershirt and with open sores on his face and chest), an unsmiling boy of perhaps eight years, and an even more sullen woman who reminded me very much of Steven Kelman's East German hostess in his book *Behind the Berlin Wall*, and whom the fates had chosen to be named (inappropriate to the point of hysteria) Rosi. I checked the bookshelf in our room for Stalinist literature. Steven had found some in his room, as I recall.

Rosi showed us how to operate the toilet and bath, but, alas, explained (through a mixture of sign language and vaguely comprehensible Hungarian monosyllables that she seemed to think anyone should understand) that there would be no hot water until Friday, three days hence! We made use of the toilet and washed up a bit — Martin called it having a "bird bath" — but skipped the cold bath for the moment.

Figuring out how to flush the toilets of Europe can be very challenging. Some have handles, some have buttons, some have ropes, and some have floor peddles. The ropes are generally hanging from the ceiling, but the buttons and handles can appear just about anywhere, from the top of the toilet to the wall behind it. Some you pull, some you push, some you turn. Nevertheless, I am proud to say that I left no toilet in Europe unflushed, although the chain in my friend Wout's student apartment in Delft, the Netherlands, threw me at first. The trick was to pull it *very quickly*. And whistle "Dixie," it sometimes seemed.

Martin was hungry; I wanted a beer. After obtaining a set of keys from Rosi, we carefully made our way downstairs (the elevator door was inscribed with graffiti reading, "I love U2"), outside through the maze of buildings, and to a bus stop, making mental notes of any conceivable landmark along the way that might help us find our way back.

At the bus stop we decided it was crazy to go into Budapest at 11 p.m., when we were both quite tired already. There were lights about ten blocks down the street, so we walked toward them, passing along the way an intersection underground (an area beneath the roadways containing not only walkways but a number of shops) that was built around Roman ruins excavated during the digging for the underground.

One of the lights down Korvin Otto street did, indeed, belong to a neighborhood pub, as we had hoped. Unfortunately, they didn't serve food. I went ahead and ordered what turned out to be a decent Hungarian beer, and Martin ordered something nonalcoholic — a seltzer, I believe — very odd for a journalist.

A young man walked up and asked in Hungarian where I was from. Somehow I understood what he asked. As soon as I said "America" he put his face to mine and gave me a warm hug. He didn't let go of me until the proprietress chased him off, mistakenly thinking he was annoying me. Unfortunately, a much larger and much, much more intoxicated man with terrible breath also couldn't get enough of us, and the proprietress wasn't nearly so successful in getting him away. He bought us some stiff schnapps and insisted we drink. I did; Martin poured his out when no one was looking. The beer had been pleasant, but the schnapps only made me drunk. I couldn't believe that one little glass could be so potent. The man was wanting us to have another, but I let the bartender know I didn't want him to pour it. The drunk man's feelings were hurt. Another young man at a nearby table intervened on our behalf, as did two older men across the room. Eventually, eight or ten drunk Hungarians were arguing loudly around us — in Hungarian, of course — while we watched with amazement. I was laughing. In the middle of this scene, Martin leaned across the table and asked me in a loud voice, "Who's crazier here, us or them?" This question sent us both into hysterics. We couldn't stop laughing. We were in some workers' pub in the distant suburbs of Budapest, surrounded by some of the most besotted people I've ever seen in my life, and we were nuts for being there. Martin's question would follow me around through much of the summer.

We left to find food, discovering to our delight that there was something next door called the Boszorkandtanda Restaurant. We hadn't noticed it before because it was downstairs, below street level. It's not uncommon in any European country to find some of the best restaurants stuck away in alleys, or hidden upstairs or downstairs beyond dark, narrow stairways, but this one was hidden especially well. According to the hours posted on the door, it also closed in thirty minutes, so, once inside, we asked the woman who greeted us if we might eat. She said we could. In a few minutes she came to our table carrying identical plates of food. We had never ordered. Perhaps we could eat as long as we ate what she brought. Maybe it was all they had. Fortunately, it was quite good: stuffed pepper, meatball, and potatoes in a sweet, tomato-based sauce. Together with another beer, the meal cost less than three dollars. If nothing else, Hungary is cheap.

Our hostess asked where we were staying, then gave us a card for her private accommodations with attached nightclub. Everyone in Hungary seems to have something going on the side.

We walked back to our lodging and did, in fact, get quite lost trying to find it. Eventually we ended up at yet another pub tucked inside one of the identical high-rises, where we showed a man the card Rosi had given us. He pointed us in the right direction. Two or three times, in fact. I got the feeling it was not every day that he felt so useful.

Outside the door to our building, we ran into some Swedish girls who told us matter-of-factly that they were leaving Budapest the next day because there was nothing to do there but eat and drink (the Swedes are wonderful, but they can be so unimaginative). They asked how long we were staying. I answered, "Four days." They said that was too long. Martin said he was leaving tomorrow, and they said that was about right. Upstairs, we had no luck whatsoever in mastering the multiple locks on Rosi's door. There were three of them. I thought I unlocked all three, but the door would not open. I then went back and tried each again, but the door remained locked. With three locks, there were eight possible combinations of lock and unlock that I could be dealing with, and it might take an hour to get the damn door open. Rosi eventually let us in, not overjoyed to see us.

Ψ

Martin and I made our way to city center the following day without difficulty, each bought a twenty-four-hour pass good on all city transit, and set out for the Citadella across the Danube on Gellért Hill. A stupid bus setup combined with an unhelpful driver delayed us a bit. The trouble was that the only stop on top of Gellért Hill isn't quite at the top. You assume there will be another stop at the summit, but there is not. Nor is there a stop as the bus descends the hill. Thus, because we didn't get off at the one stop, we ended up back at the hill's base, and had to wait half an hour for the same bus to complete its round and return. We didn't feel like climbing the hill, mainly because Martin had his pack with him, planning as he was to leave town in five hours.

Liberation Monument on top of the hill has some very nice "social realism" statues honoring the Soviet "liberators." I don't know exactly how the Hungarians feel about them, but it will be a shame if the statues' beauty is not sufficient to overcome their symbolism, forcing their removal, for they're quite impressive. The Citadella Museum, however, isn't worth even the measly fifteen-cent admission charge. Inside this "museum," which is really just the inside of the old fortress, there is a hotel and youth hostel known as Hotel Citadella. IBUSZ had told us it was full, but the view from the top of the hill was so spectacular that I checked inside anyway. Yes, it was full. Of young Turks.

After we'd scanned the panoramic view of the Budapest skyline from all sides of the hill, we returned to Pest, across the river. We strolled along the Vaci — a pedestrian-only shopping street that contains an innocent statue of a young boy urinating. For Eastern Europe, Budapest has a wide variety of things to buy. The only item I bought this outing, however, was the English-language *Daily News*. The English section is small and tucked inside the German section, so many English-speaking tourists never realize it exists. But it does, and it's worth the twenty-four cents they ask for it. The *Daily News* had less propaganda than one might have expected — certainly less than its equivalent in Turkey. There were a number of Romanian newspapers available at the newsstand, which surprised me, considering the deteriorating relationship between the two countries. Every one of them had then Romanian president Nicolae Ceausescu's name and photograph emblazoned across the front page, which didn't surprise me a bit.

Before Martin left me to go across town and catch his train, he offered to give me a sweat shirt, since it was a bit cold in Budapest, especially at night, and he knew I had only short-sleeved garments with me. I thanked him but declined.

Then, I found myself alone in the capital of Hungary. My first move was the same as it is in many large cities: I determined how to get to the main art gallery. In this case, it was the Museum of

Fine Arts, which was good, but not great. The collection of old propaganda posters at the smaller Mücsarnok Palace of Exhibitions and Branch Galleries across the square was more memorable. The woman on duty was very friendly and allowed me to take photographs. The Mücsarnok also had an exhibit called "Seven Young Soviet Painters" that was worth seeing for the artists' boldness, if not especially for their artistry. The literature accompanying the exhibit explained that the artists were not accustomed to being given a public forum, and that, in fact, such a forum within the Soviet Union was still unlikely. The artists had been invited by the Mücsarnok as a group, because of their similar styles, to come as guests of the museum and "complete half-finished works outside the Soviet Union or produce the works completely in Budapest." I enjoyed the sentence in the free brochure describing their work as originating from the "galloping intellectualism of the art of the seventies." Even more enjoyable was the quotation from the exhibition curator, Marina Safit: "In my opinion, with the results of the events of the 1960s and 1970s universal art, new colossal regions of human existence and consciousness melted into the aesthetic sphere. These regions are like an unfolding, astonishing virgin America, where even Indians do not live."

Having satisfied my craving for arts that are like a virgin America where even Indians do not live, I next began my search for a Hungarian gay bar. I had the ripped-out pages from *Spartacus*, an international gay guide for men, as well as information from my friend in Vienna that the main meeting place for gays in Budapest had remained the same for the last twenty years — a bar and coffee house called Egyetem (the stress is always on the first syllable of Hungarian words, by the way).

I must be careful what I say regarding *Spartacus* for the simple reason that I once worked for them when they were based in Baarn, the Netherlands, and I'm not too crazy about them. I think it is fair to say that their listings for Germany are good, but for most of the world they are hopelessly out of date. However, in a place like Eastern Europe, where bars such as Egyetem survive far longer than most of their Western counterparts, and where meeting places for gays do not often change, *Spartacus* can be fairly reliable. In any case, it is currently the only thing available.

I was actually looking for one of the other bars listed in *Spartacus* when I accidentally stumbled upon the Egyetem. I had not been looking for it because the guy in Vienna had told me it wasn't a gay hangout during the day. He was correct, but I stopped in anyway for a place to sit and do some catching up in my journal.

The first thing I noted in my journal while sitting at Egyetem was that U2 was apparently a very popular band in Hungary. Besides the message on the glass door of my lift, I'd seen the band members' photos on posters advertising a "U2 Club," and I'd watched people watching a U2 video on the screens at the Metro platforms.

After leaving the Egyetem, I located two bars listed in *Spartacus*: the Gösser bar near the Egyetem and the Olympia club across the river in Buda. The Gösser absolutely was not a gay bar. The attractive bartender at the Olympia told me that after 8:30 p.m., when he went off duty, the place became a disco.

I decided to go back to Pest and try the Egyetem later in the evening, but before doing so, I discovered a quaint place to eat underground near Buda Castle. This time I was given a menu, but it was in Hungarian (or German, perhaps — I often can't tell the difference) only. I ordered the *Geschmorte Hirschkeule mit Gemuse und Heidelbeere* because it was the only listing with both a *mit* and an *und*, so I assumed it would consist of at least three items, and chances were pretty good I would like at least two of them. It turned out to consist of a tasty but unidentifiable meat, plus beets, rice, carrots with a bit of corn and peas, and, of all things, potato tots, with wild cherry sauce — or something like it — and bread. It was pretty good, but the bottled mineral water I ordered with it had a disagreeable flavor and sulphurous odor.

After eating, I checked back on all three bars to see what the crowds were like. All looked uninviting, so I went to the Danube promenade and sat on a bench. Within minutes, two attractive young men had sat down beside me. After a while, one got up to leave, but the other made a motion with his head in my direction and persuaded him to sit down again. To break the ice, I asked if they spoke English. So begins the story of my adventures in Budapest with blond Attila and, especially, dark-haired Adam — *another dark Adam dreaming,* another dreamy dark Adam, I kept thinking when I looked at him.

Both boys looked about eighteen (but claimed to be twenty-one), were well dressed, and were not overtly gay. Attila was about six feet tall; Adam was about five-foot-nine and had a small scab across his nose. They asked if I had been to Egyetem. I couldn't understand them until Attila leaned toward me and said, "Homosexual?" under his breath, carefully forming the word into a question. I said I had been there, but it didn't look very homosexual.

"At night," said Attila.

I asked about the Gösser and Olympia. They told me the Gösser was definitely not gay, but Olympia was "almost gay," and that the main gay bar in Budapest besides Egyetem was called the Local, located in another part of town. I don't think this is the same bar as the final bar mentioned in *Spartacus,* the Szarakhaz, near Deli Pu station. Attila said he had never heard of the Szarakhaz. Both Attila and Adam confirmed what I'd been told by several others, that the main social gathering places for gays in Budapest were private parties — which makes it damn difficult for foreigners to meet them. One suggestion is to telephone the gay organization founded in May 1988 — HOMEROS, phone 66-0043 — and see if they will provide you with information regarding social events. The group sponsors a video club every Friday at Cinema V-95, next to the Hotel Royal on Lenin Korut. There is also an AIDS organization that might be of help — the Magyar AIDS Alapitvány, phone 22-2804.

Attila told me that he and Adam used to be lovers, but now they were only friends. Their relationship began when they were fifteen. I asked how it was to be gay in Budapest. Attila shrugged at first, then said you have to be careful. He pointed to Adam and said the scab on his nose came from a scuffle with three soldiers, part of the soon-to-be-dissolved Hungarian militia. I asked if people in Hungary accepted gays. Attila said no.

After a while they asked me to go with them to a place called Muscali. It was on one of the main streets, but was a bohemian haunt with many gays, punks, and assorted weird youth. Here it was determined by Adam that he would be spending the next few days with me. I had watched a subtle process in which the two boys tried to size up which of them interested me most. Despite the fact that Attila spoke much better English and I did most of my talking with him, they judged correctly that I was more attracted to Adam. That established, Adam went fast to work. From Attila: "He wants to know if you want company for the following days." Then, more to the point, from Adam: "We go to Egyetem, then you, me, two, go private home [he meant my lodging] and perverted sex."

Hell of a way to put it, Adam.

If an American had said that to me, I'd have probably run away. But I understood there was a language difficulty here, and I did like the omission of the verb at the end of his sentence; it was a lot less threatening without an action word. Still, it didn't sound like a sane idea, although I had come overseas partially to have such unusual adventures. But there was in my room the extra bed that Martin and I had talked about subletting — and Adam was pretty damn cute — so I agreed.

"If the woman asks," I said, "tell her you're my guide."

"No problem," Adam answered. "It is okay."

Attila thought Adam's clothes might be a problem, although I saw nothing unusual about them. Adam was wearing a nice silk coat, but it was dark in color and didn't seem that extraordinary. He shrugged off Attila's concern.

I picked up the tab at both the Muscali and the Egyetem, as I knew they expected me to, since I was the wealthy American. They had no money, I did, and the tab for all three of us was about four dollars. Still, I guessed correctly that there was a form of prostitution involved here exactly like the guy in Vienna had told me existed in Prague, and I didn't especially like it. At the Egyetem, Adam had leaned into my face and said, staring in my eyes, "Sex, no money. You homosexual. Adam homosexual. Adam want sex with you. No money."

So I asked him. "Usually, is it for money?"

He didn't understand. I put the question to Attila.

"Yes," he said. "I think usually it is for money."

Adam and I left Attila at Egyetem, which was, in fact, quite gay at night, and went home by Metro and bus. We tried to eat at the place where I'd eaten the night before, but for some reason it was "private" this evening. It was difficult conversing without Attila, but we managed to understand each other up to a significant point.

Ψ

Thursday, June 22. One day till hot water. Slept until about ten a.m., the latest in a while. Washed in cold water again. Adam followed. We left the house without the other occupants seeing us, took the bus to the Metro, then the Metro to the center of town. We stayed underground while I drank a cup of coffee and Adam had a beer. A couple was arguing loudly in front of us.

"Gypsies," Adam said scornfully.

My only previous experience with Gypsies was in 1983 in Zadar, Yugoslavia, when as a younger and less assertive tourist, I had been browbeaten into buying a wooden donkey by a Gypsy who had grabbed hold of my arm and wasn't going to release me until I agreed to the purchase. There are about 480,000 Gypsies in Hungary, about 729 of whom are musicians in Budapest's restaurant orchestras. Originally from somewhere in India, the Gypsies have been a thorn in the side of communist governments across Eastern Europe. Their extreme independence makes it virtually impossible to make them conform, and conformity above all has reigned in the East. Despite my bad experiences with them, I admire their independence. I'm also reminded that they died along with the gays, the Jews, and the Communists in the gas chambers of Hitler's Germany.

Next, there was a long delay because Adam ran across a friend who tried to persuade me to change money. An English-speaking doctor intervened to translate, only to decide he wanted to exchange money with me as well. They were offering seventy forints to the dollar, whereas the official rate was sixty-one. I wasn't interested; Hungary was cheap enough already.

While Adam talked to his friend, I looked at all the boys standing around the Metro. It was obvious that many of them were waiting for passing strangers, just as Adam and Attila had been waiting along the Danube promenade (there had been other boys there, too). Apparently the promenade and the Metro stations (especially Nyugati station) are the primary areas for this activity. Perhaps some of the boys only wanted to exchange money. Their looks, as they caught your eye, often suggested more.

Hungarians are crazy about Western things — videos, cars, clothes (they have been making their own Levi denim jeans since an agreement with that company in 1978, but the Hungarians are still willing to pay twice as much for imported ones, the only difference being the label), music — and, apparently, sexual partners. But despite all the boys around looking for willing Western men, Hungary appeared to be an excessively heterosexual country, just as the countries due west of it — Austria and Switzerland — have long had a reputation of being among the most priggish in Western Europe. Heterosexual couples are very affectionate in public in Budapest — especially the younger ones — but gays, while visible, don't make a show. Nor do you see gay magazines in newsstands. It isn't Amsterdam, Stockholm, or Athens, that much is certain.

Finally, I tore Adam away from the Metro and took his photograph with the red star atop parliament in the background. I had no idea at the time that the star would not survive the year.

Adam agreed to lead me to the American embassy, where I wanted to check for mail or messages. Adam was suspicious. I don't think he liked anything having to do with government, whether his or someone else's, and thought perhaps I planned to turn him in for something (I can just see myself going into the American embassy and proclaiming, "This young man had sex with me last night. Arrest him!"). The embassy staff searched me with a metal detector, then told me I had no mail.

Adam had a full day planned for us, from castles to opera. In music, he liked Iron Maiden and *Don Carlo*, which happened to be at the Budapest State Opera that evening. His love of opera came as no surprise to me, as the Hungarians are known for it. There are more opera houses in Budapest than in New York City.

Before we began this busy day, however, we had to eat. Adam was hungry. We went to the Havana Bar, a fancy, expensive place by Hungarian standards. I sat horrified as Adam ordered a four-course meal consisting of the menu's most expensive items. It wasn't going to cost that much, by American standards, but it was more than my budget allowed. Our meal began with bowls of almonds. The waiter wouldn't leave us alone, refilling water and beer — but the meal itself was awful. At least mine was. Adam seemed to like his.

I told Adam I needed to go back to my room for more traveler's checks and I'd meet him later. He wanted to come with me. On the way, he got into a heated argument with a woman on the bus because his coat accidentally brushed across her face. She was sitting and we were standing in a crowd; thus, I thought it a bit ungracious of her to complain. I expect it did have something to do with the fact that his coat was silk. Perhaps it signified that he was something other than an ordinary worker. Whether it signified to her that he was gay, or a boy of the streets, I can't say, but it was obvious something about him bothered her a great deal. Adam was overly defensive and wouldn't let it drop. Several other passengers joined in the argument, siding with the woman.

Hungarians seemingly like to argue, just like the Greeks and Italians. I don't. Nor do I like listening to others argue. I wanted off that bus.

Ten minutes later, I wanted back on that bus.

Rosi and Adam had some exchange, which I, of course, could not understand. All I could observe was that Adam was smiling and trying, successfully I thought, to be charming, while Rosi was being herself. She began speaking to me and signaling with her hands that she wanted me to give her something.

"She wants the key," Adam said.

I refused to give it to her. From the shelf she picked up a book that Martin and I had picked up ourselves the night when I was looking for Stalinist literature. It was an IBUSZ rule book. She turned to a section in English that said guests were not allowed in the room unless prior permission was given from the host family. I turned to the section that said hosts must provide lodgers with one hot bath per day. She couldn't read the English, so I tried to find the appropriate listing in Hungarian. Meanwhile, she dialed someone on the phone. I didn't know if she was calling IBUSZ or the police. Neither did Adam, who was insisting I give her the key, collect my bags, and go. I was too stubborn for that. My defense was sound, I thought. I'd paid for that extra bed, so I had found someone to use it. Whoever she had called, she had finished talking to them and was holding the phone for me to take.

Not only was it IBUSZ, it was the same woman who had helped Martin and me at the accommodations window. She said my host wanted her key back because I had a man in my room. I told her I knew that, but that since I was paying for both beds, I didn't see what the problem was. She told me it was against the rules. I then told her that the apartment had no hot water, which was also against the rules, and that I didn't want to stay there anyway. If I could get a refund, I said, I would be quite happy to give this harpy her key. She told me that could be arranged, but I must return to her window at Keleti Station for the refund.

I did just that, and not only got my money back, but bought a ticket for a train leaving for Zagreb, Yugoslavia, at 11:47 that night. This wasn't as easy as all that, of course, although the IBUSZ woman did let me cut in line when I went to her window for my refund.

"Must I wait an hour in line?" I asked, for it looked as if it would be at least that long.

"No," she said, "I remember your situation. Tell me exactly what happened."

"Well, first he kissed me," I wanted to begin, but decided against it.

Ordering the train ticket did involve an hour's wait in line, only to be told that I must return in an hour to pay for and pick up the ticket. Great system.

Adam, who had insisted on carrying my backpack to the station for me, wasn't pleased that I was leaving. I understood that his concern was more one of finance than any particular attraction to me. Without me, he'd be obliged to find someone else. It was a bother. I gave him the pack of cigarettes he asked for and said good-bye.

After checking my pack, I returned to IBUSZ, having correctly guessed that the hour I had to wait could easily be wasted standing in the line. Nonetheless, there was bad news: The train left from another station! I decided to leave my pack where it was, buy some postcards, and write them over a beer. Buying postcards proved to be difficult. I had to go all the way to Felzabadulas, the main tourist area, to find them. There, I sat and spent the last of my Hungarian forints. There's no sense taking it with you; the stuff is worthless outside of Hungary. Once I arrived at the Deli Pu station, I found my train waiting at the track three hours before departure.

2

Gay Rights in Eastern Europe

Radio Budapest was good that night. So good that I actually enjoyed the first part of my overnight train ride. Rolling through the black stillness of the Hungarian countryside at night, listening to clear-channel radio playing Dire Straits' "Once Upon a Time in the West" almost made me wish I weren't leaving. I had planned to spend much longer in Hungary. What went wrong? Had I panicked?

On reflection, my decision to leave had a lot to do with the lines at the IBUSZ office when I went to get the refund for my room. One does not go on vacation to stand in line. But the decision had a lot more to do with the fact that I'm an impulsive traveler. Martin and I had talked about this on the train, actually. He had experienced difficulty finding a room in Vienna, and with a Eurail Pass in his money belt, decided the easiest thing to do was just hop on a train and go somewhere else. This possibility of hopping on a train and going some other place is a feature of Europe I greatly appreciate, and the fact that it did not apply to anywhere I happened to be once I'd left Vienna was perhaps my biggest regret of the summer. As David Bowie once put it, back in the days when David Bowie could put it, "Sometimes I feel the need to move on, so I pack a bag and move on."

In retrospect, I wish I'd simply gone to another Hungarian town. Although Budapest is a city of 2.1 million people, the next largest cities in Hungary, Debrecen and Miskolc, each have only one-tenth as many inhabitants and would no doubt have provided a different perspective of the country. I should, therefore, be careful to stress that all my observations are based on Budapest alone, and just as one can't judge America by New York City, I doubt if one can judge Hungary by Budapest — even if one-fifth of Hungary's population lives there.

The Swedish girls were essentially correct: Although Budapest's two million citizens make it the largest city in Central Europe, there appears to be little to do there but eat, drink, and have sex. They didn't mention the sex, but should have. William S. Burroughs once said, "Homosexuality is a worldwide economic fact. In poor countries ... it is one of the big industries, one of the main ways in which a young boy can get somewhere." I'm sure that is true, although I take exception to his use of "homosexuality" rather than "homosexual prostitution," which are not the same animal. In any case, I felt that in Budapest I had seen more of the latter than the former, and like my friend in Vienna, I didn't really care for it.

Like East Berlin — a city I didn't visit this trip because I'd been there before, and once was plenty before the walls came down — Budapest seems to have no soul.

At the moment, Americans are being told repeatedly of Hungary's good points. Indeed, there are many. It is, and has for some time been, the most liberal of the Warsaw Pact nations. Its film industry alone is enough to set it apart, having produced such great directors as Istvan Szabo (*Mephisto*), Miklos Jancso, Pal Sando, and Karoly Makk, and such recent anti-authoritarian treasures as *Daniel Takes a Train* and two excellent 1982 releases — Peter Gothar's *Time Stands Still*, and Makk's *Another Way*, about two lesbian journalists during the 1956 Hungarian revolt. *Another Way* (*Egymasra nezve*) is based on Erzsebet Galgoczi's semi-autobio-graphical novel, *Within the Law* (*Torvenyen Belul*). Golgoczi has for several years been an official within the Hungarian Union of Authors.

Hungary was also the first Eastern bloc country to join in condemning Romania for human rights abuses, and joined NATO countries in boycotting Romania's Fourteenth Communist Party Congress in November 1989. During the final years of the dictator Nicolae Ceausescu's reign, Hungary offered political asylum to Romanians and tolerated anti-Romanian demonstrations in its streets. This should be heartening to gays, as there was no country in Europe more repressive to gays than Romania under Ceausescu (pronounced *Cho-SHESS-koo*). Any form of homosexuality was strictly forbidden, and the government's tactics in rounding up and imprisoning gays were as brutal as those in Hitler's Germany or Khomeini's Iran. Even attempting to engage in a homosexual activity was punishable with a prison sentence of up to five years. Shock therapy and castration were only two elements of torture used to keep homosexuals well within their closets. Any possible meeting place was carefully watched by members of the secret police. Even the cleaning ladies at public toilets were on the look-out for possible contacts being made there. In 1981 the German gay magazine *Rosa Flieder* carried an interview with a Romanian gay who said the suicide rate among gays was shockingly high (a friend of his had recently killed himself), and that gays could not even trust each other, for anyone might be an informer. Bucharest State Opera director Emil Kiman was sentenced to eighteen months in prison simply for being gay (reports from those who lived through imprisonment in Romania contain details of stand-ing naked in ice water, legs and arms spread out in leg irons and handcuffs, while being beaten regularly). Political opponents of

Ceausescu frequently were charged and convicted of alleged homosexuality to get them out of the way.

The June 1985 report of the Eastern Europe Information Pool (EEIP) in Vienna contained the following testimony from a Romanian gay male:

> "I have not had any contacts with other gays since I was denounced to the police by one of my friends. I was summoned to the police where I was requested to work as an informer ... The only evidence they had was the fact that I was already thirty and still not married. When I refused to work as an informer, six men beat me up so badly that I could not go to work for a week ... My current life consists of my work and sitting home alone in front of the television. But I still do not feel secure. I keep waiting for someone to knock on the door ... The only man I am allowed to love ... is Ceausescu. There are many homosexuals in Romania, maybe more than the Kinsey statistics dictate. Gay life, however, is unbearable! They only leave you alone if you work as an informer for them and immediately denounce the guy you slept with the night before ... Please write somewhere about our hopeless situation here..."

The EEIP also learned that eight Romanians were arrested in the city of Arad in July 1987. By torturing them, the police obtained the names of their friends and arrested fifty others. One of those arrested jumped out of a window at the police station, killing himself.

Romania is also the country that officially reported only three cases of AIDS, even as hundreds of Romanian children were dying in hospitals from the disease.

Despite this, I had intended to visit Romania (my trip was obviously before the revolution) — being cautious to the point of paranoia. But when the wife of the West German consul was brutally beaten by a Romanian security agent and the official government response was that the woman had deserved it, I changed my plans. There are things worse than spending a vacation standing in line, and spending a vacation in a donjon of despotism certainly qualifies. One does not go on vacation to get arrested.

I had wanted to see with my own eyes the razed villages (razed because traditional values and customs kept getting in the way of Ceausescu's program of "systemization" — they are being replaced with apartment blocks), the Palace of the People in the center of Bucharest that Ceausescu was having erected as a monument to his cult of personality, and the restaurants with nothing to order but soup. Philip Glazebrook wrote in *Journey to Kars*, "Although I don't set very great store by food when I'm traveling, the nastiness of Romanian food had begun to irritate me. Nor was there much choice. A Romanian waiter conceives of no higher pleasure than to lean over your shoulder and strike out with his pencil whatever dish you have just ordered from the menu." Glazebrook is a joy to read. He writes as Vladimir Nabokov's Charles Kinbote, from the hilarious gay-themed masterpiece *Pale Fire*, might have written had he been English instead of Zemblan.

The oppression in Romania did not come as a surprise to those who had followed developments in the country over the years. Many Americans had an inaccurate perception of the country because Romania did not participate in the 1968 invasion of Czechoslovakia, maintained ties with Israel (an increasingly dubious distinction), and refused to participate in Warsaw Pact maneuvers or allow Soviet troops on its soil, and because Romania alone of the Eastern bloc countries did not boycott the 1984 Olympics in Los Angeles. But independence from Moscow is not synonymous with *good*. Ilka Chase, in her strange 1967 book *Fresh from the Laundry*, noted even then that Romania had a firmer grip on its citizens than Bulgaria. That firmer grip included such decrees as closing two thousand bars and taverns in a crusade against alcohol, requiring that Romanians register all typewriters with the government, banning abortions and insisting each family should have five children (women were forced to undergo annual gynecological examinations to check for illegal use of contraceptives), forbidding free travel, requiring Romanians to address one another as "comrade," and prohibiting contact with foreigners. That last law was another reason for my decision to avoid the country: Had I gone and attempted to discuss gays (or any other subject, for that matter) with the Romanians, I would have been putting every person I talked with in danger — if any were willing to talk in the first place, which is unlikely.

Ceausescu had effectively taken Romania out of Europe, making it a third-world country.

Even before the revolution, however, the border between Romania and Hungary wasn't as secure as the Romanian government would have liked. Besides the much-publicized escape of the gymnast Nadia Comaneci, the Associated Press reported that others who had crossed the border included eight shepherds and their herd of 1,140 sheep.

Romanians, by the way, apparently prefer that the name of their country be spelled with an "o" (Romania) rather than a "u" (Rumania), because it ties them to their ROman heritage, rather than to their RUssian allies.

But back to Hungary and gays: Budapest was the site of a private meeting of gay activists from Eastern Europe held in November 1987 and attended by representatives from Poland, East Germany, Czechoslovakia, Yugoslavia, and, of course, Hungary. Yugoslavia was actually the first European communist country to publicly host gay events in modern times. Ljubljana, capital of liberal Slovenia, has allowed an annual gay and lesbian celebration since 1984 and played host to an international gay film festival in 1986. But the Hungarian conference was an important step in establishing a network of East European gay rights organizations.

The Third Regional Conference of Lesbians and Gay Men from Eastern and Southeastern Europe, with the same five countries attending (as well as representatives of the ILGA and the EEIP), was held in Budapest April 21–23, 1989. The meeting was hosted by the Hungarian national lesbian and gay association, HOM-

EROS (offices at Kertesz Utca 31, H-1070 Budapest) — the first officially recognized homosexual organization in East Europe. HOMEROS began in the fall of 1985 and applied for official status the following year through the offices of the Ministry of the Interior. The application was rejected without explanation, so the group submitted a new application the following year to the Ministry of Health and Welfare. On January 13, 1988, that office announced that the organization would be allowed.

The group's full name is the Homosexual Association for Leisure and Health Prevention. There had been no legal barriers to forming an organization prior to 1988, but the requirement that members of all organizations must be submitted to the police effectively prevented it. That requirement was apparently dropped, for a spokesman from HOMEROS was quoted in the March 5, 1988, issue of the Hungarian weekly *Kepes 7* as saying, "A member does not have to deal with the public; everyone's anonymity is guaranteed; no one is forced to identify him/herself."

After the constituting general assembly of the organization took place May 8, 1988, the new president of HOMEROS was interviewed on Hungarian television, along with a host of international guests including the ILGA secretary general, members of the EEIP, and gay activists from East Germany and Poland.

A member of HOMEROS told the EEIP,

"There was a large positive echo. For the last two weeks we have done nothing but give interviews. Articles appeared not only in the Hungarian press, but also in other Socialist and Western countries. There were also radio and television programs in which our members took part. After one of the radio programs, a telephone number at the Ministry was announced for persons who would like to contact us. Hundreds of people called up and completely blocked the switchboard."

Even before the formation of HOMEROS, Hungarian authorities tolerated the existence of the Egyetem café and homosexual activities in public baths. Gay fiction was published, and films with gay themes were not only shown in Hungary, but made there.

The *Kepes 7* interview asked the HOMEROS official about the gay meeting places such as the Egyetem, and received this reply: "They came into being by necessity, and they look that way too. An American professor visiting me last year asked me to take him to these places. We were horrified at the atmosphere there: isolation, loneliness and boredom. We hope that our organization will be able to offer a more interesting and better form of entertainment."

HOMEROS works closely with the Hungarian State AIDS Committee, organizes disco evenings twice a week, and has started a second gay rights group in Győr.

Ψ

Strides forward have been made in Poland and East Germany, as well, although the main instigators for change have been diametrically opposed in the two countries. In Poland, gays have found the communist officials more sympathetic to their cause than officials of the very conservative Catholic Church (no one is quite certain yet where Solidarity stands on the issue, but its policies seem to be heavily influenced by Catholic officials — no cause for optimism). The government, even before the Communist Party lost control, allowed the establishment of local gay organizations in Warsaw, Gdansk, Wroclaw, and Lodz. The Warsaw group, WRH, applied for official status in March 1988, with their request presented by a certain Professor Kozakiewicz, a member of Parliament and head of Poland's Association for Family Promotion. *Perestroika* has since made it possible for almost any organization to be officially recognized. Official registration of the other existing gay organizations is now under way, and the Chicago monthly *Outlines* reported in its January 1990 issue that the first officially recognized nationwide organization, Lambda, was formed October 28, 1989, during a gathering of gay activists at Warsaw University (at this point Lambda appears to be using the address of the Wroclaw organization: *Grupa ETAP*, P.O. Box 812, PL-50-950 Wroclaw 2; phone 71-24-90-21).

The gay group in Gdansk, which produces Poland's only gay newsletter (*Filo*), has taken advantage of the relaxed laws to print as many copies as it can afford. Previously, the group was only allowed to print one hundred copies.

Under Polish law, homosexuality is treated no differently than heterosexuality. The age of consent is fifteen for both. However, in the past the authorities were known to keep "pink lists" (a registry of known homosexuals code-named "Operation Hyacinth"), and gays were sometimes blackmailed into becoming police informers.

Compared to other countries in Eastern Europe, the number of books, articles, and plays available with homosexual themes has been quite large. The most surprising series of articles on gays in Poland was probably that published by the scout (as in Boy Scouts) magazine *Na przelaj*. The magazine said young Poles were not getting sufficient sex education in school or at home. After the articles appeared, the magazine received hundreds of letters from Polish youth saying they knew they were gay and did not wish to repress their feelings as former generations had.

Even the Catholic newspaper, *Kierunki*, has helped the cause a little, publishing the late member of Parliament Jerzy Zawiejski's *The Diary*, which contains more than a few love letters to the man he shares a grave with.

A gay nightclub called Na Trakcie opened in Warsaw in 1985 (address: Krakówskie Przedm. 41) and a male strip show opened the same year at a nightclub called Rusalka in Szczecin. The September 1985 issue of the magazine *Polityka* commented, "The stripper takes off his underpants and dances on the stage for several minutes. Not only the 'weaker sex' applauds. It's no wonder. The dancer has what we called 'homosexappeal' before the war."

One of the biggest problems for gays in Poland is the acute housing shortage. With married couples having to wait years for an apartment of their own, it is next to impossible for single gays or gay couples to obtain a place. The 1985 *EEIP Report* says, "One can find old people at the bigger train stations who are willing to rent out their apartments to 'newly found' gay couples while the children are at work and the grandchildren at school."

Ψ

In East Germany, it was the Episcopal Church that began allowing gay organizations to form under the limited protection it could provide, until the government finally wised up in 1986 and declared that gays should be treated the same as their straight comrades — the first such announcement to come from a communist nation (so far, the government of Arkansas, where I live, has done nothing of the sort). Well prior to their revolution, on December 14, 1988, the East German *Volkskammer* (Parliament) took the next logical step to assure such equality by invalidating Paragraph 151 of the penal code, which had set a higher age of consent for homosexual acts. East Germany thus joined Albania in having the lowest age of consent for homosexual acts (fourteen) in all of Europe.

East Germany's gay movement is far more active than that of any other East European country. In fact, it puts the movements in many Western countries to shame. There are more than twenty gay groups operating in East Germany's Episcopal churches in various cities, and there are another eleven gay and lesbian clubs not affiliated with the church.

The gay movement began in 1981 with an informal meeting in Leipzig that soon led to the first formal group, which met in the *Evangelischen Studentengemeinde* — basically a Protestant student union. The positive attitude the Episcopal Church has taken toward gays in East Germany has had a correspondingly positive effect on the way East German gays view the church.

A major activity of the gay organizations up to this point has been annual commemoration ceremonies at former concentration camps for the gay victims of fascism, and the construction of a memorial to them. A ceremony took place on July 2, 1983, at Buchenwald, although authorities stopped another ceremony scheduled at Sachsenhausen. The excuse was as petty as they come: The wreath had not been registered.

East Germany has by far the best-organized lesbian movement. It probably began with *Lesben in der Kirche* (Lesbians within the Church), founded in Berlin. A second lesbian group was formed in Jena in 1987, and in 1988 groups were formed in Dresden, Leipzig, Magdeburg, Erfurt, and Halle. The group in Jena publishes a lesbian journal.

Humboldt University in Berlin now offers an interdisciplinary degree program in which students may work on a graduation thesis in lesbian and gay studies. Some of the more interesting papers have included a theological study of the curing of souls for lesbians and a study of lesbian existence and theological anthropology (try doing that at the University of Oklahoma).

Ψ

Czechoslovakia, despite the fact that Prague owes much of its beauty to the cultured, if ineffectual, homosexual Emperor Rudolf II (1552–1612), had not done much until recently to encourage its gay citizens. In fact, as recently as 1987, the police in Bratislava were attempting to register all the homosexuals they could find living in that city. Nevertheless, a gay organization known as Lambda-Praha (Prague) applied to the government for official recognition before the 1989 revolution, and received it early in 1990. The Czechoslovakian Home Office suggested the group represent gays throughout the nation; therefore, the name was changed to the Union Lambda.

This organization now operates a gay switchboard (422-52-7388), publishes a bulletin, holds meetings (at either the Café Na Chmelnici or the Vinarna U Petra Voka wine cellar), and keeps track of the growing gay movement around the country.

A second gay organization in Prague is the Movement for Emancipation of Homosexual Citizens. Jan Lány, a spokesman for the Union Lambda, described it as more radical, saying its members were quite eager to do almost anything to help the movement, but lacked the official contacts necessary to accomplish as much.

Lány described the situation for gays in Czechoslovakia as similar to the situation for gays in Austria or Bavaria — or Victorian England. He said there was a "type of hypocrisy" and blamed it in part on the strong Catholic influence in the country.

"You can do just about whatever you like," he said, "but you are not supposed to speak of being gay."

Lány is employed as a high school teacher and has written an article for a Czechoslovak youth magazine in support of equal treatment for gay partnerships. He says quite a number of students, including some of his own, come to the Union Lambda meetings.

"I don't use a lot of propaganda at school, but if there is a leaflet, and the students see the leaflet and want to come, then of course it is okay.

"I always try to be very correct [concerning students]. When I have been involved with a student, it was always after they left school."

Lány says the school authorities know about his being gay, but that it is not a problem. "I am really quite content with being gay. I am accepted by my neighbors, by the people at the school — even by the parents of my partner."

Very little had been seen in print in Czechoslovakia regarding gays until very recently. Only a few books with homosexual themes or topics were printed (Plato's *Dialogues* and Oscar Wilde's *The Picture of Dorian Gray* are two that were). But in January 1990 a new youth magazine began devoting two pages each issue to gay news.

An unofficial gay disco (U Petra Voka, at Na belidle 40, Prague-Smichov) opened in Prague in 1980 and instantly became a must destination for gays all over Eastern Europe. A second bar that often threw parties for gays eventually was closed, but a mixed bar known as the Tea Club soon took its place. In Brno, a student opened a gay disco in his parents' house.

Condoms are widely available in Czechoslovakia. The Institute of Sexuality also provides free water-based lubricant to anyone who takes the trouble to stop in and ask for it.

Ψ

While East Germany, Poland, and the Yugoslav Republic of Slovenia seem to possess the greatest hopes for gay equality, with Czechoslovakia and Hungary lagging more than a little bit behind, less has been heard from gays living in Albania, Bulgaria, Romania, and much of Yugoslavia. In Albania, this can be expected, since the rest of the world rarely hears anything from *anyone* living within Fortress Albania. As for Bulgaria, the EEIP has been unable to locate anyone in this country who is openly gay. The 1983 *EEIP Report* came right to the point, stating, "No people are known in Bulgaria who declare publicly to be gay. Western lifestyle (and the degree of Western tolerance towards homosexuality) is considered evidence of Western decadence even by Bulgarian gays. Communist propaganda has done a good job!"

The EEIP found a more liberal attitude at the Black Sea resorts, where nudist beaches were created to satisfy East German tourists. In the summer, the Black Sea beaches have been popular destinations for gays throughout Eastern Europe, and the EEIP says contacts were not difficult to make. There are no gay bars or cafés in Bulgaria.

February 2 is known in Bulgaria, by the way, as the "Day of the Homosexuals," when gays supposedly congregate at the spa outside of Sofia known as Gorna Banya. "Go to Gorna Banya" is an insult in Bulgaria, with a meaning somewhere between "Go to hell" and "Go fuck yourself."

Males in Bulgaria are subjected to strong macho indoctrination. They are expected to get married and have many children. The social and governmental attitudes have effectively prevented any type of gay culture in the country.

Ψ

The laws in virtually every East European nation are currently in a state of flux, but it might nevertheless be helpful to review the legal status of gays in each country, pending changes brought about by the 1989 revolutions.

Among all East European countries, homosexuality is officially illegal only in Romania, the Soviet Union, and the Yugoslav republics of Serbia (including Kosovo, but not Vojvodina), Macedonia, and Bosnia-Herzegovina. But when it comes to the subject of gay rights, only the citizens of East Germany seem ready to accept it. In Poland and Czechoslovakia, the Catholic Church is the main obstacle. In Hungary, the obstacle seems to be that indefinable stuffiness on the subject possessed by the Austrians and Swiss, as well — a sort of Central European homophobia, I'm afraid (in Austria, alas, it is still technically illegal for gays to form organizations).

Comparing ages of consent for gays, the age is a reasonable fourteen in Albania and East Germany; fifteen in Poland; sixteen in the Yugoslav republic of Slovenia; eighteen in Czechoslovakia, Hungary, and the Yugoslav republics of Croatia, Montenegro, and the semi-autonomous region of Vojvodina; and twenty-one in Bulgaria (one wonders if people mature much slower there and in Great Britain, where the age is also twenty-one).

It is interesting that whereas the age of consent for heterosexuals in Bulgaria is fourteen, and fifteen in Czechoslovakia — considerably lower than the homosexual age of consent in those countries — in Albania, of all places, homosexual sex is treated less seriously than heterosexual sex. Although the age of consent for both is fourteen, sex with a female minor is punishable by up to fifteen years in prison, while sex with a male younger than fourteen brings five years maximum. Apparently homosexuality was fairly well accepted in Albania until at least the middle of the nineteenth century. Edward Carpenter, using information from Johann Georg von Hahn's *Albanesische Studien* (1854), wrote in *Ioläus* (1917) that "the Dorian customs of comradeship still flourish in Albania," and that "it appears to be a quite recognized institution for a young man to take to himself a youth or boy as his special comrade ... The relation generally, though not always ends with the marriage of the elder."

The December 1987 issue of *Gay Times* (London) quoted Albanian defector Ilir Bulka, the former translator for long-time leader Enver Hoxha, as saying that Hoxha had several homosexual affairs in the 1930s while a student in Paris, that his wife and Albania's top leaders knew he was gay, and that he became increasingly paranoid and anti-gay over the years, fearing this "secret" might be used to depose him.

Article 99 of the Albanian Penal Code says simply, "The perpetration of illicit acts with persons under the age of fourteen will be punished with a prison sentence of up to five years." Article 239, which provided up to ten years in prison for any homosexual act, was abolished in June 1977.

In Hungary, Article 199 of the constitution says, "A person who has reached the age of eighteen and engages in illicit sexual practices with a person under the age of eighteen of the same sex has committed a crime and will be sentenced to a prison term of up to three years." The age of consent for gays was twenty until 1978, when it was lowered to eighteen. Homosexual acts between consenting adults were decriminalized in 1961.

Ψ

A few things about the Hungarians themselves are worth mentioning. The thing I appreciate most about them is that they are avid readers. On many street corners in Budapest, there are book stalls, all of which are constantly surrounded by customers looking at what's new in print. During my visit the country was experiencing "Nagy-mania." Books favorable to former Premier Imre Nagy, who was executed by the Soviets following their massive attack against Budapest in 1956, were available for the first time as Nagy was officially re-tried and exonerated, and his body was exhumed from an unmarked grave and re-buried. Hungarians, per capita, buy twice as many books as Americans. Along with Iceland, Hungary has one of the world's most literate populations. It is also one of the world's most alcoholic, and most suicidal.

Alcohol consumption represents about fifteen percent of household spending. Hungary ranks first in the world in per capita consumption of hard liquor, third in wine, and fifth in beer. When Hungarians go out in the evening they use public transport or taxis, for they know they will drink, and driving after any drinking whatsoever is strictly illegal. The law is strictly enforced.

Nations come and go from the top of the suicide list each year. Some people think Sweden perennially heads the list, but this simply is not true. What is true is that Hungary and neighboring Austria show up near the top of the list year after year.

Another interesting statistic about the Hungarians is that the top five percent of the wage earners take home eighty times as much money as the bottom five percent. This unfortunate gap between rich and poor is about the same as that of many capitalist countries. But the Hungarian hierarchy long ago gave up on economic equality for its citizens, if it was ever a genuine goal. What the Hungarians discovered (or perhaps merely admitted) before any of the other East Bloc countries was that people produce more under private ownership. Although eighty percent of the arable land in Hungary is farmed by collectives, the members of the collectives are also allowed to farm small private plots using the collective's equipment. The twenty percent of the land in these private plots soon accounted for half of Hungary's agricultural output. The central planners got the message, and have never pushed for true communism since. In many ways, Hungary, along with Turkey, is the most capitalistic place I've seen.

I'm certain it is possible to go to Budapest and thoroughly enjoy yourself. A friend of mine who now lives in Seattle did it this very summer. She flew out of Amsterdam the day after I flew in, so we got together for one enchanted evening and I pumped her for information on Budapest and Istanbul, the only cities mutual to our itineraries. She had stayed with a family friend in Budapest, and I think this was the key to her enjoying the city. She had not told this family she was gay, and said she was glad she did not, because her current traveling companion had told them he was gay, and they were horrified.

A gay Hungarian wrote in the first *EEIP Report* (1982), "Homosexuality is considered abnormal ... It is just unacceptable to be gay in Hungarian society." Indeed, the HOMEROS member interviewed by the EEIP, said that as far as attitudes toward gays in Hungary are concerned, "Society is certainly less tolerant than the authorities."

It was this, above all, that bothered me about Budapest. For a European city of two million people to have only two small gay bars is shocking. Even Little Rock has six. The International Lesbian and Gay Association and *Spartacus* both contend that the attitude of Hungarians toward homosexuality is intolerant and that homosexuals in Hungary are afraid to express their feelings openly. Everything I observed indicates that both conclusions are true.

You don't want to grow up gay in Hungary.

Ψ

I managed to sleep a little that night on the train, until we reached the border. Again, it took five Hungarian officials to check my visa, and they came at ten-minute intervals while the train sat stationary. Once on the other side, it took only one Yugoslav to check me in. I was glad to be out of Hungary.

Rating: One falling red star.

3

Bosnia and Herzegovina

Yugoslavia is one of the most beautiful countries in Europe. This was my second visit (Daniela, my Seattle friend, and I had visited it six years earlier), but my first journey south of Croatia. I brought with me memories of scrub mountains, resembling those of New Mexico or central Spain, rising up from an Adriatic coast of tourist-brochure villages tucked inside bays, and a myriad of islands dotting the western horizon, some of these islands with moonscape terrain (the Kornati chain and the eastern half of Rab, for instance).

I also brought with me memories of the more majestic peaks of Slovenia (going down the coast is like going from Switzerland to Spain with nothing in between — the forested mountains of Slovenia suddenly being replaced by the barren or scrub-covered hills of Croatia); the university-like atmosphere and excellent Modern Art Gallery of Ljubljana; the likenesses of Josip Broz Tito adorning many a wall and mountainside (they sometimes make profiles or spell out his name with stones); the youth hostel that had no curfew and allowed Daniela and me to stay in the same room; the incredibly cheap prices; the noisy beer drinkers whooping it up on my train one day while the conductor simply ignored them; the summer evenings sitting on a rooftop in the resort town of Boric (near Zadar), drinking homemade wine with my delightfully pleasant, middle-aged, unmarried host couple while being entertained by Ana, Lydia, and Fran, the three shyly cute children who were with them (but not theirs), and who had just begun studying English — "How old are you?" Daniela asked Fran. "Fine, thank you," he replied. I remember that Fran got a big kick out of my name, which apparently sounds like the Serbo-Croatian word meaning "to shoot a gun," and I remember being asked to dance first by Fran, then Ana, and finally by a wonderful woman who was probably close to seventy years old. It was one of the most magical evenings of my life.

I also recalled the long waits in line to buy bus tickets; the hot, dusty buses (for some reason Yugoslavs, and Turks as well, rarely open windows on buses even in the most oppressive heat); the extremely bad service at most restaurants; the disemboweling of goats that took place on the front porch of one house where I was staying; the slime-covered beaches of the northern Adriatic (pollution is a problem on both the Italian and Yugoslav shores), and the Gypsy who would stop at nothing to sell me a wooden donkey.

In Ljubljana, we had encountered a sort-of-gay hangout. It was actually just an area of a large student tavern — the Kaverna Union — frequented by hippies, gays, punks, gay hippies, gay punks, and various other interesting peoples of the Yugoslav counterculture. I don't remember much about the evening except that at one point a fight broke out when, it appeared, a gay customer asked the wrong question of a straight customer. What I remember most is that the crowd rose to the gay man's defense, and the other man was shown the door. I also remember being distressed by the early closing times all over Ljubljana — about eleven p.m.

I have noted already that homosexuality is completely legal in Slovenia, and that the age of consent is a reasonable sixteen. Until

1977, homosexuality was illegal throughout Yugoslavia. Since that time the republics have been allowed to establish their own laws regarding sexuality. It only makes sense that Yugoslavia's gay movement would begin in liberal Slovenia.

There is a gay student group known as Magnus operating out of the Student Culture Center (SKUC) at the university in Ljubljana. SKUC organized an exhibit called "Magnus: Homosexuality and Culture," shown April 23–29, 1984 — Yugoslavia's first public presentation dealing with homosexuality. More than one thousand people visited the exhibit, which included several films and a large selection of gay books and magazines from the West. Media coverage of the event — which was paid for in part with public funds — was good. Radio Ljubljana covered the opening press conference and followed that with a three-hour discussion and call-in program. Local newspapers and the national papers *Start, Nim,* and *Polet* carried articles on the exhibit. SKUC also began a magazine and devoted the entire second issue to gay themes. It was thus a logical step forward when, on June 23, 1984, Yugoslavia's first gay social club was formed, taking the name of Magnus. The group became an official part of SKUC on December 4, 1984, and is treated the same as any other student organization.

Magnus operated a disco for a time, but a gay commercial disco soon opened. Since it was allowed to stay open much later (until three a.m.), the Magnus disco, which had only been allowed to stay open until midnight, closed.

The second Magnus exhibit took place May 13–25, 1985, and was given coverage by Yugoslav television. The 1986 exhibit featured a film retrospective of English director Derek Jarman.

Magnus is currently putting its energies into its *Gayzine* publication, which first appeared in March 1985 (it is distributed in Ljubljana, Zagreb, and Belgrade), and is attempting to establish a gay library and to produce a gay guide to Yugoslavia. Magnus also works closely with a recently formed lesbian organization known as Lilit. The lesbian group already has its own magazine, *Lesbozine,* with money for printing supplied by the Socialist Alliance of Slovenian Youth and a couple of Dutch organizations.

Magnus reports that it has had no problems whatsoever with harassment from heterosexual Yugoslavs. The authorities did cancel the gay congress scheduled in Ljubljana for May 25, 1987, however, saying gay gatherings were a public health hazard due to the threat of AIDS! As a result, Slovenians have begun an initiative to adopt a constitutional amendment guaranteeing equality regardless of sexual preference.

You can telephone Magnus through SKUC at 61-319662 (ask to speak to Bogdan or Aldo — or just ask for information on Magnus). The town of Bled also has a gay switchboard (61-551208).

Practically all gay bars in Yugoslavia are really mixed, with a majority of the clientele being straight. I understand, however, that since my visit to Ljubljana, the gays and punks have gone their separate ways, each with their own venues. The attitude of society regarding homosexuality is not bad, by East European standards, but could certainly improve. It is the traditional macho culture of the Slavs that is the main stumbling point. Yugoslav gays feel compelled to remain in the closet; thus, many marry and limit their homosexual activity to anonymous sex with strangers. Among the positive aspects, it should also be noted that in the republics with anti-gay laws, these laws are almost never enforced.

There are gay beaches in Yugoslavia, but for the most part they are only frequented by foreigners. I was told there was one on the island of Rab when I was there in 1983, but had no luck finding it. Nor did Daniela and I have any luck finding the straight nudist beach near Zadar.

Unlike Hungary, you do not need to obtain a visa in advance to visit Yugoslavia. You simply show up at the border and they give you one on the spot, free, valid for three months. Also unlike the Hungarians, the Yugoslavs generally do not try to pry every dollar from your pocket. Although their economy is no better than that of Hungary (the Yugoslav currency devalues at an astonishing rate: the one-hundred-lira notes I'd brought from my previous trip were now worthless — unless you had a hundred of them, then you'd have about seventy-five cents — and the currency devalued by almost fifty percent during the three months I was in Europe this particular summer), the Yugoslavs do not harass foreigners to change money. Nor do you find a great many of them willing to prostitute themselves.

Yugoslavs are, in fact, poorer than Hungarians, with a per capita income of $3,109 compared with the Hungarians' $4,180. (Neither, however, are nearly as poor as blacks living in the Mississippi Delta region of the United States. In Lee County, Arkansas, for example, the per capita income for blacks is $1,923.) Yugoslavia is also Europe's only entry among the world's ten largest debtor nations.

This time around, I was heading for the poorer, more conservative Yugoslav south — the embattled province of Kosovo with its Albanian majority, and the northern reaches of Alexander the Great's homeland, Macedonia, a land divided between Greece, Yugoslavia, and Bulgaria following the Balkan Wars (1912–1913).

Ψ

Zagreb, my first stop in Yugoslavia this trip, was an unfortunate selection, for it seemed to be the city of choice for every tourist wishing to make a quick dip into Yugoslavia to say they had "been there." I knew I was in trouble when I arrived at the train station and found it crammed with young travelers who had spent the night there, unable to find a room. I exchanged one hundred dollars in traveler's checks, which came to 1,628,000 lira. I received this 1,628,000 lira in 20,000-lira notes, which meant I was given a stack of more than eighty bills. It might as well be Monopoly money. Put inside my money belt, the notes added at least an inch to my waistline. Fortunately, all the walking I'd done on the trip thus far had reduced my weight by five to ten pounds, so there was room between jeans and skin for the wad of bills.

A young woman began a conversation with me, not wasting much time in getting to the line, "I'm going to try the youth hostel. I don't usually stay in them, but I'm tired of being alone." It seemed like an invitation, but I declined to bite. I had been with friends and family for much of my journey thus far, and was looking forward to spending some time being lonesome.

I was told there was no agency in Zagreb to help tourists find rooms, so I set out in the rain to see what I could find. I know well the look of desk clerks who are tired of being asked for rooms when the situation is hopeless, and I got this look everywhere I went. At the same time, I'd been looking over Zagreb and I wasn't impressed. Of course, it was raining and I was carrying a heavy pack, hadn't had much sleep, and was even trying to fight off a cold — all of which can make even the best of cities seem unpleasant. But whatever the situation regarding Zagreb's appeal, the fact remained that there were no rooms. I returned to the station and bought a ticket to Sarajevo, which was more in the region where I wanted to go, in any case.

I have been on crowded trains before, but the train from Zagreb to Sarajevo was unbelievable. The first bad luck was at the station. They had two trains back to back on the same track. I thought it was all one train and was waiting for it to leave to make room for my train. When only half of it left, I realized, too late, my mistake. The train already was packed to overflowing. I tried four doors before finding one with enough room for me to squeeze on board. There was no room for my pack except above or below my body, so I sat on it, crammed with five other sardines in the entry corridor. Every time someone walked by, a major shuffling of people was involved to make room for them. Invariably, they stepped on my blistered feet. It looked as if transportation in Yugoslavia was even more nightmarish than before — and that was, indeed, the case. Later I would meet a couple from Michigan who, although traveling on a tight budget, had broken down and rented a car for the Yugoslav leg of their journey because they couldn't take any more of the public transit. I also met several people who were cutting their trip short for the same reason.

After two and a half hours, I did get a seat. At the very next stop, however, half the occupants of the compartment got off and were replaced by the most obnoxious family I was to see in Yugoslavia. There were five of them, and they crowded into the three vacant spaces. Then, when one of the original occupants got up to use the WC (rest room), the adults encouraged one of the children to take his seat. When he returned, he simply got his luggage and left. Five minutes later, the other original occupant did the same, with the same result. I held out for a while, but was miserable with this cabal from hell and badly needed to push my way through to the Pullman car for something to drink. I saw them grab my seat as I left, and wished the conductor spoke English so that I might have a chance of complaining. English was suddenly scarce. The "Do not flush toilet while train is in station" sign in the WC was written in five languages, none of them English. I could make out enough of the Italian to understand the familiar imperative, but I speak no language other than English. I'm not proud of it. Still, if *I* can get by in Hungary, Yugoslavia, and Turkey with only English at my command, so can you. You can get by even better if you know German, the only other language (except the native ones, of course) that is very useful in this part of the world.

The train journey soon improved. Although I stood for the last three and a half hours, the scenery was nice. Many families working the fields would stop to watch the train go by. The children would wave; I'd wave back.

Pulling into Sarajevo, I was praying the room situation would be better than in Budapest and Zagreb. It was. I didn't see a room-finding service, so I went outside the station, where a taxi driver tried to talk me into a ride. When he finally understood that I had nowhere to go, he led me back inside to a woman at the information desk. The woman first told me in English, then the driver in Serbo-Croatian, that if I could wait five or ten minutes, she should have a room for me. The taxi driver ruffled my hair and left. Pleasant fellow. Less than a minute passed before the woman came from behind the counter with a man who, she told me, had a private room, spoke English, and could take me to the room in his car. This was three-fifths of heaven. I took care of the other two-fifths with two questions: "Where is it?" and "How much?" The price — nine dollars — was quite reasonable, and the man told me it was close by, but up a hill. This, I didn't mind. From the train, I had seen that Sarajevo is a modern town, by Yugoslav standards, with houses beautifully situated on the surrounding hillsides. I had hoped to stay on one of those hills for the view. Once my pack is off my back, I don't mind climbing the occasional hill.

The man's name was Aleksandar Scepanovic, and the room was in the basement of his mother's house at M. Trifunovica 24 in a section of town known as Kosevsko brdo. The room, although nice, was cold and damp, which would make fighting off the cold more difficult. I took my first hot bath in four days, then went to a nearby restaurant, called the Imbiss, on the same hill. The woman behind the bar spoke English and brought me a good plate of food, but far more than I could ever hope to eat. It's an odd thing, but I find that I eat much less when I'm traveling. You would think the constant walking would work up quite an appetite, but a light breakfast and a nice dinner are all I can hold most days, and I eat less at dinner than I normally would at home. I think it has a lot to do with the fact that all the walking and the heat keep me thirsty, so I drink a lot of fluids all day, keeping the appetite in check. I offer this as explanation for the fact that I literally could eat less than half the food the woman brought, and I felt bad about it.

"Why you not eat?" she asked, after I'd pushed the plate aside.

"It's good," I said, knowing that was hardly an explanation.

"Yes, it's fresh!" she exclaimed.

One guilt trip, coming up. I'd insulted her with my lack of appetite.

I tried to explain that it was simply too much food. Actually, the meat had been far greasier than I like, but that would be the situation for the next eight weeks, through all of Yugoslavia, Turkey, and Greece. It would only get worse in Turkey and Greece, in fact, where olive oil frequently seems to saturate everything on the plate. It's especially sickening with eggplant, which they call *aubergine*. There's nothing quite as nasty as *aubergine* swimming in oil. The Turks ruined me on eggplant for life.

Sarajevsko *pivo*, the local beer, was good. I sat at a table outside and was immediately surrounded by five boys with a soccer ball. Perhaps they didn't see many foreigners on their hill. They stared at me a while, then one of them asked, in English, "What is your name?" They laughed when I told them. This puzzled me until I remembered that "Keith" sounds like some Serbo-Croatian word for "to shoot a gun." I had crossed from Croatia into Bosnia and Herzegovina, but the language of the two regions is the same. The biggest difference in people is that Muslims account for forty percent of the population in Bosnia and Herzegovina, but only about five percent in Croatia. Anywhere you have a forty-percent Muslim population, you're going to have a different culture, and that was certainly the case in Sarajevo.

I got the boys' names as well, then they stared at me a while longer. I tried not to become self-conscious, remembering another scene from Glazebrook's book, concerning the young boys of Turkey: "Self consciousness attracts an audience. Boys seeing me pass from a window clattered downstairs and ran into the road to stare, even crossed it to walk backwards just in front of me, looking up with unsmiling black eyes into my face."

"Do you play football?" one of the boys asked suddenly.

He meant soccer, which I've played exactly twice. It's a great game, which I wish would catch on in America.

A light-skinned blond boy, the tallest and cutest of the bunch, asked for my name again, then two more boys joined the five already assembled.

"What are you doing?" the first boy asked.

I had quit eating and was writing in my journal, but I don't think he was particularly interested in what I was doing so much as he was simply proud to know how to ask the question in English. I asked if they were studying English at school. Three of them were. At this point the woman behind the bar came outside and chased them all away. As he ran off up the hill, the cutest one turned and yelled, "Good-bye—" followed by some word other than my name. I hope it was a term of endearment.

All of that food and the beer cost two dollars.

Ψ

Sarajevo is a city of historical importance, if only because the pretext for starting the First World War occurred in this city on June 28, 1914, when Crown Prince Franz Ferdinand, the heir to the Austro-Hungarian throne, was assassinated on orders of the Mladá Bosna (Young Bosnia) national revolutionary youth movement.

Sarajevo is also a city of Turkish bazaars, cafés, bars, ice cream shops, and mosques. The streets are lively, particularly in the area of the largest Turkish bazaar, which is full of scenes from another era — men, buggies, and donkeys carrying large sacks of fruit, vegetables, meat, and spices to sell; and turbaned mothers washing children and sweating boys stopping for a drink at the public faucets below the minaret.

The first thing I did the next day was figure out how to get to old Sarajevo by bus. Once there, I sat for coffee, and experienced my first *Turska kava*, served in a little tin silo with grounds that you must allow to settle before it is drinkable, with a glass of water and a huge packet of sugar on the side. I also ordered a small slice of *baklava* and a donut, but both were too sugary to eat. The Turkish sweet tooth is incredible; their former subjects in Bosnia obviously still share the addiction.

A fast-flowing mountain stream runs through Sarajevo. I was walking along it when I saw a wedding procession of about thirty cars, including taxis, decorated with red roses, horns blaring, someone in the second car waving a large Yugoslavian flag, and police stopping traffic for them. After a wonderful *cappuccino*, I walked to a mosque just in time to see a funeral procession making its exit, the coffin bearers carrying the corpse shoulder high before the entire procession disappeared into a line of waiting taxis.

I could hear loud music coming from somewhere. Following the sound, I came upon an outdoor rock concert farther along the street. It ended soon after I arrived, so I made my way to the Umjetnica gallery, otherwise known as the Art Gallery of Bosnia-Herzegovina. It was closed. I love Yugoslav art and had looked forward to seeing this gallery, so I rang the bell and asked the man who answered if he could tell me when the gallery would be open. He answered in Serbo-Croatian, shaking his head and ending with a word that sounded exactly like "never." It seemed a ridiculously long time to wait, so I continued my explorations, stopping by a cool little bar called Had, which at first seemed as if it could well be a gay bar. It wasn't. In fact, there apparently are no gay bars in Sarajevo. *Spartacus* lists the bars at the Holiday Inn and the Hotel Europa as possibilities, but neither looked very likely to me.

I followed the Had bar with the equally chic Pizzeria Bambus. The few customers inside were watching the European basketball championships. I knew the Yugoslav team, Jugoplastika Split, was one of the favorites. Over the next few days, I would repeatedly encounter Yugoslavs gathered around television sets watching the games.

Waited a long time for my dollar-fifty vegetarian pizza, sipping at a Sarajevsko on tap, which wasn't close to being as good as the bottled version. Finally, the cook came to tell me there was trouble in the kitchen and there could be no food for an hour. I left, the beer still two-thirds full and unpaid for, and found another pizzeria, this one with a very nice waiter, and an oven that worked. The waiter was planning a trip to San Francisco in September. He asked where I was from in the States. I went through both pronunciations of Arkansas: the correct "Ar-kan-sah," then, following his blank look, the incorrect "Ar-Kansas," which he recognized (the trouble is that Arkansas was not named by English-speaking people; the name is a French spelling of an Indian word, just like *Illinois, Iroquois,* and *Sioux*). In most cases, the second attempt draws a blank, too, so I end up saying, "near Memphis," or simply, "the mid-South."

As a concerned-looking Tito looked down on us from the cloth over the bar, I asked the bartender for his opinion of the best place to go at night in Sarajevo. He said he preferred the crowd at the disco in the Hotel Beograd, and suggested I meet him there later in the evening. I told him I'd try.

Ψ

Went back to my hillside abode to wash up, then walked to the train station, just to be sure I could find it. From there I was lured like a moth to various outdoor clubs across the town where exotic chanteuses sang haunting Balkan songs. I sat at several, enjoying the music, although I wish they would accompany those wonderful vocals with some instrument other than a damn accordion. At the last place I sat, some man spun four bottles of beer off his table, one at a time, breaking each on the concrete floor. Although he got a disapproving look from his waitress, no one approached him to throw him out or even ask him to stop.

Making my way back to the center of town, I passed a restaurant on fire. A fire truck was present with firemen putting out the blaze seemingly in their spare time as they chatted with the customers on the outside terrace, who went on drinking their beers.

The *korso* — Yugoslavia's version of that favorite Balkan pastime, promenading — on a Saturday night is something to see. It seems that at least half the town's citizens come out to walk up and down a ten-block stretch that runs through the center of the old town. There are plenty of coffee shops and bars for stopping in, many with outside tables, always full.

People dress up for this promenade. A jacket, which I didn't have, seemed to be a requirement. The colors of choice were obviously green and black. These I had, but they were hanging up in my room to dry. Young women walked arm-in-arm. Young men leaned on each other a lot, but I saw little evidence of anything gay.

The Beograd Hotel had quite a gathering of youth outside. The waiter at the pizzeria had told me it was a "young and interesting" crowd, and I suppose I would agree, but I was too tired to stick around and check it out. I was so tired, in fact, that I got off at the wrong stop when I took the bus back to my neighborhood, then realized with a sense of panic that it had almost certainly been the last bus of the night. I had no idea how to get to my room.

I knew I was in a valley and needed to be on a hill, but I didn't know *which* hill — there were hills all around. Streets forked frequently, making directions all the more difficult. The fact that every house in Sarajevo has identical red roofs didn't help much, either. I waited in vain for another bus, then set out walking, deciding to simply climb the closest hill and see if I could spot anything familiar from the top. Fortunately, the first car to come by was a taxi, which I flagged down. Although it would have been quite a walk home, most of it uphill, the cab fare was only slightly more than a dollar.

Met another nice young man in front of my house when I arrived. His English wasn't good, but he said his name was "Mamanel," or something like that, and asked where I was going next on my journey. I told him I was inclined to go to Mostar and Dubrovnik.

"Mostar is very nice," he told me, "but Dubrovnik, I think it is..." He catalogued the supply of English superlatives in his brain, and apparently finding only the one, repeated bashfully, "very nice."

In my room, I swam through the radio waves on the AM band, picking up Radio Moscow World Service on four frequencies and BBC World Service on one.

I spent part of the following day in Sarajevo's old town, as well. Whereas Budapest is a "downstairs" town and Amsterdam is an "up- or downstairs" town, Sarajevo is a "back-in-the-alley" town: Many signs on the streets point to establishments a few yards off the main street through a walkway.

There was quite a lot of graffiti on the Sarajevo walls — everything from "We hate the reds" to "U2's the best." There were also many soldiers about, most of them looking as if they wished they weren't soldiers.

Other notes on Sarajevo: A larger percentage of the people seem to speak English as a second language here than in any other part of Yugoslavia except, perhaps, Dubrovnik. In Slovenia and Croatia, German (and Germans) dominates. It's not just a winter resort; it's beautiful in the summer, too. The sugar here isn't exactly white or brown — it's beige sugar. Yugoslavs litter worse than Americans. They're also very tall, like the Dutch, so it's no wonder they're crazy about basketball.

Ψ

Trains and buses in Yugoslavia always seem to leave at inconvenient times, bound for improbable places, following circuitous routes. The train from Sarajevo to Mostar, for instance, leaves at six a.m. If you don't want to get up that early, no problem — you can sleep the day away and take the 7:10. After that, there's nothing until 3:10 p.m. Personally, I consider noon convenient, but nothing ever seems to leave within three hours either side of noon in Yugoslavia.

Buses aren't much better, but I decided — after the infernal train ride from hell to Sarajevo — to take a bus to Mostar simply because bus tickets in Yugoslavia supposedly guarantee you a seat, whereas tickets for the trains obviously do not.

The bus to Mostar played Slavic music, which wasn't bad. Like buses everywhere in Yugoslavia, Greece, and Turkey, it had no toilet, but it did make a stop at a roadside water spigot in order for passengers to get a drink. While I was waiting in the bus station in Sarajevo, a hailstorm had suddenly appeared. The result was that on my journey, the mountain streams were full of briskly flowing

– 61 –

water. Everything was very green and the towns built on the hillsides were wet and beautiful.

The bus and train take basically the same route between Sarajevo and Mostar, but whereas the train takes a more direct approach, the bus winds its way there, hugging the curving hillsides. Even so, the bus goes through three tunnels, while the train goes out of its way to avoid one, going through only two. Construction crews working toward straightening the road held us up at one point for thirty minutes.

The most scenic part of the journey is the portion from Tarcin to Mostar. The quadruple train bridges near Tarcin are impressive, viewed from the road. The road, however, is very bumpy. Between Tarcin and Konjic is an extreme decline in altitude. With the brakes whining down the twisting road, you hope they don't give out. Further along, the Neretva River and Jablanicko Lake impress you with the truly aqua color of their waters. The bridge across the lake at Ostrozac is especially nice. First you're high up, looking down on the Neretva, then you're in the valley beside it, looking up at the mountains. The strata of the rock on the mountain faces remind you of just how geographically unstable the Balkans are, which might, in turn, remind you of just how unstable *politically* they are, as well. Every movement going east from Western Europe, west from the steppes of Russia, or north from Asia Minor has left its impact on the region, which some have referred to as the "Crush Zone."

Most countries of the Balkans are made up of a conglomeration of different peoples descended from native kingdoms or conquering tribes. Yugoslavia is the most obvious example: a country of six republics and two semi-autonomous provinces, seven major nationalities and eleven "national minorities," three official languages and numerous minority languages, two alphabets — Latin and Cyrillic — and four major religions. The fact that a single country was ever created from such a diverse mix is remarkable. That it will eventually break up seems virtually certain. A resurgence in Serbian nationalism, in particular, seems to threaten the fragile balance of power among the six republics. Slovenia seems especially likely to soon go its own way.

This instability in the Balkans was what Vincent Malmström had in mind when he stated in *Geography of Europe* that "by and large, the people of East Europe have never been as prosperous as they have during the last decades. Some of these countries have experienced responsible government — a government that cared enough about its people to do something for them — for the first time in their histories." Obviously, denying them basic freedoms wasn't doing anything *for* them, but I think Malmström's point should be considered, at least in the context of Yugoslavia. Although guilty of many shortcomings, the Yugoslav government at least has had the interests of the Yugoslavs at heart, not the interests of Athens, Istanbul, Rome, London, Washington, or Moscow.

Ψ

Unlike my friend in Sarajevo, I did not find Mostar "very nice." I was the only American I encountered there, and for once I had to consider that maybe I was the only American foolish enough to go. The bridge the tourist bureau puts on all their propaganda is nice, but the rest of the town is dirty and ugly. I didn't want to stay long.

Having read about an artist colony at the little village of Pocjtelj, and that many private accommodations could be had there, I decided to go. I'm not sure that either statement about Pocjtelj is true — I encountered neither artists' studios nor private rooms — but the decision was definitely a good one.

To get there I had to put up with the first in a series of boorish Yugoslav bus drivers. This one had photographs of topless women taped to the back of his seat, and money flung across his dash. I was afraid I would not know where to get off the bus, but the driver would not agree to tell me "when." Luckily, there was a rare sign.

I stopped to watch the many people fishing from the now much shallower Neretva River, then walked to a restaurant to inquire about rooms. There I encountered a long-haired, muscular youth with a winning smile and very good English. He told me there was one hotel in town, then — suspiciously — didn't understand my inquiries regarding rooms in private houses. My suspicions proved to have foundation when the hotel proprietress turned out to be his mother. It couldn't have mattered less, however, for once I saw the "hotel" there was no question of staying anywhere else. It was a converted sixteenth-century mosque, spread out over the side of a mountain leading up to an old castle.

The boy's mother merely sat and waited when I was introduced. I repeated that I needed a room. She stood up, plucked a mimosa blossom from the several thousand adorning the surrounding trees, handed it to me along with a key, and told me to "follow the boy." After inquiring about the price and check-out time (the answers were "about sixteen American dollars" and "no problem"), I did. The boy, in this case, was a small, silent, long-haired, blond youth wearing swimming trunks — possibly another son. I followed him up several hundred steps, well past the top of the crumbling minaret, nearly to the top of the mountain. Despite the exterior, it was a very modern room, with a view to kill for. The boy, still mute, did a routine with the lights, showing me which switch did what, then another routine with the key (showing me, one supposes, how to lock and unlock a door), and seemed in no hurry to leave. I understood that a tip was in order. Once I produced it, he snatched it from my hand, bowed, and was quickly out the door.

I was exhausted from the uphill climb with my pack. Even a light pack with only the essentials is a burden when climbing hills.

This seems like as good a time as any to say a few words about packing for such a journey.

Every travel guide will tell you to travel light. If you ignore this advice the first time, you won't the next. Still, it is amazing what you need on a three-month journey, and it is just as amazing what you can fit inside a lightweight pack.

I travel with a Lowe's Odyssey backpack. It weighs three pounds, eight ounces when empty, and has a twenty-inch internal frame. It isn't the kind of pack you would want to climb too many mountains with, but it is a good pack for walking across towns, it zips up the side like a suitcase (which makes getting to items at the bottom *much* easier than packs that only unzip at the top), and it can be converted into a large suitcase with shoulder strap in places where you might feel uncomfortable carrying a pack — Romania, for instance. It also holds up very well, but comes with a lifetime warranty, just in case.

The following list includes absolutely everything I took with me on this eleven-week trip, whether in my pack or on my person: a water-resistant money belt, three short-sleeved shirts, two tank tops, one pair of walking shorts, one pair of shorts that doubled as a swimsuit (although I did break down and buy a European-style swimsuit once I hit the Turkish coast), one pair of blue jeans, one pair of black denim jeans, two long-sleeved shirts, one Arkansas Razorbacks sweat shirt (don't leave home without it), one pair of comfortable tennis shoes, one pair of lightweight slip-on canvas shoes for the beach (they doubled as house shoes), one beach towel, four pairs of socks, five briefs, several handkerchiefs, two cloth napkins, one carton of American cigarettes, eight packs of chewing gum, two rolls of toilet paper, a camera with zoom lens in a camera bag that doubled as a shoulder bag, a pocket-size radio-cassette player-recorder (Emerson makes them), nine blank cassettes, twelve extra long-life batteries, condoms, ten zip-lock bags, one large plastic bag for dirty clothes, one smaller bag for wet clothes, a journal, five pens, silverware (spoon, fork, knife that cuts, and bottle opener), miscellaneous foreign currencies and coins left over from previous trips, insect repellent, sleeping pills (noisy hotels and hostels can ruin a trip, especially in Greece and Turkey, which are noisy enough already), sunglasses, sunscreen, soft soap (for doing laundry), a paperback novel (by Mary Renault in this case — it's nice to read something set in the land of your visit), an address list, airmail stickers, a small photo album showing the area and people where I live, various toiletries (don't forget nail clippers!), a washcloth, maps (I used Kümmerly & Frey because they show both road and rail routes), a watch with an alarm, *Let's Go Greece and Turkey* and ripped out chapters of *Let's Go Europe*, a Peruvian friendship bracelet tied to my wrist by a genuine Peruvian friend, money (most of it in traveler's checks), a major credit card for emergencies, and one pair of Levi's I had long ago outgrown.

An interesting thing about life on the road is that you begin to notice how long products actually last. For instance, a regular-size deodorant stick, used by one person once or twice a day lasts about nine weeks.

Everything on this list was intended for my own use except the American cigarettes and gum — both of which are popular in Eastern and Southern Europe and make good simple tokens of appreciation — and, obviously, the old Levi's, which I intended to either bestow on some deserving person or, if I didn't run across a deserving person of the appropriate size, sell. I used everything on the list except the cloth napkins and silverware. In most of Europe, you would use those to prepare inexpensive bread-and-cheese meals to stretch your budget, but, where I went, food was cheap enough that I ate in restaurants. Unfortunately, I sent home the long-sleeved shirts and sweat shirt while at my brother's house in Germany, mistakenly thinking I wouldn't need them as I went south.

That had been another decision to make when planning the trip — whether to travel from north to south, experiencing the increasingly alien cultures in gradations, or to go from south to north, avoiding the heat and the packed beaches of Greece in August. I don't think I made the correct decision.

My decision to go from north to south was made, I think, because I was anxious to see my friends and my brother in the north. I flew first to Amsterdam, where I saw Daniela, Mark (whom I'd met in 1984 when we were both working for the same publisher and who, with his ex-lover, Leo, fixed me up with a squat in Zaandam after we'd both left the company), and Sander, who was eleven at the time and the son of Leo's ex-roommate. I then went to Delft to visit Wout, a university student who a year earlier was a high school exchange student living with me in Arkansas. From there, I went to the Mosel Valley to see my brother.

Ψ

I was in the middle of paradise, it seemed. From my hillside perch I had a wonderful view of the river in the valley below and the scrub hills beyond it. Across the road were several restaurants, all with grapevine canopies covering the outside terraces, and pink rose bushes in front to shield them from the lights of passing cars. Music drifted from each. On my own hill, besides other rooms, were two quaint restaurants with no signs other than chalkboards outside the doors indicating you could get food and drinks inside. Altogether, it was perhaps the most romantic spot I've seen. I was suddenly sorry that I was alone; this was the type of place meant to be shared with someone special.

I descended into the valley to select a place to sit and have a drink. Two of the restaurants had suave quartets — male vocalist, bass, drums, and goddamn accordion. I don't care much for suave, except in extremely good cases like Bryan Ferry singing "Sentimental Fool" or "2 H.B.," and it struck me that no one seemed to be having much fun in those places, so I went back to the restaurant where my long-haired friend still sat. He didn't seem to be having much fun in this paradise, either, listlessly playing a game of trying to flip matchboxes into a glass. It begged the question: Is paradise boring? Two older friends were with him, as well as an attractive younger boy of about sixteen who, midway through the evening, pulled a bright pink sweater over his head, pairing himself harmoniously with the roses and altering my perception of his character. He was the only one at the table who seemed interested in getting to know another foreigner, but he spoke no English. Too, there were mosquitoes in paradise. I expect Eden had mosquitoes even before Adam and Eve bit into the kumquat.

Around eleven p.m. I strolled back up my hill, happily surprised to find the restaurant still open and willing to serve me. I had a choice of trout or mixed grill. Although I was tired, too tired already, of the greasy Yugoslav grills, trout was too risky. I hate fish staring at me from the plate.

How, I wonder, do the Yugoslavs manage to look so healthy drinking beer until midnight, smoking heavily, and eating tons of sugar and grease?

Osjecko *pivo* wasn't bad, but the mixed grill came with bread that was like American white bread with the texture of angel food cake — some of the most tasteless bread I've ever tried in vain to taste. The meal was expensive, as I should have guessed, and I had to excuse myself to my room to get more money. *No problem!*

By the way, *Let's Go Europe 1989* says there are no buses from Mostar to Dubrovnik, making it seem as if you can't get there from here, for there definitely are no trains. The book suggests Mostar as a day trip from Sarajevo, which is ridiculous, as the journey's too long. There are, in fact, three direct buses from Mostar to Dubrovnik, and any number of indirect connections via Capljina or Kardeljevo. Perhaps they meant to write "trains." You cannot get to Dubrovnik from *anywhere* by train.

Ψ

I slept late the following morning, missing the breakfast that came with the price of the room. Actually, I had been awakened at six a.m. when my duplex neighbors got up. The walls are thin — but that, the bread, and the mosquitoes are my only complaints. I awoke to a wonderful view and the smell of flowers from the hillside and from the wildflower bouquet in my room. The proprietress gave me a strange look when I went to pay and said, "You slept well, I can imagine." I asked about the mosque's history. She told me that the reception area where we stood had been the caravanserai. Oddly, the name of this romantic spot was currently the Pocjtelj Motel, an unlikely and unfortunate choice. Perhaps *motel* sounds romantic to Yugoslav ears.

I took a bus to Capljina, a nothing town, but the one where I could catch a bus on to Dubrovnik. I wandered around the place for two hours while waiting on my bus; there was nothing to see. It was extremely hot, which had served at least one purpose for me overnight: The laundry I had washed in my damp Sarajevo room was finally dry.

I saw no one who spoke English in Capljina. I saw no other tourists. I exchanged money at a small bank, where the clerks acted as if they had never been called upon to perform that task before. They at least knew the rates, however, and I discovered that 50,000-dinar notes do exist in Yugoslavia (since my visit, inflation has forced the government to introduce a 100,000-dinar note).

Got a window seat on what promised to be the scenic side of the bus (the right side, heading south), then switched to the left side to avoid the sun. I drank a Coke. Hungary had been Pepsi country, but I was pleased to find that Coke ruled in Yugoslavia.

I abhor Eastern-style toilets. At this point in my journey, I had seen only four. All had been disgusting. I was, of course, to encounter many more along the way. Once in Turkey, my wish to avoid them grew to the point that I would walk for an hour around a town trying to locate the one place to stay that had a Western toilet. For anyone not familiar with the concept, Eastern toilets are merely a hole in the floor. There are places on either side of this hole where you are meant to plant your feet and squat. There is *never* toilet paper. If the natives are lucky, there is running water in the room. Children are taught to always clean their butts with their left hands and to always eat with their right. Left-handed people traveling in these lands might want to eat with their right hands to avoid funny looks. I always carried toilet paper with me, and avoided Eastern-style toilets altogether whenever I could.

My bus to Dubrovnik took back roads, including a gravel road up a steep mountain, and narrow roads on which it barely fit, through the mountain villages. It was wonderful: a parade of flowers, goats, chickens, roosters, white rock walls, white rock houses, and lots of children and shirtless young men all stopping whatever they were doing to stare at the bus. During the ascent on the gravel road, the driver played a tape of Arabic music — a nice touch, although this driver was in every other respect as unpleasant as the other Yugoslav bus drivers I encountered. The view was breathtaking! There was once again water in the valley below — and those beautiful scrub mountains! I love them. We stopped in the middle of nowhere a lot (which made me feel almost at home), and after eighty minutes, took a twenty-minute rest stop at a café. Niksicko *pivo* isn't bad, either.

The terrain in this part of Yugoslavia is a lot like that found around Santa Fe, New Mexico. If you saw the stupid 1973 film *Scalawag*, starring Kirk Douglas made to look like he had only one leg, and a very attractive Mark Lester, you've seen it. They filmed it here, one of a number of cheap westerns made in Yugoslavia. Why not? It's cheaper and looks considerably more like the American West than does Italy. The vegetation is short and unfriendly, much like my bus driver.

At some point coming out of the mountains we left Bosnia and Herzegovina and entered Croatia. It is odd to have been in the Croatian north — Zagreb, etc. — then to traverse the length of Bosnia and Herzegovina only to come out and be in Croatia again. Why didn't Bosnia and Herzegovina get some beach?

We hit the coast at Slano and made good time from there. But I was grateful for the long, bumpy journey. It had been wonderful — one of the most scenic overland journeys of my life.

G O S L A V I A

BOSNIA
• Sarajevo
o Počitelj HERZEGOVINA
• Mostar
• Čapljina
MONTENEGRO
Dubrovnik
Kotor
Titograd
Cetinje
Budva-
Bečići
Ulcinj
TIRANE
ALBANIA
GREE

KOSOVO
• Priština

• Skopje

MACED

Pella o

GREE

4

Dubrovnik, Montenegro, and Kosovo

I was expecting an incredible view upon entering Dubrovnik, but there was none on the route we took. Instead, I found myself at a dreary bus terminal without a clue how to get to the walled old town I had heard so much about. I was trying to hail a taxi when a woman approached and convinced me I would be better off taking a room in her house for ten dollars a night and walking to the old town from there. She said it was a ten-minute walk or two minutes by bus.

It was a long walk up a steep hill to her house, but the room was impeccably kept — probably the most luxurious I slept in all summer — with handsome furnishings and a balcony with another great view. I was drenched with sweat, so I took a shower then walked twenty minutes (not ten) to the old walled city on the peninsula. It was beautiful, just as I'd heard, but far too tourist-infested for my rooted tastes. Still, I had a pleasant evening strolling through the narrow lanes, listening to live music (mostly classical) from various restaurant courtyards, and touring art galleries. One gallery had some amazing chiaroscuros, but an exhibit titled "Poetic Realism" by a painter named Mirko Horvant was the best I saw, and the sounds drifting up the stairs from the orchestra in the courtyard next door made viewing it all the nicer.

At the Spaghetti Club I got a bad waiter who ignored me, so I moved to another table of the same outdoor restaurant and got a great waiter. The air was full of swallows, the streets (no cars in the old town) full of tourists, and my glass full of Nik Gold, another nice beer. The label said it was made in Yugoslavia for export, and had been "Imported by Triangle Wholesale Co., Inc., Kenosha, Wisconsin." Obviously, something had gone awry.

I bought postcards and wrote them at another courtyard place, trying to ignore the obnoxious upper-class Americans at the table next to me. The worst was a woman who looked like Nancy Reagan and had the same annoying voice — the kind that asks a question like "How do you *do?*" with such revolting speciousness that you want to spit back, "How do I do *what?*" The kind of woman who uses credit cards not because she can't afford to pay cash at the moment or because they're more convenient but because paper money is "too nasty." She had apparently been to every haunt of the rich in the Western world, and found them all "charming." When I hear the word *charming*, I can't help but recall the opening words from the television show "Good Morning America" on April 3, 1987: *Danny Kaye, endlessly charming, dead this morning.*

To avoid climbing that hill again, I found the correct bus to take me back to my room. Amazingly, I found the place again without difficulty. I also found one of the sexiest young men I've ever seen — he looked like a young Paul Newman — meeting me, shirtless, at the door. He lived there, the woman's son. Too bad he hadn't been around earlier to show me the town.

Ψ

Although there was much more English spoken in Dubrovnik than in Sarajevo, the natives didn't seem half as friendly. I expect they see too many tourists. I should mention that my visit to Dubrovnik did not coincide with their famous summer festival. Since it was too crowded with tourists for me already, I should think a visit during the festival would be a particularly painful hell.

When I awoke, it occurred to me that I did not really want to spend another day fighting the tourists, so I showered, informed my host through her adorable son that I would be leaving, paid, gathered my things, and trudged back down the hill to the bus station. I was in luck: There was a bus leaving at noon for Cetinje via Kotor. The bus station had a water polo club in the back part of the building, with glass windows separating the two. This created a weird effect at the ticket windows, with so many cute boys in swimsuits distracting one's attention. It was too early in the day to see so many attractive boys, all looking as wholesome as the Cracker Jack boy. I wondered why they were better-looking in Yugoslavia than in America. Healthier, maybe. All of that grease, sugar, and beer.

I had not seen anything very gay in Dubrovnik. *Spartacus* had not listed an exclusively gay club, and I had not found one, either. The Orlando, which it listed as mixed, was anything but gay when I went by the night before. The most interesting diversions in Dubrovnik, perhaps, are the young men leaning against the walls along the Placa (the main boulevard in the walled city) at night. But I expect almost all of those young men are straight. There just don't seem to be that many gays in this country. Yugoslavia is probably the straightest country I've ever visited.

While waiting for noon, I had a breakfast of the largest strudel I've ever seen (about three times as large as the ones back home, but not too sweet, so I was able to eat it all), another horrible *Turska kava* (coffee with grounds, the only way one could order it), and a cute little two-tenths liter Pepsi (roughly the size of the old six-ounce bottles).

Watching the passersby, it occurred to me that white socks were "in" for men this summer in Europe. Another fashion note: Shirt-tails were invariably tucked in, even if the shirt was a t-shirt.

Ψ

I had wanted to take the "Serpentine" road from Kotor to Cetinje, which is so winding it makes you dizzy just looking at it on a map. I had read that the view from the top of Mount Lovcen is "the most startling panorama in Europe." Therefore, I was careful when buying my ticket to Cetinje to take a map to the window with me, point to the road on which I wished to travel, and ask for a bus that traveled it. Although I was assured my bus did, it in fact did not.

The driver stopped after only a half hour of driving to take a half-hour break. Rather silly, I thought, suspecting the bus drivers must have special arrangements at these cafés they haul their passengers to, willing or not. They certainly don't pick them for the clean rest rooms.

Back on the road, we wound our way along the Adriatic to Herceg Novi. I had grown accustomed to the disappearance of the English language on this trip, but the sudden disappearance of the Roman alphabet took me slightly aback.

I had entered Montenegro.

Ψ

Perast is a beautiful town with ramparts and mountains behind it, situated at the back of a cove that takes the bus forty-four miles to circumvent. Perast, Kotor, Budva, and Becici are all, in fact, located in back of bays, with calm, salty Adriatic waters in front and bold scrub mountains in back. Kotor, however, looked more than a little bit dirty. To get out of Kotor and away from the bay, the bus was forced to climb one of the imposing mountains behind it (the coastline has no road for a stretch). After checking with the driver concerning our route, I decided to get off the bus at Budva, where I could at least find another bus making some approach on Mount Lovcen.

– 74 –

However, since I was on the coast and wanting a good salty swim, I decided to stay in Budva a night before setting off for the mountains.

The Roman alphabet had reappeared in Budva, due to the town's popularity with tourists, especially Germans booking package vacations with Jugotours, the national travel agent. The information office in Budva insisted I would have better luck finding a room in the sister town of Becici. Since I'd read that the beach at Becici was better, anyway, I set out to walk there. The town is about four miles by road, but by walking along the paved walkway skirting the beach and going through a tunnel, I was able to cut it to two miles — still a good distance carrying a pack in the heat of the day. The beach was lined with tourists and things for tourists — even a small soccer arena.

I was wet with sweat when I reached the disappointing hotel village of Becici. It wasn't what I expected, nor was it what I wanted, but I was too tired to go elsewhere. Finding a reception desk proved more of a hassle than one would think possible, but these hotels were not designed for the "walk-in" tourist. Here would be my first case of feeling weird for carrying my luggage on my back. I had received enough funny looks from the people along the beach. Now, the clerk in the first hotel I tried looked at me with something close to astonishment and said, "No rooms! Always full!" This was not encouraging.

The Hotel Montenegro, however, did have a room, although the desk clerk acted as if the last thing in the world he wanted to do was rent it to me. He quoted the price in German marks. When I asked for the price in dinar, which was, after all, the national currency, he gave me the price in British pounds. I persisted with the dinar, but the price quoted was outrageous — much more than the equivalent of the asking price in marks and pounds. I then inquired about American dollars and was given a more satis-factory answer. At twenty-seven dollars, the room did not fit my budget, but I could handle it for one night.

It was a nice enough room, with cold-water shower and toilet, balcony, and clothes closet. But the doorknob came off in my hand when I went to open it, and — for the money — one might have expected hot water. There *was* a hot water tap, but the only liquid I ever got from it was cold. Fortunately, it was hot enough on the coast that hot water didn't really matter.

After two days of watching others swimming in the Adriatic, I was anxious to get on with it, so I immediately went to the beach. Adriatic beaches, whether in Yugoslavia or Italy, are not the best in the world. In the northern Adriatic, there's pollution. In the south, beaches tend to be rocky, overrun with algae, or both. But the beach at Becici is great! It must have been, once, a little piece of paradise, when the people living here didn't have to share their heaven with thousands of tourists. If you swim a few yards from shore, it is still possible to block out the other swimmers, the hotels and tennis courts and bandstands and restaurants and souvenir stands, and to look at the majestic mountains surrounding you on two sides, the wide expanse of sea on a third, and the generous stretch of beach at Budva on the fourth, and marvel at the beauty of it all. The water itself was quite clear. There were many attractive boys.

Budva-Becici, however, is a *family* vacation spot. I would no more recommend it to the gay traveler than I would Myrtle Beach, South Carolina.

After my swim, I changed clothes and went in search of food. Had a "pizza Montenegro," which contained ham, cheese, mushrooms — and an egg in the middle. The egg didn't bother me until the final bites, when a sudden surge of nausea made me wish it hadn't been there.

What a horrible evening I had! This may once have been a paradise, but the Yugoslav government has turned it into a tourist hell on earth. Bad bands were playing everywhere. Families were everywhere. I walked along the beach and back through the tunnel (which smelled disgusting) all the way to Budva, but it was more of the same, although slightly more casual. Somewhere along the way, I had a *déjà vu* that didn't quite match up — sort of an "off" *déjà vu* — and that could not possibly have happened before. *Déjà vu*'s are strange enough in themselves — to have one in a land where you have never been certainly increases the feeling that life is playing tricks on you.

Returned to my hotel just to escape the crowds. Read the "Impressions" book at the front desk and found that most British tourists hated the place with a passion (they even complained about the food!). Many wrote cute poems, sarcastically setting their grievances to rhyme. Other tourists defended the Yugoslavs and complained about the British. Finding it disconcerting to be siding with the Brits, I declined to write anything. The song "We're All Prostitutes" was winding its way through my head again. The Yugoslavs have certainly profaned their coast.

I had planned to spend two days at Becici, but changed my mind. I asked at the desk about the check-out time, but neither clerk understood the term. When I tried to explain it, they both shrugged and one said, "I don't know."

As the rates included breakfast, I went next morning to find the hotel restaurant, having read several signs that said: "Breakfast and dinner is served at 'Buffet-integral' in the hotel restaurant." What I thought might be interesting turned out to be the final insult: a dormitory-style self-serve spread of bland, cheap food. I've had better in youth hostels (better rooms, too, for that matter). I felt so sorry for people who had purchased fourteen-day packages in this abomination. Breakfast was said to be served from seven until ten, but most of the food and coffee — and all of the juice — was gone by half past nine. They were snatching up plates before people had finished eating. They took my coffee as soon as I released the cup from my hand, still half full. I went and got another cup — the last one.

I was able, finally, to get a check-out time from a beautiful young man behind the front desk who reminded me of Rupert

Graves the way he looked as Freddy in *A Room With a View*. I had an hour, which I spent on the beach dreaming about the dreamy desk clerk. I wanted to take him home with me.

I was tempted to go farther down the coast to the town of Ulcinj, having heard that the village not only had black sand beaches rumored to possess healing qualities, but had black Yugoslavs, as well. It was strange and unsettling for me to be around nothing but white people, for the area in which I was currently living is seventy percent black. I had not seen a black person since leaving Germany — and most of those had been American soldiers. Steve, my brother, told me that several of the blacks I saw in Germany had once been U.S. soldiers and were now private citizens who had decided to stay in Germany because they felt blacks were treated better there than in America. Steve seemed to think they had a legitimate point. Many older Germans have never struck me as being particularly tolerant themselves, but the younger generation of Germans — including my sister-in-law, thankfully — seem to have become almost Scandinavian in their views concerning race, sexual orientation, ecology, and economy.

However, as Ulcinj is practically in Albania and therefore not on the way to anywhere, I abandoned the idea and took a taxi back to Budva, then caught a bus to Titograd. The bus climbed the huge mountain behind Becici that I had been gaping at from the water. There was an excellent view from the top, which was absolutely putrid with the overwhelming smell of wild flowers.

Titograd was a major disappointment. There was nothing to see, very little English spoken, and all schedules and information were in Cyrillic. My choices, both bad, were to waste a day there and take another tourist hotel (no private rooms to let in Titograd, I was told), or to take a bus to Skopje, arriving at eleven-thirty p.m. I assumed this would in reality mean at least one a.m. since nothing in Yugoslavia ever runs on time.

In another fit of impulsive inspiration, I inquired at both bus and train station on how I could get to Sofia, Bulgaria. They both told me to go to Skopje and take a train from there. The train information officer spoke no English, but when I showed him Sofia on the map, he took a keen interest and would not allow me to leave until he had checked half a dozen schedules, made two phone calls, and devised a schedule from purgatory whereby I would catch a train to Belgrade in the middle of the night, wait there a day, take another train to Skopje, spend the night, and take a train the next day to Sofia, arriving in the Bulgarian capital at four a.m.

Obviously, I had to go to Skopje one way or the other, and both ways were as inconvenient as one comes to expect in this country. Still, the bus made infinitely more sense, so I thanked the man for his time, gathered my bags, and returned to the bus station.

They never take your bags in Yugoslavia until the last possible minute, even if the bus is sitting in the gate three hours before departure. I left mine sitting unattended in the station and went to find a food stand. Had a terrible Yugoslav hamburger, but they had nothing to drink, so I then had to find a lemonade stand. These little convenience stands in Yugoslavia — and Turkey, too — are convenient only in their being there. You can't take the drink with you because they serve it in a glass mug that you're obviously meant to return.

The scenery on this bus journey was incredible. There can't be many countries in the world with more natural beauty than Yugoslavia. We followed a river gorge, with mountains above us, the river below, on winding, disquieting roads. As our altitude steadily increased, the temperature began to drop rapidly. Like a fool, I had not taken this into account and was still wearing the shorts and tank top I'd put on that morning on the coast.

It didn't take us long to reach the heart of mountainous Montenegro — beautiful, haunting mountains, a world unto themselves. There was an occasional village, but mostly there was only forest. In the middle of this thick, green nowhere would suddenly appear a small boy by the side of the road selling berries — or one might see a man with a goat. When it began to rain, the scenes began to resemble those from storybooks — long-haired shepherd boys hurrying home in the rain, jumping over sudden-born streams, appearing and disappearing amongst the trees. Still, we would pass the occasional small boy on the roadside with his berries, a parka pulled over his head. I've seen few things in life that struck me with a more overpowering melancholy than these lonesome small figures in the Montenegrin hills.

The temperature had now dropped to around fifty-five degrees. Everyone else was wearing a sweater or jacket, but all of my warmer clothes were in the luggage bin below.

We came to a good-size village, at which a boy got on and took the seat in front of me. I presented my map and asked him to show me where we were. He pointed to the town of Bijelo Polje, which was slightly off the most direct route to Skopje, then came to sit in the seat across the aisle, beginning a very short but somewhat important friendship. His name was Adax. His identification card, which he showed me at once when I had difficulty understanding his surname, indicated he was seventeen. His name was printed in both the Roman and Cyrillic alphabets; everything else was in Cyrillic.

Adax was a tall, considerate boy with a take-charge personality. Noticing that I was cold, he removed his sweater and insisted I wear it. He still had a warm shirt underneath, so I gladly agreed. He then took a pair of jeans from his bag and told me to put them on. Adax saved me from freezing. Within an hour the temperature had dropped into the forties, making me feel guilty for wearing his sweater. I was still cold even with it on, so he must have been cold, also. I loved the sweater — red and black wool, from Greece. When I told him how much I liked it he seemed very pleased. He explained that every bit of clothing he owned that was worth anything had been bought in Greece.

"In Yugoslavia, clothes very bad," he said.

Adax was on his way to some kind of camp located in Croatia, but, typically, had to travel 160 miles in the opposite direction to make his connection. I gathered all this information despite the fact that Adax probably only spoke about fifty words of English. His persistence and our combined ingenuity, however, allowed us to communicate fairly well.

The scenery continued to be outstanding, and then it was dark. Adax tried to sleep by placing his feet on the arm of the unoccupied chair in front of him, sinking down in his seat, and stretching out. An inviting ribbon of skin, including his navel, became visible between jeans and shirt. His head was turned toward me, long eyelashes closed upon angelic face, lips slightly parted.

We stopped twice at terrible dives, but in neither place was there time to order anything to eat, nor was there anything resembling fast food or snacks available. Thus, I had an eight-hour ride with no food. The toilets at both stops were unusable — Eastern-style with about twenty men crowded around each hole, watching and waiting their turn.

Ψ

Police cars passed us regularly, lights flashing. Strange sights began appearing by the side of the road almost like apparitions: tent caravans, buses pulled over by police, their passengers standing outside, faces flashing orange, blue, orange, blue in the police car lights. Buses were as frequent as trucks on American interstate highways. Three times we passed police cars leading long caravans of buses. Amazed by the numbers, I began counting after the first convoy passed. There were twenty-one buses in the second caravan, twenty-seven in the third. I had no idea what was going on. Yugoslav flags waved from a few. Since Jugoplastika Split had won the European basketball championship only days earlier, I ventured a guess.

"Basketball?"

Adax understood, but shook his head in the negative and made a motion with his hands to indicate "rolling." I didn't understand. He couldn't — or perhaps did not wish to — explain.

We had entered Kosovo, a region not a part of Yugoslavia by choice, but because since the twelfth century, Serbia — arguably the most imperialistic of the Yugoslav republics — has annexed it at every available opportunity. The population of Kosovo is seventy-three percent Albanian. Kosovo also has an ancient history in common with Albania, both having been part of the region known in antiquity as Illyria. Lately, the Albanian majority has been demanding greater independence at the same time as the Serbian minority has succeeded in urging Serbia to take greater control of the region. Riots and strikes have been the predictable result. Twenty-three people had been killed during clashes earlier in the year, after which Kosovo's legislature voted to give Serbia direct control over Kosovo's courts and police. Larger demonstrations had followed.

To be fair to the Yugoslav government, however, I should add that they haven't tried to assimilate the Albanians the way the Romanian and Bulgarian governments have tried to de-ethnitize their minority populations. The Albanians of Kosovo enjoy newspapers and radio programs in their own language; over thirteen hundred of Yugoslavia's nearly two thousand schools for nationalities are for Albanians (other nationalities with their own schools include Hungarians, Turks, Bulgarians, Romanians, Italians, Slovaks, Czechs, and Ruthenians). Yugoslavia has a ninety percent literacy rate, which is not as good as that of any of its neighbors except Albania. It is, however, better than the literacy rate for the women of Greece.

There is also the question of whether the majority Albanian population has been fair in its dealings with minorities living in Kosovo. The Turkish minority, for instance, complained in 1971 of pressures being exerted during the taking of the census. Also, claims of discrimination against Serbs have prompted Serbia to attempt an imposition of more control over Kosovo. I have no inside information regarding which side is right, but the fact that Slovenia, where homosexuality is legal, sides with the Albanians rather influences my opinion.

History indicates the ancient Illyrians were just as stubborn and fiercely independent as their modern descendants. Rebecca West, writing about native girls she had observed at the Roman ruins of Salonae, said:

> I am sure of it, those little girls were being taught that they should be proud because Split was the heir to a Roman city. Yet neither I nor anybody else knows whether or not the conquest of Illyria by the Romans was not a major disaster, the very contrary to an extension of civilization ... Little girls of Salonae, try to work out this sum on your fingers. It took Rome two hundred and fifty years of war to bring peace to the Illyrians.

History also records that the Illyrians were known to offer children as sacrifices. And it was history that went flying before me as we climbed and wound through these ancient mountains. I thought especially of the young Alexander the Great, who spent his time in exile here after publicly insulting his father, Philip II, on Philip's wedding night. Of the event, Mary Renault said, "An adolescent so sexually fastidious, and with the homosexual preference which marked this phase of his life, would hardly attend for fun a drunken Macedonian wedding with the prospect of seeing his father put to bed, amid the usual bawdy jokes, beside a girl younger than himself."

At a critical point on a mountain bend, with a beautiful lake beckoning from below, our road was washed out. The driver noticed it just in time to change into the lane for oncoming traffic, which was still intact. The ticket-taker on the bus used the moment to rid the bus of some trash, tossing it out the window into the lake. Twice before on this journey he had tossed litter from the windows. I would like to have tossed *him* out the window on his head. One wonders how much longer Yugoslavia's scenic beauty will remain.

We passed bridges of all descriptions, including swing bridges across deep gorges. Even at night, I would see a small boy walking alone seemingly in the middle of nowhere. What was he doing there?

I considered whether to get off in Priština, the capital of Kosovo, since my arrival there would not be as far into the middle of the night as arrival at Skopje. I decided to wait and see what Priština looked like before making the decision. Sadly, Priština looked like an armed encampment, from the little I could see of it. The station was heavily guarded, and didn't appear to be connected to any city. A family that I assume was either Albanian or Gypsy were the only passengers to get off in Priština. This family had looked very different from the other Yugoslavs on the bus, both in their features, which were dark and wrinkled, and in their dress, which was colorful and elaborate. They had constantly been dropping things: sacks, cans, water bottles, fruit — they sent all this and more, all *manner* of objects rolling down the aisles of the bus during their stay aboard it.

5

Macedonia

I entered Macedonia in the dead of night. Ancient Macedon. Home of Alexander the Great. Readers of Mary Renault novels will understand why I entered this land with dreamy visions of young athletic lovers swirling in my head: Alexander proving his friendship for Hephaestion by letting the latter hold his life in his hands as he dangled precariously over a cliff; King Philip II (Alexander's father) and Pausanius, when they were young.

Modern Macedonia is divided between Yugoslavia, Greece, and Bulgaria. Only the Yugoslav portion is a semi-autonomous republic; thus, the only Macedonia you will find on most maps of Europe is the Yugoslav Macedonia. The "Macedonian question" is perhaps the greatest cause of tension between Yugoslavia and Bulgaria. The Bulgarians insist the Macedonians are Bulgarians. When, in a recent census, the Bulgarians showed few Macedonians living in Pirin (Bulgarian Macedonia), the Yugoslavs accused them of "statistical genocide." Exactly how the Macedonians of Bulgaria feel about this is unclear. I've read that most of them tune in Macedonian radio broadcasts from Skopje to hear news and Macedonian folk music, but I've also read that when asked if they consider themselves Macedonian or Bulgarian, most will say they are Bulgarians. It was a question I hoped to answer, if I ever made it to Bulgaria. I did try the question on Macedonians in Yugoslavia and Greece, and without exception those I asked considered themselves Yugoslav or Greek, not Macedonian. It could be, then, that *Macedonian* in our time refers only to a language and a region, not a people.

The nationality question has been a problem for Yugoslav Macedonia from the opposite perspective: The question of national identity concerning Muslim Slavs in Macedonia has sometimes strained relations with the government of neighboring Bosnia and Herzegovina.

Macedonia has, perhaps, been fought over even more than the other Balkan regions. At one time or another, Rome, Byzantine Constantinople, Ottoman Turkey, Bulgaria, Serbia, Austria, and Greece have all laid claim to it. The Byzantine conquerors were perhaps the most ruthless. As Basil II extended his empire to include Bulgaria, he took fourteen thousand Slavs prisoner, blinded them, and sent them back to Tsar Samuel, who died soon afterward, broken down by the horror of it all. In this century, Bulgaria has three times tried and three times failed (the Balkan Wars, World War I, and World War II) to regain control of Macedonia to the Aegean Sea.

Rebecca West once wrote: "Macedonia should perhaps be looked on as a museum not typical of the life outside it."

Well, perhaps.

There was a disco near the bus station in Skopje with a steady flow of pedestrians heading for its doors. Other than that, the city, including the bus station, was deader than dead. I returned Adax's sweater and jeans. He left with another boy who, I think, had come to meet him. I found a taxi and managed to communicate that I needed a room. The driver kept repeating, "Name?

Hotel? Hotel name?" I kept repeating, "No hotel. Need hotel." Eventually he ushered me inside the cab. This, of course, was not the smartest thing to do. Had it not been the middle of the night, cold, with no hotel in sight, I would never have considered giving a cab driver *carte blanche* to find my room for me. Exactly what I didn't want to happen was exactly what happened. He took me to the far outskirts of town, a fifteen-minute journey, to some dump of a hotel called Hotel Camp Saraj. When I first saw the word "Camp" on the sign, and saw tents around me but no hotel, I almost cried, thinking I was now going to be forced to pay for another fifteen-minute cab fare back into town, and still have no hotel. But there *was* a hotel, and it certainly wasn't full. It was a dump, but it was an *expensive* dump — at thirty-five dollars, it was even more expensive than the coastal resort hotel at Becici. Still, I took the room. The taxi, needless to say, was expensive, too — around ten dollars. After paying the fare, I realized I didn't have enough dinar left to pay for the room. I assumed, however, that any hotel charging those prices would surely take credit cards or Western currency, especially given the obsession for Western currency of the hotel in Becici that had quoted its prices in German marks.

The guy at the desk at least spoke good English. I asked where I could buy a beer. Nowhere. His eyes met mine, then he said, "One moment," and, from a small refrigerator behind the desk, he produced a beer that I expect he had planned to drink later himself. He gave it to me and invited me to join him in an adjoining room to watch television. Although tired, I accepted, partially because of the young man's having given me his beer, partially because it was an increasingly rare opportunity to have a real conversation in English, and partially because I remembered Yugoslav television to be quite an interesting diversion.

I remembered, for instance, watching explicit sexual scenes one would never see on American networks, American cartoons dubbed into Serbo-Croatian, and long-haired news anchors with not a thought toward fashion reading the news copy without looking up.

He was watching a music video program from Zagreb that, for some reason, was being broadcast in English. They played Tone-Loc's "Funky Cold Medina" and several Yugoslav videos that weren't bad. I hoped to see something from the peculiar Yugoslav band Laibach, but did not. Their Balkanized versions of the Beatles' "Let It Be" album and the Rolling Stones' "Sympathy for the Devil" are hysterical; their original songs, even better. Unfortunately, the station switched to a film, in French with Serbo-Croatian subtitles. I asked if Skopje didn't have its own station, broadcasting in Macedonian. The answer was that there existed a Skopje television studio that produced several programs in Macedonian, but there were no Skopje stations. This was hard to believe. After all, Skopje was Yugoslavia's third largest city, with a population of 440,000.

I led him, eventually, into a discussion of the situation in Kosovo. His opinion was that the Albanians were terrorists. He said that he was a Yugoslav first, and a Macedonian second, but that the Albanians in Kosovo were selfish for not considering themselves Yugoslavs first. On other issues, he felt that Yugoslavia was being discriminated against because of its communist government by the West European countries that would not allow it into the European Economic Community. He wanted Yugoslavia to be part of a United Europe. He also believed Italy, Greece, and the United States were run and controlled by the Mafia, and felt capitalism and Mafia-control went hand-in-hand. I gave him a pack of Marlboros and went to bed.

The beer wasn't bad. The label was in Cyrillic (it did, however, have a computer price code), so I can't tell you what it was. My room, on the other hand, was quite bad, with peeling paint and plaster, no hot water, and a much-abused mattress.

Ψ

Before 1689, when General Piccolomini of Austria ordered it burnt to the ground, Skopje had been considered one of the most beautiful cities in Ottoman Europe. Today, following the 1963 earthquake that virtually leveled the city for a second time, this city of nearly half a million people is one of the ugliest in Yugoslavia.

I suppose the new buildings were constructed with the earthquake in mind; they certainly look capable of withstanding one. Every storefront resembles a bunker; every apartment seems to be awaiting Armageddon. Aside from these concrete monoliths, there is the litter and the air pollution, which seem especially awful here. Besides the general populace discarding their rubbish on the city's streets without a care, you have the Skopje Iron and Steel Mills and the seventeen factories of the Skopje Chemical Works spewing irritants into the air. (Tell me — isn't it slightly insane to construct seventeen chemical factories in a city known to be earthquake prone?) There are other factories manufacturing furniture, buses, tobacco, glass, and cement in Skopje. The combined effect is reminiscent of what many American cities looked like before we began to give a damn. The Macedonians appear to have a long way to go, and one wonders if they will begin caring about their environment soon enough to save it.

I tried to sleep late, although Arabic music kept interfering with my dreams from about seven-thirty on. When I went down to pay I discovered that my friend had departed, replaced by a woman who hardly spoke English at all. Of course, I had no right to expect her to, but I was kicking myself for not having asked the man last night about credit cards and payment. I tried to pay with my VISA. She pointed to an American Express sign. I tried to pay with American Express traveler's checks, but she wanted nothing to do with them. Instead, she sent me out to find the Hotel Grand, where she said I could exchange money. I think what she actually said was, "You, Hotel Grand, exchange, dinar," but I knew what she meant. I asked for my passport, but she said, "No, no, no. You, Hotel Grand, exchange, dinar, passport." The problem was that it is nearly impossible to exchange money without a passport, but I wasn't sure which would be more impossible, trying to exchange the checks or trying to make her understand the problem. I decided to go on to the hotel without my passport, and hope that someone there spoke English so that I could have them call the hotel to verify my identity.

Finding the Hotel Grand, however, proved to be a considerable problem. She said it was three kilometers, which turned out to be a nasty lie. It was actually about five miles, but I never found it, in any case. I kept asking directions, and kept getting conflicting information. I ran across one "exchange office," but the man at the counter said he couldn't help me.

"Hotel Grand," he said, making a motion with his hand as if to shoo me out the door.

I pointed to the lettering on the window and said, "Exchange office."

"No exchange," he said. "Hotel Grand."

After I had walked almost two hours, I found a young man who spoke decent English. He told me I had been badly misled and was far from the Hotel Grand. Infuriated, I turned around to retrace my steps. I hopped on the first bus that came along, not knowing where it was going. If it departed from my road, I planned to get off at the first stop and go back. For once, however, my luck was good; the bus took me within half a mile of the Hotel Camp Saraj. I walked back past the children dressed in colorful native clothes and the donkeys and chickens that had been my first view of Skopje that morning, then had a wild scene at the hotel desk, demanding my passport while the woman behind the counter demanded dinar.

A compromise was reached in which I agreed to ride with the dirty laundry to the Hotel Grand, exchange the money, and then be on my way. The driver would hold my passport until I handed over the dinar, but would accompany me to the exchange window.

Why I had to stay in the one hotel in Eastern Europe not frantic for Western currency, I don't know. I did, at least, see a large slice of life in Skopje that morning. What I missed on my two-hour walk, I got a glimpse of while making the laundry run.

Even here, the young were rather fashion-conscious. It seemed totally beside the point, amid the surroundings, but you could tell quite easily that *fa-fa-fa-fashion* ruled their lives.

The laundry driver did not take me on to the train station, as I hoped he might. I walked, arriving just in time to miss the only train to Sofia. I had not eaten since the awful "breakfast-integral" at Becici. At the station I found a restaurant and ate enough food for two meals, contemplating what to do. The train schedules were all in Cyrillic, but I stared at them until I felt fairly certain there was a train leaving for Thessaloníki, Greece, at five p.m. It was either that or find a place to spend another night in Skopje, a hideous thought. I bought a ticket, even though I would again be arriving in the middle of the night.

The park opposite the rail station, which *Spartacus* lists as "very cruisy," was peopled only by two very old men sitting on a bench, with looks of malevolence on their faces. I wondered what they were thinking.

There are, of course, no gay bars in Skopje.

The train was two hours late, but while waiting on it I had the good fortune to meet a couple of travelers who spoke English and were also bound for Thessaloníki. Gina was from California and had been traveling in Europe for three years. Of Italian ancestry, she had a beautiful dark complexion and looked more than a little like Gabriela Sabatini, the Argentine tennis star. Donach was from Ireland and planned a three-year journey to Australia, via Turkey, Saudi Arabia, and India. Both were twenty-four and quite friendly. They had met earlier in the day. With them was a muscular Austrian named Gregor, but he was going to Athens, whereas Gina and Donach were headed for Thessaloníki.

I can't say I made the best of first impressions on Gina. She offered me a drink of her orange juice, which I accepted. But when I tried to take the carton from her, I grabbed it in the middle, not realizing how full it was, and the pressure sent sticky juice all over her arms, legs, and carry bag (an hour later a drunken English boy would spill a cup of coffee on the same bag, sending poor Gina into a near rage).

An old man told us that a vacant railway car sitting up the tracks would be added to the train once it arrived and that we could beat out the hordes waiting to board the train by claiming seats on it now. Without waiting for us to think it over, he grabbed most of our packs and began walking toward the car. We grabbed the other bags and followed. We gave him a large tip, which is obviously what he expected, but when our train arrived and nobody came for our car, we got nervous and abandoned it, making a run for the train. It turned out the man was telling the truth. After we'd frantically run to the train, squeezed on, and watched the boy spill coffee on Gina's bag, we had to wait while an engine was dispatched to fetch the car. We got off the crowded car we were on and hopped aboard the new arrival while it was still moving. Carrying packs on our backs, it was a dangerous thing to do, but I think we'd all had our share of standing on Yugoslav trains. We secured a compartment for the four of us as the throngs clambered on board behind us.

Gregor kept buying us beer, all the way from Skopje to Thessaloníki. I managed to buy a round, with *kebabs*, but Gregor bought three or four rounds, shrugging off our protests by saying he didn't like to drink alone.

We arrived in Thessaloníki at one-fifteen a.m. A guy named Nick approached us in the station and talked us into staying the night at his place for about eleven dollars each. There seemed to be something strange about him, and it wasn't just his Australian accent or Cheshire grin. I don't think any of us would have accepted his offer had we been alone, but we were tired and were counting on safety in numbers.

Thessaloníki, like all Greek cities, is noisy. The Greeks seem to thrive on noise. Cars seem to have no mufflers. Horns sound for no reason other than the general thrill it provides the driver. Conversations are carried on, whether at a distance or in close quarters, at volume levels usually reserved for the partially deaf. Loudspeakers blast music into the night. Children shriek. In "On a Greek Holiday" Alice Bloom wrote that the two things one would most want to avoid in Greece during the summer are "the intense heat and the unworldly, unimaginable, unforeseeable amount of din." She went on to report that "two Greeks together produce more noise than 200 of any other Western nation."

As we sped through the bustling street, the car horns blaring, the flashing lights and crowds of people struck me as unlike anything I'd ever seen except in Mexico. Our taxi, which Nick was paying for since none of us yet had drachma, played Greek music very loudly. For the moment, I enjoyed it. It seemed as if we were in someone's film.

Nick's place was modern enough, although dirty. The rub was that he'd told us he had plenty of beds, when in fact all he had was two mattresses. Gina got one. Without asking for it, I somehow got the other. I still didn't sleep very well, but it beat the train station floor, and Nick *did* have hot water — the first I'd felt since Sarajevo.

Nick fixed breakfast hurriedly the next morning, explaining that the banks closed early. He told Donach and me that we didn't have time to shower, but we both took one anyway, although mine was so quick that Nick thought I only washed my hair. While we were eating, a woman banged on the door calling Nick's name. He said it was his aunt and that we should ignore her. We tried to. He gave us information, including pamphlets, on Greece and Turkey. He claimed his job was "helping tourists." We never trusted him, but with the exception of misleading us about the bed situation, he did us no harm.

Nick went with us to the bank, naturally, and then showed us to the youth hostel, not upset at all that we weren't going to be using his services for another night. The hostel did not open until seven p.m., so we left our packs there and went walking.

I wanted to find the statue of Alexander on the waterfront, so we walked toward the sea. The water was dirty and stank, but the statue of Alexander was impressive. From there, we went to the Archaeological Museum, which was worth seeing if only for the treasures discovered in 1977 at the royal tomb in Vergina, believed to have been the tomb of Alexander's father, King Philip II.

Back on the streets, we marveled at the clutter of antennae adorning every roof. Cable television obviously had not come to Thessaloníki.

I had no trouble getting in the youth hostel without a hostel membership card. I don't usually like to stay in them because of the early curfews, but at four dollars a night, it wasn't a bad deal. Returned to the streets of Thessaloníki at night, amazed by the life pulsating through every crevice of the city (and amazed, too, at Donach's carefree penchant for walking into the path of speeding cars).

Greek boys are fine, make no mistake. I would have liked to have found a gay bar, but had no information on where to find one (*Spartacus* doesn't list one, although it does list a gay cinema, the Ilion Cinema on Vardaris Street), and couldn't have gone in any case, since the youth hostel locked its doors at eleven. In fact, after walking for two and a half hours, we had to run half the way back to the hostel in order to get a shower by the ten p.m. cutoff time. Spend a day and night walking through Thessaloníki in the summer and see if you want to go to bed without a shower. In a hot room with five other guys, you hope they all feel the same way.

Ψ

I would be using the sleeping pills just about every night from now until I left for home two months later. Greece and Turkey are the noisiest countries I ever hope to see. I thought I'd never go to sleep that night in the youth hostel, even after taking the pill. The crescendo of noise lessened only gradually, but it picked up again with a crash and bang about six-thirty a.m., and there was no sense even trying to sleep after that. I got up and walked next door for coffee, over which I extracted all the information we would need for the day from *Let's Go Greece*. I got Donach out of bed at eight, and Gina joined us about nine. Each reported having slept in fits and starts, not only because of the noise, but also because of the heat and bedbugs.

After checking each other's plans, it was decided the three of us would go to Istanbul together, since we had all planned to go there at some point during the summer anyway. My only hesitation was that I wanted to see Bulgaria, having already obtained a visa, and now I would be more or less bypassing it. I decided I could see it at the end of my trip if I still wanted to then. We checked the bus schedules to Istanbul, then caught a bus for a day trip to Pella, where once stood the palace of Philip II and Alexander.

I don't know why I expected mountains, knowing it had once been a port city (it's about twenty miles from the coast now). The physical landscape did not match my expectations. It wasn't very pretty, and there wasn't much to see. You've got to assume, however, that it didn't look the same twenty-two hundred years ago, when Alexander roamed the area on his horse, Bucephalas.

The mosaics, nevertheless, were impressive, as was the mere idea of being there. As we walked through the ruins, I related stories from Alexander's life to Gina and Donach. Gina was surprised by the bisexual element that kept recurring, but Donach told her it was accepted at the time.

"That's strange," she said, "that they accepted it back then but we don't now."

I let it go at that.

Ψ

Plutarch dates Alexander's birth to July 20, 356 B.C., citing as his source Hegesias of Magnesia, an early Alexander biographer whose work has not survived. The ancient Macedonians are said to have been from a blond Dorian tribe. Plutarch describes Alexander as blond, "shading to ruddy on the breast and face," and with a "droop of the neck to the left and the melting eye." His "melting" eyes were gray, his hair, thick and wavy. He was clean-shaven. Legend has it that he ordered the entire Macedonian army to shave because he didn't like facial hair. The memoirs of Aristoxenus tell us that Alexander liked a daily bath and that a pleasant scent came from his skin. Arrian simply states that he was very handsome.

Historians agree that Alexander loved physical pursuits, and was himself extremely athletic, although he did not care for specialized Olympic physiques, preferring the more balanced classical appeal of Greek sculpture. Alexander loved music and theater, and liked staying up late and sleeping late. He also loved books, and slept with a copy of *The Iliad* beneath his pillow (he kept a dagger there, as well). The friendship of Achilles and Patroclus apparently served as a model for his own relationship with his lifelong friend, Hephaestion, whom Curtius describes as being taller and even more handsome than Alexander. Alexander thought so highly of Achilles that he claimed to be a descendent of his through Neoptolemus, founder of the Molassian dynasty (Macedonian kings also claimed descent from Hercules, whose myths include at least fifteen episodes involving male lovers). According to Plutarch, Alexander said of Achilles, "[He was] happy in having a faithful friend while he lived and a glorious herald of his deeds when he was dead," referring, of course, to Patroclus and Homer, respectively. Although Arrian saw the purpose of his life as being Alexander's "glorious herald," it wasn't until the twentieth century that his legend received the literary attention it deserved. Mary Renault brought the triumph and passion of Alexander's life into the hearts of modern readers with her brilliant novels, *Fire from Heaven* and *The Persian Boy*, and the nonfiction biography, *The Nature of Alexander*.

Renault believes Alexander came to be king as an indirect result of a homosexual relationship of his father, King Philip II. Philip's one-time lover, Pausanius, was jilted in favor of a younger man, whom Pausanius insulted at a drinking party, calling him a paid whore. To prove that he wasn't, the new favorite ran ahead of Philip in battle to certain death, leaving behind a note explaining what he had done. To avenge his death, friends of the king got Pausanius drunk, then threw him in the stable and invited the slaves to fuck him. Pausanius, according to this story, saved his revenge for many years, but eventually murdered Philip, giving Alexander the throne.

It is clear that Alexander valued friendship above all else. His near-fatal fit of grieving at the death of Hephaestion is proof enough. Plutarch says of his other friends that those who asked for anything were "treated so generously that most of what he owned in Macedonia he distributed and spent," and that some friends thought he was foolishly generous, refusing to accept his gifts. Renault wrote: "He grew up with a religious faith in friendship, making it a cult, publicly staking his life on it. The real loves of his life were friendships, including his sexual loves."

Arrian, reporting information from Alexander's earlier biographers, tells us that when Hephaestion died, Alexander "flung himself on the body of his friend and lay there nearly all day long in tears, and refused to be parted from him until he was dragged away by force," that he "lay stretched upon the corpse all day and the whole night too," that he cut his hair short in mourning (as Achilles had when mourning Patroclus), that he ordered sacrifice "to be always offered to Hephaestion as a demi-god," and that he "sent to inquire of Ammon if he would permit sacrifice to be offered to him as a god; but Ammon refused." Further, Arrian says that Alexander ate nothing for three days, but lay on his bed alternately weeping and "in the silence of grief." Later, Alexander held Funeral Games in Hephaestion's honor, in which three thousand men competed. Plutarch adds that he had an enormously expensive funeral pyre prepared in Babylon and proclaimed a period of mourning throughout the East.

Ψ

At the indoor museum, I managed to take a few photographs before the guards intercepted me and insisted I stop. Donach had gone crazy with his camera at Pella, taking photos of every column and mosaic outside. The mosaics were, indeed, something to see — especially those in the museum. The lion hunt mosaic depicts a scene believed to involve a young Alexander with his friend Krateros when Alexander slew his first lion. It is amazing how colored pebbles can so deftly portray muscle tone, in both the lion and the two nude youths. The deer hunt mosaic is just as astonishing, with the nude hunters even more attractive than those depicted in the lion hunt. The mosaic of Dionysos riding a leopard isn't bad, either.

We took the bus back to Thessaloníki. I checked the schedules to Sofia, in case I was able to go later on. The bus cost about one-fourth the price of the train, but they only ran two buses per week.

Our bus to Istanbul was a nice one, but arrived in Thessaloníki two hours late. I listened to the Voice of America on my radio headphones for a while, then switched to Gregorian chant music on another band once V.O.A. began broadcasting in Romanian. Across the aisle from me a friendly-looking guy sitting beside his girlfriend was also fidgeting with his radio dial. I was impressed enough with the chants to suggest the radio frequency to him, but it turned out he was listening to shortwave. He switched bands and found the station. When he let his girlfriend have a listen, we began a conversation, and that's how I came to know Richard from Chicago, who was presently teaching English in Spain, and his girlfriend, Ester, who was from France. Gina, meanwhile, was talking to people all around us. She had a natural talent for meeting people that made me envious. It was clear she would always have friends wherever she was in the world.

While messing with the radio, I noticed that Radio Moscow Foreign Service was being jammed across the AM dial. In fact, after leaving Yugoslavia, I was never again able to pick up one of their signals.

We passed near Arethoussa in the region of Lake Volvi, where a thirteen-year-old Alexander once studied, with Hephaestion and several other boys, under a forty-year-old Aristotle. If I had been in a car, I would have driven to the spot, for I had directions, of a sort, to the ruins of the school and to the hot springs where Alexander once bathed. For those interested, these directions may or may not get you there, but it's worth a try: Go to Karpanos, take the second turnoff, go right at the T-junction by the church and school, and incline right through the orchards past the bend to the natural amphitheater, where lie the ruins. Aristotle is said to have written Hephaestion enough letters in later years — when Hephaestion was on campaign with Alexander — to fill a book, though none of the letters have survived. We know of them only from other historians having mentioned them. What *has* survived is a fragment from one of Hephaestion's letters to Olympias, Alexander's mother, in which he tells her, "Stop quarreling with me; not that in any case I shall much care. You know Alexander means more to me than anyone."

Kaválla looked like a nice port city in which to spend a couple of days, but we stopped instead at Xanthi, which is nicely situated with hills behind it, but not as attractive as Kaválla. Alexandroúpolis — which is *not* named after Alexander the Great, by the way — was bustling, but we didn't see much of it. We were now in Thrace, the legendary birthplace of Orpheus and home of Eurydice.

The border crossing was a ridiculous hassle. At one a.m. the entire bus was unloaded and everyone made to collect their bags from underneath. They gathered our passports, then we stood outside with ferocious bugs biting our legs for almost an hour, until a Greek guard lazily looked through our open bags. Our passports were thrown on a table for us to grab, which did not go over too well with some of the older passengers, who couldn't see well enough in the dim light to tell which were theirs. I took it upon myself to match passport to older traveler, and was thanked profusely. We put the bags back in the bus, drove maybe thirty yards, then had to get out and repeat the process for the Turks. I had been a little worried about prescription drugs, such as the sleeping pills, but the Turkish guards only played at looking through our bags — they couldn't have cared less what we brought across, it seemed.

During the delay, we were able to change money; therefore, when the bus stopped at two-thirty a.m. for us to eat, we all had money for the occasion. This would be my first experience with the Turkish custom (actually, they do it in Greece, as well) of going back to the kitchen to select your food. It's much better than trying to decipher a menu in a foreign language. Gina had met enough people by this time that we were eight at the table — six of whom would end up helping me celebrate a birthday in Istanbul in a couple of days. The restaurant tables were outdoors, but for some reason the bugs that had made a meal of our legs on the Greek side of the border were not bothering us here. There were, however, half a dozen cats climbing around on the tables. Like the Egyptians, the Turks appear to love cats — they're everywhere. You rarely see a dog. Personally, I prefer the warm goofiness of canines. The abundance of cats and scarcity of dogs in Turkey would begin to annoy me after a few days.

I A

Bosphorus Strait

Istanbul

ACE Tekirdağ
Alexandroúpolis
Sea of Marmara
ceabat Gallipoli
(Gelibolu)
Çanakkale Bursa   T   U
TROY

an
a Ayvalik
Bergama

6

Istanbul — Sultanahmet

I didn't get much sleep on the bus. Of the eight of us now more or less grouped together, only Gina slept soundly, leaning on me through much of the night.

I had hoped we would go through Edirne. My only real interest in the city was that it had been founded by the Roman emperor Hadrian (he named it Hadrianopolis) during one of his many tours. Hadrian, generally regarded as the noblest of the Roman emperors, made it a point to travel through every Roman territory without the trappings of his position. Of the many early Roman emperors known to be bisexual (the first fourteen, apparently), Hadrian alone is thought to have preferred males almost exclusively. His love affair with the youth Antinoüs was known and admired throughout the empire during his reign, and the beauty of Antinoüs was celebrated by painters and sculptors everywhere (see the statue at the museum in Delphi, Greece, and you will surely understand why). Antinoüs drowned crossing the Nile in Egypt — whether accidentally or on purpose, history is uncertain.

The burnt-orange Aya Sofia was constructed in A.D. 532 by the emperor Justinian (who in A.D. 533 was the first to forbid homosexuality in Byzantium). For many years, until St. Peter's Cathedral was built in Rome, the Aya Sofia boasted the world's largest dome.

Like Achilles and Alexander before him, Hadrian went mad with grief when his young lover died.

I gather from what I've read that the museums and statues in Edirne are devoted to the city's Islamic past (it served as the Ottoman capital in 1363), not its Roman. In any case, I could not have seen much of Edirne at three-thirty a.m.

There was a beautiful view when we first came over the coastal mountains to the city of Tekirdag. The lights on the road below made me think it was a bridge, which fooled me into thinking we were looking down upon Istanbul. Actually, the Sea of Marmara was to the right of us and Istanbul almost one hundred miles east. The landscape looked fluid in the early dawn.

We arrived in Istanbul about six-thirty a.m. The eight of us were immediately besieged by several taxi drivers, all asking ten thousand lira (five dollars) per cab to take us into Sultanahmet, the old sector of Constantinople where we had made up our minds to stay. We tried to haggle, having been told by everyone that you simply *must* haggle in Turkey, but they wouldn't budge. I looked around for a *dolmus*, for I had read that the *dolmus* — a minibus carrying ten or twelve passengers heading in the same direction — was the cheapest method of traveling short distances in Turkey. This information is true, but there was not a *dolmus* in sight. With the negotiating for a taxi deadlocked and eight sleepy tourists staring at each other bleary-eyed, wanting someone else to decide what to do, a driver grabbed my pack and took off in a trot, leaving me no choice but to follow. I yelled for him to stop. He didn't. He was going so fast through the crowd, I didn't have time to consult with the others or turn to see if they were following me, for fear of losing sight of him. The bus station, like every other part of Istanbul, was swarming with people. Walking in a straight line anywhere was absolutely impossible. I had half a mind to tackle my pack-snatcher when I caught up with him, but his years of experience darting through crowds kept him well ahead of me until we reached his cab. Instead of jumping on him, I simply hurled insults at him, pissed off not only because he'd taken my pack without my permission, but also because I thought I was now very much alone in Istanbul, and I had rather liked Donach, Gina, and the people from the bus.

But I wasn't alone, for Elena (from New York) and Samuel (from Paris) had tailed me, and Gina was following them. Cheered slightly by their arrival, I stopped cussing at the driver and allowed him to cram our packs into the small trunk of his taxi. Then, we ourselves crammed into the small cab and were immediately whisked away on an absolutely insane eighty-mile-per-hour race through the early morning streets of Istanbul, shortly to be deposited in the middle of Sultanahmet, with Aya Sofia and the Blue Mosque towering majestically on either side of us. It had been one jolt after another, and seeing these two architectural wonders standing in such close proximity was the biggest jolt of all. The burnt-orange Aya Sofia (also referred to as Santa Sophia and Hagia Sophia) was constructed in A.D. 532 by the emperor Justinian (he was the one who first passed laws in Byzantium — in A.D. 533 — forbidding homosexuality, possibly because several of his political rivals were homosexual). For many years, until the building of St. Peter's Cathedral in Rome, the Aya Sofia boasted the world's largest dome. The Blue Mosque is a seventeenth-century attempt by Sultan Ahmet I to eclipse Justinian. Today, facing each other across the courtyard, they epitomize the face-off between Christianity and Islam that has been taking place in this part of the world for centuries. Symbolically for Turkey, however, the Blue Mosque continues to serve its original purpose, while Aya Sofia has become a museum.

We had not enjoyed the opportunity, of course, to establish a meeting place with the other four people in our group, which included Donach. We waited a while, during which time we watched several more taxis screech around curves carrying frightened tourists, some cars with their trunks full of packs and their trunk lids flapping stupidly up and down — but none arrived with our companions.

A couple of Turks wanted to show us rooms. Unfortunately, they were wanting to show us rooms in opposite directions. We let them work it out among themselves, and finally left with a very polite older gentleman, who told us if we didn't like his rooms we could come back where we were and go with the younger man to his hotel.

The hotel he took us to had just opened and had huge wreaths of congratulatory flowers in front of the building to prove it. One was from the local Coca-Cola bottler, we noticed with mild amusement. Still, the rooms were not exactly what we had in mind, so we told him we would look around and come back if we were interested. As we approached the square where the taxi dropped us off, who should we see but the young hotel hawker with the other four members of our party in tow. We did, eventually, take a room at the Pension Side run by him and his two brothers — after much looking around comparing prices and relative comforts.

One major consideration was water. The water system in Istanbul is designed to serve two million people, while the city has almost six million full-time residents, not to mention tourists. Some hotels have their own reservoirs, which helps somewhat, but these hotels are hard to find, and just because a hotel has a private reservoir doesn't necessarily mean the management will always find water to fill it. Curiously, the only hotel with a reservoir we could find in Sultanahmet was also the dirtiest hotel we found in Sultanahmet, so we took a chance on the other, cleaner hotel without a reservoir. It was nice enough, but besides the water shortage, they also had problems with their doors. While we were waiting for a room to become available, another couple checked out because their door would not open and they were tired of having to climb in and out through a window. We didn't get that room. The room we did get was probably the nicest in the hotel — four single beds were lined around a corner with three huge windows looking toward the Blue Mosque. Gina, Donach, and I were sharing this room with Jeff, an American who was meeting a woman the next day with whom he planned to travel across Turkey. The others in our party had chosen another hotel, although Richard and Elena, unhappy with their choice, would switch the next day to ours.

On the advice of another hotel guest, we first went to the nearby Interyouth Hostel to obtain Youth International Educational Exchange (Y.I.E.E.) cards. These cards are necessary to obtain student discounts in Turkey because the country does not honor the International Student Identity Card (I.S.I.C.) recognized by virtually every other country one might choose to visit. I had not intended to get a card, since one is supposed to be a student and under the age of twenty-six, and I was neither. But when neither Gina nor Donach was asked to produce proof of either, they urged me to give it a try. Nothing to it. This one-dollar card probably saved me seventy dollars over the course of my stay in Turkey, for it gets free entrance into a considerable number of museums and sites, including Topkapi Palace and the Archaeological Museum in Istanbul, and the ruins at Ephesus and Bergama. Sure, it's dishonest producing a student card when one is not a student, but it's also dishonest for Turkey not to recognize the international student card used in most other countries. I can rationalize with the best of them.

The Interyouth Hostel is a world unto itself, with its own Turkish baths, rooftop bar and café, t-shirt shop, travel agency, and the only reliable international telephone service I found in all of Istanbul (the post office at the Istanbul Hilton, for instance, won't allow you to call collect, insisting that you buy tokens to pay for your call — grooved tokens that must be inserted into grooved slots so rapidly, if you're calling America, that it's impossible to do that and talk at the same time). Any night of the week you can find youth from all over the world on the hostel roof drinking beer and talking loudly over the incongruous Western rock and roll that the hostel blares into the night over loudspeakers. It's not much of a Turkish experience, except for the fact that it's probably the most commercialized youth hostel you will ever run across, and it's in Turkey. Donach's Irish sensitivities did not disappoint me — he hated it.

Ψ

Istanbul is one of the world's most incredible cities. It's hard to know where to begin when trying to transfer its essence to paper. Above all, I think, it is sound and smell. Minarets equipped with loudspeakers blare calls to prayer half a dozen times a day, the muezzins intonating in those sorrowful, droning, Middle Eastern, Middle Ages, snake-charmer vocals. It is this constant reminder that you are no longer in the company of Christians, more than anything, that will make you feel you are far, far from home, the stranger in a very strange land. The novelty of it thrills you at first, but after the second day of being awakened before dawn by the calls to prayer, you are cursing Islam, ready to strangle the muezzin.

As in Greece, the noise is often deafening. Cars honk for any reason or for no reason. Mufflers, if they exist at all, don't muffle

– 106 –

— especially on the motorbikes. Everywhere you go, someone wants to sell you a carpet or a leather jacket or postcards. They want to give you a shave or direct you to a restaurant or shine your shoes — even if you're wearing tennis shoes. They have this white paste that, they tell you, will make your Reeboks look like new. It will actually make your Reeboks look like shit; it will make your Reeboks look as if someone has covered them with white paste. But if you hesitate, you're lost — they will already have slapped a dab of paste across the toe of your shoe, giving you the choice of submitting to their "shine" or walking around Istanbul with one scuffed Reebok and one Reebok with a shiny white toe.

Methods are subtle. To get you into a carpet shop, a young boy may first tell you he is brushing up on his English. "You from America? — Where in America? — America good. How long you in Turkey? — You like Turkey? — You come from America, now, please, you come with me, we have tea. — Apple tea, if you like. — You follow me. My uncle's shop over here. He give you tea." Before you know it, you're sitting in his uncle's carpet shop, drinking his tea, answering the same questions ("You from America? Where in America?"). Then you're shown carpets. It's the same thing over and over every minute of every day that you're on the streets of Istanbul. The first time, of course, you end up looking at the carpets. After that embarrassing or aggravating experience, you pretend you don't understand English, or try to brush off the initial questions without being rude. When that doesn't work, you become rude. Even if in every other way you are in love with Istanbul, this constant badgering will wear on you. It will also make you suspicious of the motives of every Turk you meet. This is difficult and unfortunate, for the Turks seem to be divided evenly into two camps: those who are among the nicest, friendliest people you've ever seen on this God-forsaken planet, and those who will go to any lengths to rip you off. Unfortunately, the first three sentence fragments either group will say to you are the same, and if you listen to more than three

Street vendors in Istanbul sell everything imaginable, from *kebabs* and roasted corn on the cob to clothes, toys, and jewelry.

sentences from the latter, it's often difficult to extricate yourself from their presence.

I'd much rather talk about the first group.

Where but in Turkey have I stayed at a hotel in which the owner tried to talk me into staying in his country and drove me to a job interview he had set up at a university? This same hotel owner went dancing with Gina and me in the evenings and, when we left Istanbul, drove us to the bus station.

Where but in Turkey have I been befriended by a handsome soldier who spent virtually his entire week's leave with me, giving me rides in his father's boat and generally taking care of me?

Where but in Turkey have I encountered a young waiter who was so concerned with my happiness that he stayed at my table through much of the meal in case I should need anything — except when he left momentarily to run down the street and pick for me a flower?

Where but in Turkey has a total stranger, a handsome straight boy who knew he would never see me again after that evening, insisted on showing me all over town and absolutely refused to let me pay for anything?

That is Turkey. The fact that all these good people live side by side in the same country with some of the world's most disgusting slumbuckets just attests, I think, to the general yin and yang of life: Where there are hills, there will be valleys. If you want the dull security of the plains in life, spend your vacation in Nebraska. It was another, better-known chronicler by the name of Paul Bowles who wrote from India in 1952, "Security is a false god; begin making sacrifices to it and you are lost."

Bowles probably wouldn't have mentioned sounds and smells way back there somewhere, then waited so long to discuss the smells. But I have, so let me correct that.

The Egyptian spice market. The Grand Covered Bazaar. *Çiçek Pasaji* (the "Flower Passage," an area of restaurants in the new town). The Yerebetan Cistern. The Galata Bridge fish market. Charcoal fires and rosewater. *Nargiles* (water pipes). The *hamam* (Turkish baths). The Bosphorus and the Golden Horn. *Turska kava. Kebabs.* Stuffed mussels. Fried-mackerel sandwiches. Leather shops. Tea gardens.

I could go on. Of course, the *sights* of Istanbul are something to behold, as well. The French romantic poet, Lamartine, wrote of Istanbul, "There God, man, nature and art have together created and placed the most marvellous view that the human eye can contemplate on earth." All of those minarets against any sky, but especially against an early dawn sky or against the hazy purple-and-orange light of dusk, are something you won't soon forget. It's also unlikely you will forget all of those attractive Turkish boys walking around with arms slung across each other's shoulders, or walking down the streets holding hands (especially, for some reason, the soldiers). They lean on each other a lot, too. Sometimes they even grab hold of the hand slung across their shoulder to hold it in place.

And then there's the *feeling* you have, being on the very edge of Europe, looking across the Bosphorus strait to Asian Istanbul and Anatolia, surrounded by Islam, in a country surrounded by enemies. Turkey gets along with absolutely none of its neighbors. Not Russia, nor Iran, nor Iraq, nor Syria, nor Greece, nor Bulgaria. Enemies all, even if Greece is Turkey's partner in NATO. Turkey doesn't even get along with its own peoples. The Armenians (what's left of them) are unhappy. The Islamic fundamentalists — devotees of Iran's late Ayatollah Ruhollah Khomeini — are (by definition) unhappy. The Kurds, increasingly, are most unhappy. Guerrilla warfare rages throughout Eastern Turkey, and, occasionally, in the streets of Istanbul. That boy who is trying to shine your Reeboks is a Kurdish orphan. His parents were killed by government troops. That young man scrubbing your back in the *hamam* longs for the day when Islamic law returns to Turkey and Atatürk's Westernization is history.

Most Turks, however, although Muslim, are moderate in their approach. They will tell you, "One must not be too Muslim."

But it's hardly just the ethnic minorities or the Islamic extremists who are unhappy. *Every* Turk, it seems, has a grievance. You can see it in their eyes, you can hear it in their tortured music. And, if you spend enough time with them, they will tell you. You will hear their story of the injustice done to them by their own government. The fear of police and military personnel is not a *Midnight Express* myth, as some Western tourists returning from a week of partying in a coastal tourist resort will tell you, but is very real. Of the sixty or seventy Turks whom I talked to in depth during my month in Turkey, I found *not one*, be they adolescent, student, businessman, elderly, rich, or poor, who supported the government of Prime Minister Turgut Ozal (he has since taken the position of president). Even my soldier friend intended to vote for the Social Democrats, when and if elections are held. Most Turks actually seemed to favor the Socialists (the Communist Party is outlawed, of course), but did not believe the military — in whose hands true power lies — would ever hand over the government to a Socialist. They are instead planning to vote for the Social Democrats, hoping those candidates will be acceptable to the powers that be. Indeed, the Social Democrats may very well be acceptable. Like the crumbling communist governments to its north, Turkey is suffering from severe economic mismanagement. Ozal has been accused of mortgaging his country to the United States in return for a loan from the International Monetary Fund. For the calendar year 1988, Turkey's returns of grants and payments of principal to the U.S. was $720 million greater than the grants it received from the U.S. It is by far the most favorable economic relationship the U.S. enjoys with any country (compare, for instance, the $1.8 billion *deficit* in our grant exchange with Israel the same year). Even the military may soon be convinced that a change must come. The unpopular Ozal is waiting as long as possible before calling elections.

But what about gays in Turkey? There is more information available than one might expect, thanks mainly to Turkish author Arzlan Yüzgün's book, *Homosexuality in Turkey, Yesterday and Today*, published in 1986. Within two years it was in its third printing.

There is, of course, a history of bisexual and homosexual activity in every Islamic country. And, like in all Islamic countries, you cannot understand the attitudes of society regarding homosexuals, or the attitudes of homosexuals regarding homosexuals, without knowing something of the country's culture and religion.

In Turkey, little has survived in writing of the country's homosexual past. The author Resat Ekrem Kocu is one of the few early sources. We know that before Islam, the Turks practiced Chamanism, and that the high priest of this religion, the Chaman, was forbidden sexual contacts with women. Instead, he enjoyed sex with men and boys. In Ottoman times, several emperors, including Emperor Murad, were homosexual. An Ottoman poet, Hamumizade Ihsen Bey, wrote a poem in which a boy is told his arms are like scarfs — "It's wrong to embrace them/but impossible not to."

With the conversion to Islam, homosexuality was forbidden in Turkey, and those who continued to practice it were tortured and killed. However, some sects, such as the Hanefi and the Sufi, refused to go along with these rules. The founder of the whirling dervishes, Mevlana Jalalu'ddin Rumi, was almost certainly himself homosexual. More recently, Kemal Atatürk, the "father of the Turks," had a known homosexual minister in his government. Although Atatürk made many laws forbidding many things, virtually prescribing the lifestyle to be led by the Turks, he proposed no laws against gays.

On the very negative side, there was also the letter of Alexius Comnenus to Count Robert of Flanders in the early twelfth century asking for his assistance in the war against the Turks, in which he said the Turks sodomized men of every rank — "boys, adolescents, young men, old men, nobles, servants, and, what is worse and more wicked, clerics and monks, and even ... bishops." Literature of the nineteenth century indicates sex between Turkish women to be commonplace, particularly at the *hamam*, but there seems to be no evidence that the same was true for Turkish men. The baths *are* contact spots for Turkish homosexuals today, but police raids seem to be on the increase.

Although Islamic Sufi literature used homosexual eroticism in describing the relationship between man and God, most Muslims now frown upon homosexuality, and those in Turkey are no exception (Sufism, however, lives on today among millions of people in central Anatolia, the Middle East, Iran, India, Pakistan, and Bangladesh).

Of the estimated two million gays in Turkey, six hundred thousand are estimated to be living in Istanbul, where tolerance is higher than in any other part of the country. Turks elsewhere will tell you the *only* homosexuals in Turkey are in Istanbul and the popular resort of Bodrum. You can smile when they say it, but as far as you're concerned as a tourist, it may as well be true. It is doubtful you will find any native Turk willing to engage in a homosexual act except in Istanbul, Bodrum, Bursa, and perhaps Izmir or Ankara.

The two bars *Spartacus* lists for Bodrum — Café Sebil and Romans Café Beledye — apparently no longer exist, but there is a gay bar in Bodrum just off the main shopping street, on a side street connecting it with Atatürk Caddesi. There are several gay bars in Istanbul, which I'll mention later. I did not go to Bursa, but was told there were quite a few gays there, as well as a fledgling — and very secretive — gay rights organization. However, there are apparently no gay bars in Bursa. The remainder of Turkey is too Islamic, and homosexuality is absolutely taboo. Don't let those young men holding hands as they walk down the street or belly dancing sensuously with one another fool you; Turkish men can be some of the gentlest, most affectionate men on the planet, but they are usually not gay.

Although homosexuality is not mentioned in the Penal Code, I met only one Turk who supported equal treatment for gays or thought that gays were anything other than "abnormal." In general, the population maintains a hostile attitude toward gays, and the police are especially hostile toward persons who are openly gay.

When Yüzgün's book was printed, Turkish conservatives asked the government to ban it. They only partially won the battle, however: The book was not banned, but had to be sold in a wrapper that hid the cover.

Yüzgün investigated 223 homosexual men in Turkey and printed statistics on what they told them. Among his findings:

- 40% of the men said their parents knew they were gay.
- 34% were known to be gay by their co-workers.
- 56% found it difficult to be openly gay.
- 96% complained of police harassment.
- 41% had been taken to a police station for reasons relating to their homosexuality, and 61% of these reported having re-

– 113 –

ceived humiliating treatment at the hands of the police (including 13% who said they had been "close-shaven" by the police).

- 72% dared to assert their rights at the police station.
- 31% had been forcibly taken to a holding institution, such as a venereal disease clinic, and held there several days.
- 94% had been in court as a result of their sexuality.
- 50% had been propositioned on the streets.
- 60% had been attacked on the streets.
- 48% thought it might do some good to report a crime inflicted upon them; 49% did not.
- 81% wanted a gay rights organization and were willing to help create one.
- 55% lived with their parents.
- 84% were bachelors, 10% were married with children, 4% were widowed, and 2% were married without children.
- 74% had regular income.
- 55% had no property, 24% owned a house, and 1% owned a shop.

The conservative government now holding power in Turkey passed a law giving police the authority to arrest homosexuals without warrant. If a couple is arrested and one is under age, the adult could be convicted of "incitement to homosexuality" and the minor would be barred from protesting. Yüzgün and several others formed the Radical Party, which, although not officially recognized as a legitimate political party, succeeded in having this law removed.

Turkish men love to talk about sex when they are in the all-male confines of pubs. Even in straight pubs, gays are usually not hassled, for Turks consider the pubs to be almost sacred regarding privacy and tolerance. Turkish newspapers do not shy away from stories on gays, either, but almost always sensationalize the articles. In Jale Simsek's article "Turkey, a Country with a Long Homosexual History" in the *ILGA Pink Book*, she lists some recent headlines, including: "The lover of her husband turned out to be a faggot," "She committed suicide when she found out her husband was a homosexual," "In Istanbul dozens of homosexuals were arrested at a nightclub yesterday evening," "Male prostitutes are more appreciated than female," "The police have arrested some 'walking viruses' suspected of spreading AIDS."

Spartacus says that in the early 1980s, the police arrested transvestites, transsexuals, and effeminate men, who were "brought back to their home towns or villages with cropped hair, and then sent off to some other town."

Curiously, two of the most popular singers in Turkey are transsexuals. Bülent Ersoy was banned from public performances and radio play following his sex-change operation. Ersoy lived in exile in Frankfurt until 1986, when he was allowed to return to Turkey. That was the year Turkey enacted a law giving its citizens the right to appear at the court of justice in Brussels. Ersoy and author Aziz Nesin were among the first to bring cases against the government.

Contemporary Turkish authors who frequently mention homosexuality in their work include Gulden Dogiogku, who discusses lesbian relationships among women whose husbands have gone overseas for work; Atilla Ilhan, who also writes about lesbian relationships; and Bekir Yildiz, whose themes are homosexuality in rural Turkey, and man-boy relationships.

Filmmakers have not yet dealt with homosexuality in Turkey (there is, of course, *Midnight Express*, but that's hardly a Turkish film), although Yüzgün has been approached about a possible screenplay on the life of a male homosexual, and the actress Mujale Ar has made films on the sexual hypocrisy in Turkey. There are plays about homosexuals, however, including Ali Poyrazoglu's *The Flower Has Opened, My Son; Lunatic Club;* and *Give Me My Right, Hakki.*

In Istanbul, gays who are open about their sexuality generally cannot find work except in the "gay ghetto" occupations of shop assistants, waiters, musicians, sewer workers, hairdressers, or prostitutes. Astonishingly, transvestite prostitutes are licensed by the government. Having sex with them is not generally construed to be homosexual activity, so long as you are on top. My Peruvian friend tells me that in his country if you fuck a man, you're not gay, but if you get fucked by a man, you are. The Turks seem to share much of that attitude.

Recently, a group of gay professionals in Istanbul instigated a confrontation with the police — it wasn't difficult to get themselves arrested for no legitimate reason — in order to demand, at the police station, an open trial, which was their right. The judge at their trial reprimanded the police — an encouraging development for gays throughout Turkey.

On the subject of AIDS, most of the news is far from encouraging. Simsek quotes Radical Party chairman Ibrahim Eren as saying, "It bothers me that a subject like AIDS is used by the authorities as a weapon against homosexuality. The mayor of Istanbul, B. Dalan, proclaimed AIDS to be the punishment of God. Until now three people have died of AIDS, none of them homosexual ... At the moment blood tests can't be done in Turkey. They're sent to Switzerland..."

Eren, by the way, participated in the conference on homosexuals in Europe organized by the Green Party in the European Parliament, March 5–6, 1987.

Ψ

Watching afternoon prayer in the Blue Mosque is fascinating. You must be dressed "properly" to enter any of the more than two hundred mosques in Istanbul. This usually means only that your limbs must be covered. Some mosques have black scarves that you can drape over your body should you arrive in shorts and muscle shirt. Some insist that females wear these scarves on their heads when they enter. All mosques insist that you remove your shoes at the door before entering. In the Blue Mosque you can take photos of the Western infidels sitting underneath the "Please do not sit in mosque" signs.

You will find the women worshippers kneeling in a roped-off area at the back of the mosque; only the men are allowed in front. The status of women in any Islamic country is usually something just above that of farm animal. In strict Muslim households, men always walk in front of women when they go down the streets. The women work in the fields all day while the men congregate in game rooms to play a strange game resembling a cross between Scrabble and dominoes. The women, of course, are expected to finish their field work in time to have dinner on the table, but the Turks usually don't eat until eight or nine in the evening, so there's really no rush. Women must also keep their heads (and in some cases their entire faces except for the eyes) covered at all times in public, and they sit in the back of the wagons with the other farm animals.

I'm afraid I'm not exaggerating.

After an hour in the Blue Mosque, I separated from Donach and Gina and toured the Topkapi Palace. Because the types of things it houses are not things that interest me a great deal, I wasn't as impressed with the palace as others seem to be. Among the exhibits are halls devoted to porcelain, jewelry, the Sultans' treasures, Islamic holy items and documents, costumes of the ruling class, and early hand-written religious texts (most with beautiful gold-laden illustrations — these were what I found most interesting). You can also visit the former harem.

At the bottom of the hill on the Golden Horn side of the palace I accidentally came across the entrance to an outdoor festival. I stood and watched the people going in — all Turks, no tourists — and finally decided I would simply have to find out what was going on. After figuring out where and how to get a ticket, I entered the grounds, conspicuous because I was the only person inside wearing shorts. The first thing I came across was an exhibit of photographs depicting the suffering of the ethnic Turks being evicted from Bulgaria. The Bulgarian government had been trying for years to force the Turkish minority, which accounts for more than eleven percent of the population of Bulgaria, to change their religion, their language, and even their first and last names. Until 1968, the one million Turks were not permitted to leave the country. When Bulgaria finally changed its mind, Turkey, fearing a swarm of immigrants, refused to give entry permits to all but a few. Now the Bulgarian government was confiscating their land and forcing them across the border. Turkey, which already had three hundred thousand unwanted Kurds from Iraq and Iran living in refugee camps on its southeastern frontier, now had to find food and shelter for 320,000 more refugees from Bulgaria (most eventually chose to return to Bulgaria after Bulgarian leader Todor Zhivkov was ousted). It was an odd position for such a notoriously repressive government to find itself in, but they were trying to make the most of it from a propaganda standpoint. By constantly reminding the natives of the enemies on every side of the border, the Turkish government attempts to justify the tremendous military presence inside. The fact that the Turkish military spends more time training for counter-terrorist campaigns and riot control techniques than it does on possible foreign invasions is something every Turk knows, but usually won't admit to a foreigner.

Past the photographs were rows and rows of stands selling everything imaginable, from *kebabs* and roasted corn on the cob to clothes, toys, and jewelry. There was also an amusement ride area, with a huge sign over it that said "Luna Park." I skipped that for the moment and followed the crowd to a stage on which a comedian was telling jokes I could not understand. Later, a wonderful Turkish singer backed with a full orchestra would be on the same stage.

I finished walking the length of the festival. It was at least a mile long, curving around the base of the hill. There were thousands of people, but never did I see another tourist. I sat down at the only vacant table I had seen at any of the outdoor beer gardens, and soon was joined by a Turkish journalist who had lived in London the last three years. We had an interesting conversation spanning American-Turkish relations (he considered Turkey a puppet state of the U.S. and didn't like America), the Bulgarian situation, the role of Islam in Turkey, the Armenian question, and, finally, gays in Turkey. He told me there were many homosexuals in the Taksim district of Istanbul.

After buying me a beer and fried clams and talking for two hours, he left, so I walked back to the stage to catch the concert. A man approached me for no reason whatsoever, asked a few questions, then introduced me to his wife and children. Nearby was a woman who had her baby in a makeshift hammock, swinging it back and forth like the world on fire.

Later, after I had returned to the hotel and taken a much-needed nap, the gang woke me up to go with them to the Sound and Light Show at the Blue Mosque. It was essential we go tonight, they said, because the show was in English tonight, but would be in German and French on the nights to follow.

The Sound was terrible, terrible, inaudibly terrible, so it didn't really matter what language it was in. The Light was okay, but we all felt we could have done better. At some point during the show Gina was felt up by a kid she described as an "eight-year-old." It upset her to the point of tears; she had been hassled by Turkish men all day long.

After the show a very cute Kurdish boy engaged us in conversation for about twenty minutes, probably just to practice his English, which is considered a key to success by many entrepreneuring Turks. Most families can't afford lessons for their children, so the kids are encouraged to learn what they can on the street.

We polished off the night with *mahallebi* (cold rice pudding) and apple tea (sometimes derisively called "tourist tea" by the Turks when they're talking to each other, but who nonetheless seem to like it quite well themselves) at a nearby café, then had a beer at the youth hostel before returning to the Pension Side, our hotel.

Ψ

Happy Birthday to me. Had a Turkish card from Donach and "the bus people" waiting for me when I woke up. Jeff took off to meet his "bride." I really think Jeff may have been gay — he was even thinking of becoming a priest. The woman he was planning to escort across Turkey was older than he, but they were going to pretend marriage. They had even purchased cheap rings.

The rest of us decided to venture out of Sultanahmet, so we walked across the Galata Bridge to climb Galata Tower for a view of the city. The bridge was something else — more than a dozen fish restaurants underneath the bridge at the ends, and each restaurant with a man outside pointing to the fresh catch in the display window, insisting you come inside.

"We're looking for breakfast, not fish," I kept saying. They didn't seem to think the two were necessarily anomalous.

One restaurant gave Gina a card printed in German, English, and French — but the information wasn't quite the same from one language to another. The English copy emphasized that the restaurant was clean, the fish were fresh, and that they stocked a wide variety; the French copy emphasized the ambience; the German emphasized that prices were low. It was psychological marketing, via stereotype.

On top of the bridge were, besides hundreds of cars and pedestrians, many peddlers selling all the things one usually sees along the streets of Istanbul. A man was demonstrating a knife sharpener that with a few strokes could make a dull knife (he demonstrated its dullness by rubbing the blade along his tongue) sharp enough to cut through glass (after cutting through the glass he threw both pieces over his shoulder into the Golden Horn). I suppose the saddest of the street venders in Turkey are those poor old men and small boys sitting beside a scale. You see them everywhere, patiently waiting to weigh you.

Throughout the streets, especially in the area of the Egyptian spice bazaar, man is the beast of burden. You see them with anything and everything on their backs, colorful and anachronous, reminiscent of the "Consider Yourself" scene in the movie *Oliver!* The males not toting some weight would hoot and leer at Gina. I understood why some of the guys at the youth hostel were upset because Turkish men showed neither respect for their girlfriends, nor regard for the fact that these Western males were alongside their girlfriends. The Turks still felt at ease to make disgusting suggestions, whether the women were accompanied by men or not. In America, it would have started many a fight.

It's almost funny, however, what the Turkish males (and I'm referring to heterosexuals here) have done to themselves. By adhering to their stupid religion, these children of a misanthropic god have oppressed their women to the point of making them hideous. How many Turks did I meet who told me that they loved Western girls because Turkish girls were ugly? Too many. They turn their own women into farm animals they don't want to touch, then stand around lusting after Western women they can't have, or getting erections from pictures of belly dancers gracing practically all the Turkish newspapers. Add to this the Islamic insistence on virginity before marriage and the scorn for homosexuality and you have a nation full of sexually repressed males. It's not a pretty sight.

From atop Galata Tower we could see women all over town doing laundry on the rooftops while small children played games around them. There seemed to be some activity on every roof. In Istanbul, space is precious. Connecting the roofs, connecting the buildings, was the most tangled mass of wires in the world, I expect. Apparently every cable and wire is above ground in this city, held up by any available building or post.

Donach and I took a taxi to the American Express office at the Hilton, where I tried without success to deal with stuffing tokens into the phones. Gina had decided to visit more mosques, and it was clear that it really didn't make much difference whether Donach and I were with her or not, she was going to get hassled either way. Despite this, I really think Gina liked Turkey more than either Donach or I.

We walked all the way back to Sultanahmet from the Hilton, taking our time, having a look around Taksim. I saw the VAT 69 club, which I knew was gay, and we stumbled across a great little café at the end of a dead-end street. The café was called "Sam Burgers." We had the *döner* sandwich, with Sam (we supposed) taking good care of us, bringing us extra tidbits of meat from time to time and cleaning our table at the slightest drop of crumb or tea. Sitting outside, we had an unsettling view through a small grate of the shirtless men working in the sweatshop below Sam's. They seemed to be sewing jeans, and occasionally stared up at us as though this odd arrangement of our bodies in space was the most natural on earth.

A curious thing about our tea at Sam's — every time we ordered it, Sam summoned a small boy who disappeared around the corner of the building two doors down for about one minute, returning with two cups of tea. I expect he was getting it from someone's house.

Ψ

My birthday night on the town began with Donach and Gina at one of the fresh fish restaurants under the Galata Bridge. I decided on the mackerel and fresh mussels. Donach paid. Just as he finished taking our photograph for the fourth time, we were joined by Richard, Ester, Elena, and Samuel. After more photographs, we moved to a beer joint, still under the bridge, and had quite a nice time. I talked with Samuel, mostly, and mostly about France and French filmmakers. It was the first time I had ever discussed the films of Louis Malle with someone from his home country. Americans know Malle primarily through *Atlantic City, My Dinner With Andre,* and *Au Revoir les Enfants,* but perhaps his best work — and certainly my personal favorites — are two earlier French films, *Murmur of the Heart* and *Lacombe, Lucien.*

Eventually everyone left to go back to their hotels, but I told them I wasn't quite ready for that, and set out across the bridge toward the gay clubs of Taksim. VAT 69, off Istikial Caddesi at 7 Imam Adrian Sokagi, was closed. The most popular gay bar and the only gay disco in Istanbul, it is only open on weekends. Another club mentioned in *Spartacus*, Valentino's, was no longer gay. I wanted to tell them they should change their name, but instead followed their suggestion to try Club Marilyn next door. Marilyn's was gay (it may be the same as the club listed as "1001" in *Spartacus* — both are on Siraselviler Caddesi), but was also horrible. There were many transsexuals and transvestites — they seem to be quite the thing in Turkey — providing the entertainment. It was, for the most part, the typical lip-sync drag show you can find in cities of any size across the American South, but with a peculiar Turkish twist: The lip-syncing queens were accompanied by accordion-playing queens. This was worth one good laugh, after which I found a table and ordered a beer. The drink arrived on my table at about the same time as one of the entertainers. Finished with her performance, a particularly shapely singer came over, sat down on my table, and got straight to the point. She wanted me to pay one hundred dollars to have sex with her. I wouldn't have considered sex with her had she paid me two hundred dollars, and I started to tell her so, or at least offer her five bucks to get off my table. But decency took over and I simply said, "No." Her friends at a nearby table had been watching and, I suppose, read my lips. In any case, they began laughing, which sent her storming off indignantly toward the bar.

I went to the upstairs bar to avoid further accordions, and picked exactly the wrong person to ask if there were not some other gay bars close by with a different type of crowd. The person I asked was the club manager. He was nice enough, considering, giving me the name of Pub 14, where, he assured me, I would find "boys with moustaches." I didn't recall asking for a place where I could find boys with moustaches. I had merely wanted the name of a place where I could find boys without dresses. I asked him about the gay scene in Turkey. He said it was "only in Istanbul" and was "still very young." If he was offended at all by my not liking his club, it showed when I asked for my bill — fifteen dollars for one beer and the "entertainment." I was quickly learning never to order *anything* in Turkey without first asking the price. I barely had money left for the remainder of the evening, and told the man so when he went outside to hail a cab for me. He asked how much, I told him, and he said I shouldn't worry, that I had enough for cab fare to Pub 14 plus one beer, which turned out to be exactly the case. I suppose he thought that once I was there I wouldn't need to worry about getting home. I decided I would deal with that problem when the time came.

Pub 14 has the same address and phone number (1-562121) as another club listed in *Spartacus* — Ceyland. The guide also lists a bar under the name of "Efes Pilsen," which is the name of Istanbul's leading beer. There are, of course, Efes Pilsen signs outside practically every bar in the city.

Pub 14 looks perfect — exactly like a bar of this type should look. It is simply a medium-sized rectangular room with an elliptical bar and chairs all around. Glasses and bottles are kept under the bar, with nothing blocking the customers' view from any side of the bar to another. The lighting was just right, the decor was nice (the posters were extremely sexy, but not obscene — much like the posters Scott Madsen did for Soloflex), and so were the colors. Sort of marine-green, gray, and silver. The music was decent, too.

The clientele, unfortunately, wasn't nearly so worthy of raves. I don't know if gay bars for Turks of average incomes exist in Istanbul, but I doubt it. Perhaps none of those beautiful young men one encounters throughout the day leaning on each other and holding hands are gay, but I doubt that, too. Perhaps there is simply no point, from a businessman's perspective, of opening a gay bar for gays with no money. Around the bar at Pub 14, at any rate, was a collection of wealthy, jaded, unfriendly Turks of no interest to me. I drank one beer, then went outside to find a taxi.

Once at the Pension Side, I had the driver wait while I went upstairs for money. The door to the hotel was locked, but a ring of the bell eventually brought one of the brothers newly awakened to open it. I went upstairs, where I encountered an attractive, tall, blond (it almost goes without saying, but not quite) Swede, whom I'd met the day before, stumbling around drunkenly. He followed me into my room, talking loudly. Gina sat up in bed and told him to get out and close the door behind him. On my way back downstairs with the money, I encountered the Swede's even more attractive traveling companion, who was from San Diego, and whom I had also met the day before, going to bed. He had been wearing a "Smiths" t-shirt the previous day, which is how I had come to have a conversation with him. The Smiths, a now-defunct English band, had a gay lead singer named Morrissey and were known for their blatantly gay song lyrics. But they had a considerable heterosexual following as well, and I was left to suspect that the San Diegan was of this category, if only because he and the Swede were also traveling with two females and seemed decidedly more interested in the women than in each other.

I paid the taxi driver, including a hefty tip for waiting, then went back upstairs, where I once again encountered the Swede.

"Can you help me?" he asked.

Don't you love it? He took me into a room and showed me two women trying to sleep in one single bed and the San Diegan on the other.

"Come on, Jonas, let us get some sleep," the San Diegan said.

I ushered Jonas out of the room and shut the door, thinking it was too bad that he didn't just get in bed with the guy. Jonas explained that a third female had the key to his room but was still out somewhere in Istanbul. I went downstairs and got the manager to let him in his room, then went sleepily back to my own.

7

Istanbul — Hamam and Taksim

I had not shaved in a week. Richard said I looked like Indiana Jones. Whatever I looked like, I didn't feel the greatest when I awoke the next morning to the sounds of some man yelling loudly in Turkish outside our window.

Hotel management had us move to a smaller room with three beds since Jeff, our fourth, had left us. It wasn't nearly so nice, but we were spending so little time in our room, it didn't matter. After washing some laundry in a basin downstairs and hanging it to dry on lines strung across the roof, I joined Donach and Gina for breakfast and a trip to the Grand Covered Bazaar. Breakfast in Turkey almost always meant bread, cheese, tomato, cucumber, and black olives, with tea. Luck would bring you a soft-boiled egg, usually boiled hardly at all and often too disgusting to eat. I always asked for the egg to be cooked longer, which, if they bothered to heed me, would bring to my plate a decently soft-boiled egg.

In the Covered Bazaar you can find just about everything except your way out. Over four thousand shops cover fifty acres under one roof. It is, in effect, the world's largest mall. Merchants hawk silver and gold coins, baubles, shovels of copper filigree, Farsi texts, hookahs (yes, *hookahs*), icons, daggers, flintlock guns with mother-of-pearl handles, pipes, ancient pocket watches, spices, antique copper pots, inlaid wood, chess sets, hand puppets, onyx, jade, and — of course — all the carpets and leather coats you could ever want. The tourist brochures put out by the Turkish Culture and Information Office tell you, "There's no reason not to buy an item too large to bring home on the plane: trustworthy merchants will often ship anywhere in the world." Heh, heh, heh.

I'm not a big fan of malls, so after splitting from Donach and Gina, I didn't spend much time at the bazaar. Half of my time there was spent trying to find a way out.

My next stop was one I had been looking forward to — the Archaeological Museum. I knew only three pieces housed in the museum, but those three were plenty — the Alexander sarcophagus, a head of Alexander, and a statue of Alexander that, to judge from photographs, was absolutely sensuous.

My student card gained me free entrance. The courtyard contained any number of aged sculptures, weather-smoothed to the point of not being museum quality and therefore relegated to the lawn. Amidst these large, featureless slabs of marble was a tea garden.

The Alexander sarcophagus was even more impressive than I had imagined. What I couldn't imagine is how an object this large had been carried from Babylon across Persia and Syria to Egypt after Alexander's death. Diodorus said the catafalque was pulled by sixty-four mules, each wearing a crown, a collar of gems, and bells of gold. Supposedly, the gold sarcophagus was eventually melted down for coin by Ptolemy IX. So what is it doing here? Good question.

The Alexander sarcophagus sitting in the Archaeological Museum was commissioned by King Abdalonymus of Sidon. After Alexander had overthrown Sidon's King Straton, he had left

A detail from the remarkable Alexander sarcophagus in Istanbul shows a young Alexander seizing a stag by the antlers.

it up to Hephaestion to find a suitable successor. Hephaestion discovered a distant relative of the royal house working as a gardener in the outskirts of the city. The gardener, Abdalonymus, was a man of good character, and Hephaestion saw no reason he should not be king. In gratitude, the new king commissioned a marble sarcophagus. Although it was never actually used to hold Alexander's body, it is a remarkable and lasting tribute. It was discovered in an astonishingly preserved state in a vault at Sidon. The reliefs on one side show Alexander at the Battle of Issus, where he defeated Darius. The other side shows Alexander conducting a lion hunt with several Persians in his company. In one scene, a Greek and a Persian are involved in hand-to-hand combat, the Greek naked, with only helmet, sword, and shield, battling a man fully clothed and turbaned in Persian style. The scene is especially striking because of the eye contact between the nude Greek and the turbaned enemy. Another scene of the young hero grabbing a stag by its antlers is quite similar to the Deer Hunt mosaic at Pella. The body lines, muscle definition, balance, and proportion of the nude male figures are among the best I've ever seen — right up there with Michelangelo, Anton Hanak's *Der Gigant* (in Vienna), and an awesome bust by an unknown artist in Florence's Uffizi Gallery.

But of all the bad luck, the other works I had come to see were on traveling exhibit in Denmark! The desk clerk did not know when they would return. Three-fourths of the museum's exhibit space was temporarily closed.

As it was the fourth of July, the day after my birthday, and as I hadn't called home in a month, I waited until a late enough hour in the day that it would be after dawn in the central U.S., then went to the Interyouth Hostel and put a call through to America. One of my dogs was missing. This was depressing news — my dogs were brothers, and I didn't see how Huck would get along without Tom.

On an impulse while walking by a Turkish barber, I stopped in my tracks and went inside for a shave. It was shaving as an art form, and all for a buck fifty. The shave was actually three lathers and shaves, followed by a brief facial and shoulder massage, after-shave lotion, cream, and powder.

Enjoyed an *adana kebab* (the spicy hot *kebabs*), then went to the hotel to meet the others for a trip to the Turkish baths. Gina had the only existing key to our room, so I wasn't able to get in until she got back. Passed the time on the roof talking with a very nice and very shy Pakistani medical student named Ali (which seems to be the most common name in Islamic countries — that and Mehmet). The boy was so exceptionally polite and so obviously pleased to be in the company of a friendly American that the conversation made me tingle. Later, when a Turk would tell me that the Turks were unlike other Muslims, *especially* the Pakistanis, because, unlike the others, the Turks were clean (his specific example was that Pakistanis entered toilet areas with bare feet —

something, he said, a Turk would never do), I would think of Ali sitting opposite me on the Pension Side roof, muezzins calling the faithful to afternoon prayer throughout Istanbul, as the sun reflected off the hundreds of domes and minarets, and I would smile a sad smile and dedicate it to cruel prejudice.

We had obtained from the hotel management the names of two genuinely Turkish baths, both supposedly better and cheaper than the tourist-infested baths around the hotels. Neither was far away, but they were in working-class neighborhoods not detailed on our maps. We set off on foot, certain that we were at least heading in the correct direction. Samuel had stayed behind, saying he didn't like the idea of someone giving him a bath, but Elena, Richard, and Ester were with us. The street scenes we encountered were different than any we had come across in Istanbul. Children interrupted their games to greet and follow us — among the first children I had seen in the city who weren't either working some miserable job or trying to part some tourist from his or her money. Women gathered to talk in doorways. Men drank tea or beer at outdoor tables. Cats were everywhere. As Elena kept saying, it frequently looked like a painting by Brueghel. She and Donach, photographers both, were cursing themselves for not bringing cameras, but I was glad they had not. I'm sure these natives were more pleased to see the gleam in Elena and Richard's eyes than they would have been to see the flash of their cameras. It seemed these Turks did not often see tourists navigating their narrow, winding, hilly streets.

Even more surprised to see us were the employees of the baths. The women's bath, unhappily, had closed at five, but Gina and Elena felt comfortable with the neighborhood, so we left them with it and went inside. Our hotel had been right about the prices — an assisted bath and full massage was only five dollars here, whereas the baths in the tourist district of Lâleli charged seventeen. They were correct about the quality, as well, for what we were about to experience was something the three of us will never forget.

First, they took our shoes and gave us rubber thongs, then they led us upstairs to a small room and gave us each a towel. We stood stupidly, assuming we were to undress and put on the towel. Donach and Richard left their briefs on, but took them off when I suggested that they were certain to get wet. We were then led into a room with four marble basins and left to ourselves. The room was exceptionally hot — especially the marble floor. The building itself had a marble interior top to bottom, was very old, and contained several rooms — including the one we were in — with a perforated dome at the top, through which steam escaped, as if one were standing inside of a huge Byzantine incense burner. Three of the four basins were filled with water. We assumed, since there were three of us, that someone had filled them for our use, although we were puzzled regarding their differing temperatures. One was quite hot, another was cold, and the baby bear's basin — mine — was just right. We had not a clue what to do, but began wetting ourselves from the basins, Donach and Richard adding water from the taps to make theirs a practical temperature. A young Turk entered the room next to ours. As I was the only one in position to see what he was doing, I watched him as inconspicuously as was possible and reported his actions to my comrades.

The first thing he did was take the provided bowl and dish the water from his basin. I reported this with necessary chagrin: We had been bathing, evidently, with someone else's dirty water.

After running fresh water into the basin, the Turk sat down on the marble floor and began soaping himself. We had no soap. As it turned out, he was enjoying a self-bath, not the assisted. Still, we certainly felt stupid at the time.

We were then led into individual, smaller rooms with a basin in each. These had soap in them, so I began to lather up. Two men then came to attend to Richard and me, while Donach got his treatment where he sat. I got the youngest and best-looking attendant, although I suspect Richard got the one best at his job. I didn't complain.

Richard and I were placed on a marble slab in a large room, first face down, then face up, and given a very rough massage. Richard is a nice-looking fellow, short dark hair, medium height and build, and soft-spoken. He generally carries himself with unassumed dignity, wears glasses, and is very much the thoughtful type — a type, you understand, that seems incongruous with being walked on while prostrate on a marble slab. But he did, in fact, get walked on. I saw it happen. I don't think I was walked on myself, although there were many times during this fifteen-minute massage when I didn't know quite what was going on. I can tell you that my masseur, despite his small, wiry build, had extremely strong hands, which rubbed, twisted, and pounded on my body unceasingly. He bent my legs back double. He threw his full body weight quite suddenly into the center of my chest, causing some loud, hollow animal sound I had never heard before to come rumbling from my throat. Soon, I heard the same sound come from Richard. The leg massage, however, was the only part that was painful, and this was undoubtedly because four weeks of walking the streets and climbing the hills and mountains of Europe had strained my calves to the limit. The lower-stomach massage was the strangest, and must have been even stranger for Richard. I wonder if his masseur looked into his eyes as mine did while performing this praxis.

While we were on the slab, Donach was being walked on in a tub full of water, unable to breath at times, as he told us later. Richard and I were led back to the small cubicles and scrubbed. My masseur used a rough cloth that scraped away old skin, and two shades of tan along with it. He twice scrubbed every part of my body except the face and most private parts, then used his hands for a softer massage-scrub that felt terrific. This was followed with two shampoos and much rinsing. There were water taps running constantly. Obviously, Istanbul's water shortage did not extend to the baths, which possibly had their own reservoirs. (But even this possibility doesn't explain how they could afford to be so wasteful with it.)

Next the three of us were taken to a conventional bathtub — the same one in which Donach was nearly drowned — and made to get in together. We barely fit, and I was happy to have been put in back, so I could lean against the tub. They grabbed Donach, in front, and dunked his head under the tap, then repeated the procedure with Richard, directing Donach out of the tub and back in behind me. Then I got mine, as Richard made the circuit. When we were back in our original positions, they left us sitting there.

"Rub-a-dub-dub," I said. "Three men in a tub."

"I think I'll take a photograph and send it to my mother," said Donach.

We sat there a while, then were taken back to the cubicles, where pails and pails of water were dumped in rapid succession over our heads: the rinse cycle. Next we were led into another room and each given two dry towels. One, they tucked expertly around the waist. When I saw the attendant wrapping Richard's second towel around his head, I wondered if we were about to get the spin dry. In fact, the towel was handsomely tied into a turban, making each of us look like we had come to the Halloween ball dressed as Yasir Arafat or Saudi Arabia's King Fahd. We were led back to the small rooms and dried off by a large, jolly man who flapped the towels around our heads while repeating, "Babi, Babi, Babi." I suspect they had begun to play with us, but it was all in fun. The towels were then re-tucked, and we were taken back to the room where we had undressed, and given pillows in case we desired a nap.

There was only one bed, but we flopped down on it all at once, feeling akin to Jello brand gelatin, but each agreeing that it had been quite wonderful and he had never felt cleaner. We sat in a state of near-stupor until Richard decided he should try to find Ester. We dressed, tipped, and paid — and that was the end.

When we reached our hotel, we found Gina and Ester sitting outside playing backgammon with Sadat, one of the brothers who owned the hotel. Sadat began talking to me about the advantages of teaching English in Istanbul. He claimed that because there was a shortage of teachers, most were paid well and had excellent benefits. He also offered to drive me to a school the next afternoon to check on possible openings. I accepted; it would be an interesting experience, if nothing else.

Gina, Donach, and I later went with Sadat to the festival below the palace. As we walked there, Sadat, who isn't at all bad-looking, had his arm through mine in Turkish custom most of the way. It's the little things, like that, that one comes to appreciate in a foreign land.

Sadat proved to be great fun. He was also generous, and insisted on paying our admission. Too, he showed himself to be compassionate, as tears filled his eyes while looking at the photographs of the Turkish refugees from Bulgaria. "Please, let's go," he said. "I don't like."

We went to Luna Park and rode a ride that takes you up and drops you, giving you the thrill of an astronaut in training. It was great fun — especially with Sadat, who acted as thrillingly frightened as a child and absolutely refused to let go of the guardrail.

Dinner followed. Donach and I ordered something that looked delicious, but turned out to be lamb intestines. To please Sadat, who had suggested the dish, I ate it. Two of his friends came by while we were eating and suggested we go up the hill to the festival's outdoor disco. One of these friends knew little English and was therefore very quiet. The other not only had a good command of English, he was also exceptionally good-looking. Both smiled constantly — infectious smiles that made you appreciate their company. Unlike Sadat, his friends drank beer. The cutest one, Kamil, was studying political science at the University of Istanbul. The other, Mehmet, was also a student. They told us Sadat's grades had not been good enough to get him in.

The disco was a blast. The Turks dance extremely free-form, with the emphasis on having fun rather than on appearance.

Naturally, in Turkey, the crowd was almost totally male; therefore, it was almost totally males dancing together. Some danced very seductively. We joined in, forming a kick squad at one point — step, step, step, kick, kick, in unison, arms across each other's shoulders. When an appropriate song began, the Turks even convinced Donach, Gina, and me to try belly dancing. Watching those attractive Turkish boys belly dancing seductively with each other was something else. If I hadn't already picked up some knowledge of their customs, I would have assumed they were all gay. One boy in particular seemed interested in showing me what he could do, and Kamil was an expert, too. Sadat and Donach shimmied back to back. A total blast.

Gina and I had often remarked that all Turkish music sounded the same to us. Occasionally I would hear a song I liked, but usually the droning vocals were almost more than I could stand. At the disco, Gina asked Sadat what one of the songs was about.

"It is a song about the night," Sadat answered, quite enthused. "It is a woman whose lover has left her, and now it is the night and she is lonely, so she is singing about the night."

Remember that.

The festival closed at midnight, before we were ready to leave. Back at the hotel, I tried *raki* for the first time. It's the national drink, and tastes exactly like *ouzo*, the national drink of Greece. It probably is the same; they both taste like licorice, which seems dreadful at first but grows on you after a while. They serve it with a glass of water, with which you dilute it to suit your taste.

Ψ

We spent two more days in Istanbul. Had we only spent one, my lasting impression of the city would be a great deal more positive. The fifth of July was a relaxing day, relatively. I went to the school with Sadat. They did not need teachers, but said Bosphorus University did. Went back to the hotel, where Donach told me the others were taking the Bosphorus cruise at twelve-thirty. He had decided to stay behind and go with me at three p.m, which is when we had all decided to go the day before. We had twenty minutes to catch them, so we took a taxi. A tremendous traffic jam, not uncommon in Istanbul, made this a ridiculous decision, so we left the taxi in the middle of six lanes of cars and ran the distance to the pier.

The cruise was a disappointment, which began with the boat itself. Unlike on most cruise boats, passengers were not allowed on the upper deck. The lower deck was glassed in, except for a bench on either side. We went outside the glass, anyway, and found places to sit, although they were uncomfortable. The cruise was also disappointing in that it did not actually go to the Black Sea, as advertised, but stopped just short of it. The main sights of interest were an old castle, two grand restaurants with tables on verandas at the water's edge (one in particular, in unpainted gray wood, looked genteel enough to have been in Charleston or New Orleans), and the many cute boys in swimsuits all along the way, both in the water and on passing boats.

We were given fifty minutes to mess about in Anadolufeneri, the final port-of-call on the Asian side. It was an uninteresting tourist village, but it *was* the first time I'd set foot in Asia, and I managed to have a good time wandering about the back alleys with Elena and Samuel. We climbed a hill toward a castle, but were thwarted by a sprawling military complex. The attractive soldier boys were listlessly laying about, watching us watching them. It was tempting to take their photo, but taking photographs of Turkish military installations is strictly forbidden, and the fear of Turkish prisons is certainly enough to help one fight off such frivolous temptations.

After the cruise, Gina and I went through the Egyptian spice bazaar and Süleymaniye Mosque. We had to wear black scarves over our legs at the mosque (and Gina over her head, as well). I discreetly recorded a portion of the prayer.

Back outside, we had our shoes shined against our will by a difficult Kurdish kid who said it was free (we still declined, we

An ancient castle overlooks the Bosphorus strait, which splits Turkey between Europe and Asia, and connects the Sea of Marmara with the Black Sea.

thought), then demanded five dollars. Gina was furious and stormed off. I gave him a pack of Marlboros, which didn't please either Gina or the Kurd.

Sitting at a café, Gina and I commented again on how the music there sounded just like all the other Turkish music we had heard. She then struck up a conversation with a Turkish man at the table next to us. Perhaps he had been listening to our conversation; in any case, he asked if we liked Turkish music. We looked at each other and evaded the question by asking him what the song playing at the moment was about.

"It is a song about the night," he said. "A man's lover has gone away, and now the night makes him very sad."

Ψ

Gina, Sadat, and I returned to the festival that night. We spent some time at the outdoor stage, watching an extremely talented Turkish chanteuse, then went to the disco. Sadat's friends were there again. Kamil sat by me and kept his hand on my leg the entire evening, except when we danced, sometimes fidgeting nervously with my leg as if it were his own.

He didn't remove his hand even when Gina commented that the only males in America who danced well were gay. She said one of her best friends in California was gay and she often went dancing with him at gay clubs. Sadat and Kamil didn't understand, so Gina repeated her sentence, substituting *homosexual* for *gay*. Sadat's face lit up and he said, "*Really?*" as if it was the most incredible thing he had ever heard. Kamil asked Gina to repeat the word *gay*. He said homosexuals in Istanbul were very good belly dancers. I asked how he knew and he said that they danced in special clubs, but had to stay in certain areas of the city — mainly Yesilcam, the "Turkish Hollywood," and Sablabat, both in the Beyoglu-Taksim area. I never was clear whether he meant they had to stay in these areas for their own safety or whether they were actually forbidden to go elsewhere. I told him that I was certain not every gay in Istanbul was a belly dancer, and asked if he thought there were many gays in Istanbul. He said yes.

Gina brought up the matter of how unusual it was for Americans to see males dancing together and touching each other in public so often. Kamil was surprised to learn that American males didn't do it — and he kept his hand on my knee. If it hadn't been for the fact that he and his friend had their eyes on two Turkish girls the whole evening (they said they couldn't ask the girls to dance because the girls were with their brother, who didn't like them), I might have wondered if the hand on my leg meant something beyond casual affection. I asked Kamil how gays were regarded in Turkey. He said they weren't accepted and they had many problems with the police. I asked for his views on the subject. He said he thought gays should be treated the same as anyone else. In the entire month I spent in the country, he was the only Turk to tell me that.

We danced a little and stayed for another drink, closing down the festival. There was no one around but workers and soldiers on our long walk out of the park. The soldiers, with their automatic rifles, helmets, armbands, and fierce eyes, were more than a little frightening. I was glad not to be alone.

It was the next evening that I certainly shouldn't have been alone.

I slept late, had breakfast with Gina, then took a bus halfway up the Bosphorus to the university with the teaching positions open. Sadat had called ahead to set up an interview. I met with the director of the English program, who seemed quite enthused about the prospect of me teaching there, and more or less offered me a job. The trouble, she said (that the director was a woman had come as a total shock to me, she being the only woman in a position of authority that I encountered in Turkey), was that she would not be able to let me start working until February, due to extensive bureaucracy. I was relieved, not wanting to be forced into a decision on the spot. She gave me forms to complete and mail back to her, telling me that once she received the papers, I could probably expect a letter offering a position in about four months. I never returned the forms.

The Turks had been especially nice to me this day, showing me how to get around. One student took me in a taxi and paid the fare. Another student paid my bus fare, for you were supposed to have a ticket before getting on the bus; I didn't, and there was nowhere nearby to buy one. He gave me his extra and refused to let me pay him for it. The bus driver told me where to get off and how to get to the university from there. The campus was certainly pleasant, if damn near inaccessible. As it was atop a hill, you had to either walk up or take a taxi from the bus stop. On the way up or down you passed a very nice swimming pool for students and faculty.

I found my way back to the Taksim district and tried again to locate the gay area. Again, no luck. I suspect they only come out at night in Istanbul.

So, that night, I returned. My big mistake. I was walking toward VAT 69 to see if it might be open, when a well-dressed young man offered me a cigarette and started a conversation. His English was very good. He said he would soon be going to New York and would like to talk to me about America. Could he buy me a beer? Well, okay. He asked if I was gay. What made him think that? I asked. His answer was that most men who walked by themselves through Taksim at night were gay. I pointed to half a dozen playboy clubs along the street and told him I didn't think so, but, yes, I was gay. I asked if he was, and he answered yes.

I suggested we go to VAT 69, but he said he knew a nicer place just two blocks away. I followed him to something called the Carnaval Club. We went downstairs to what looked like a nice enough, if rather empty, club. Only three or four other humans were present. One of them, female, came over and told the boy I was cute, that she liked me. He ordered two beers, then confessed that he didn't like beer. Why did you order one? I asked. He said it was the proper thing to do.

We talked about America. He kept rubbing my leg. Finally, he said that when we finished our beers, he wanted to take me to a gay sauna. I told him he was very attractive and nice, but that I didn't want to go to a gay sauna. He implored, saying it was only eight dollars each for the whole night. I put off giving an answer. He urged me to hurry and finish my beer. When I did, he yelled something in Turkish to a waiter. I assumed he was asking for the check. He then stood up and said, "Come with me. We pay." I thought it unusual for us to be leaving our table to pay in Turkey, but followed him nevertheless. I then thought it very odd that we seemed to be headed in the direction of the toilets, but at the same instant I made up my mind to stop and head for the door, two large men appeared behind me and ushered me into a small room in back — the extortion room.

There were two other men, not as large as the others, waiting in the room. Counting the man I'd come in with, there were five of them and one of me. One of them proceeded to produce an itemized bill for 750,000 lira — about $375. They held the bill in front of my face without giving it to me. The only charges I could understand were two beers at 40,000 lira each — twenty dollars a beer. The rest was in Turkish. Naturally, I refused to pay. They began attempting to stick their hands in my pockets, saying, "No money, no problem. Money, you pay." I pointed to the man who had brought me there and told them he was paying. They said something to him, he answered sullenly, and one of them slapped him across the face, but not hard enough to do any harm. They told me he had no money and repeated, "No money, no problem. Money, you pay." It was clear they meant to continue the charade that the boy was not employed by them. I made a movement for the door, but they grabbed me, held me, and again tried to go through my pockets.

It was then that I became enraged. I knew I was in a dangerous situation, but the realization that they had used gay-baiting to pick their target filled me with fury. I wondered how many other frightened gay tourists, with more money in their pockets than I, had forked over the 750,000 lira. I began kicking and trying to throw punches, wishing for the first time in my life that I knew a martial art. With four of them against me (the boy kept playing his part, telling me to give them the money, but never admitting he was in with them), I didn't stand a chance. They soon had my arm twisted behind my back in a position near the breaking point, and one had his arm pressed against my throat so that I couldn't breath. I was then forced to let them go through my pockets. They took the three 20,000-lira notes they found there, but gave me back the small change. They took the unopened pack of Marlboros and opened pack of gum, but gave me back the lighter. One of them stuck his hand down my pants and up my shirt to feel for a money belt, but I had left it at the hotel. They then released me. One of them began talking rapidly in Turkish and waving the money in front of my face. I grabbed it, stuck it in my pocket, and again tried to reach the door. Again, they blocked my path. The second mugging was exactly like the first, except that they threatened to break my fingers and roughed me up more, trying to instill in me the appropriate sense of danger, I suppose. Then, they let me go.

Outside, there were quite a few policemen about. I approached several, but all looked bored and said, "No," when I asked if they spoke English. Finally, I found one who also said he spoke no English, but asked, "Problem?"

"Yes," I said.

"Club Carnaval?"

"Ye—"

How did he know that?

The cop and another officer took me back to the club. We didn't go downstairs, but to a back room on the street level. These cops obviously knew their way around the place.

I was becoming suspicious, so I wasn't surprised when two of the men who had just robbed me greeted the officers with a friendly handshake.

They took out a price list and showed it to the officers, who looked it over, laughing to each other. They showed me that the price of a beer was 40,000 lira, that the price list had the official government seal of approval at the bottom, and said, "Bill eighty thousand lira. You pay seventy thousand lira."

I protested that I had never agreed to pay for any beers and reminded them that they had initially given me a bill for 750,000 lira. The officers, not speaking English, *asked the fucking gangsters to translate*. There was some discussion then, and the next thing I knew I was being given a 20,000-lira note from one of the men, who said, "You pay only one beer. Okay?"

"Not okay," I said, and he snatched the note back.

We remained at an impasse for several minutes, the police basically siding with them, until one of the cops took the note, gave it to me, and led me outside. "Good-bye," he said, in a tone that made it clear he was tired of me.

I walked out of the area, feeling that all of the cops in the district were probably in on the scam, and found another cop who looked nicer than the others. He didn't speak English, but kept asking passersby, until he eventually found two young men who did. I related the story; they translated. They then told me the policeman was not interested in helping me, but they would show me where the station was, if I wanted to go fill out a report.

"We show you, but we don't go in because we no like police," one said. They also told me that I would probably spend all night at the station filling out forms, but that nothing would be done. I decided to press on anyway, still enraged by the entire affair. It is a particular foolishness of mine that I sometimes expect justice to triumph in this world.

We walked back to the same street the club was on. The station was just around the corner from the club — probably actually adjacent in the back. It all fit nicely together. "Problem?" — "Club Carnaval?"

Several cops were listening to the two men relate my story when the two cops who had accompanied me into the club came up and intervened. It was agreed by everyone except me that I had simply paid for a beer.

"It's not much money," one of the men with me said.

"This happens in Istanbul, New York, everywhere," the other said.

"I've never been robbed by the police in New York," I answered.

One of the cops who didn't understand English showed me a gun. He didn't point it at me; he simply took it out of its holster and waved it in my face. I left.

In a furious haze, I retraced my steps to VAT 69. I asked the price of a beer and was told eleven thousand lira — $5.50. The interior looked dirty. I decided to leave.

It wasn't my night, top to bottom. Waited with several others over an hour for a bus that never came. Gradually, people gave up and hailed taxis. I did the same.

Back in Sultanahmet, I went to find a beer with a sane price tag, still mad as hell. I was intercepted by Donach and Richard, who were sitting on a bench in the middle of a dark square drinking beer themselves. I bought a round and joined them, blurting out the story of my evening. We sat on that bench for two hours, talking about travel, books, girlfriends, life — and how we had spent one too many days in Istanbul.

8

Gallipoli

Donach and I ate a farewell breakfast with Richard and Ester the next morning. They were leaving for Kars in Eastern Turkey that night via a Black Sea cruise to Trabzon. They had hoped one or two of us might go with them, but it made more sense to Gina and Donach's plans to go south, and I was in the mood to spend a few days at some nice Aegean beach. Donach planned to go east only as far as Antakya, in the south, then cross into Syria. From there, he hoped to make his way to Saudi Arabia, then take a boat to India. Gina had to be back in Italy for a job in a month, and wasn't sure how far east she would make it. While we were eating, she was trying to make up her mind whether to go with Donach and me to Gallipoli (Gelibolu), or travel with an Australian woman who wanted company but didn't want to travel in a group of four.

As we were finishing our meal, she joined us and said she was coming. Sadat then drove us to the bus station. It had rained that morning, flooding the streets. Istanbul has a terrible drainage system. Or, rather, a nonexistent one. There are no underground drains, so the water runs wildly down the streets until it eventually finds its way to the Bosphorus or Golden Horn.

The bus station was a dizzying conglomerate of offices from about forty different companies. They were located on either side of a highway far too busy to cross; thus, a tunnel went underneath. Sadat let us off and told us we needed the cluster of offices on the other side of the highway. The offices on one side were for buses to and from Asia; on the other side, for buses remaining on the European side of the Sea of Marmara. We went through the muddy tunnel, which smelled as if the entire nation had at one time or another used it for a toilet, only to find that Sadat had been wrong. We had to go back through the damned thing.

The stations were a maze of signs advertising bus companies and destinations: Edirne, Tekirdag, Thessaloníki, Sofia, Çanakkale, Izmir, Ankara, Konya, Samsun, Bursa, Malatya, Erzurum, Van, Gaziantep, Marmaris, Sivas, Malkara, Uzunköprü. We needed the Çanakkale bus to get to Gallipoli. Despite the many companies, we found little difference in prices. It was then only a matter of finding which bus left first.

On the bus, before leaving the station, a man got on with a serving tray full of watery juice, handing them out. After we'd taken one, he asked for money. We had, of course, assumed the juice was courtesy of the bus company. Gina and I refused to pay, replacing the juice from which we had each taken one sip. Donach went ahead and drank his, then when he paid for it, the man refused to give him change, indicating that he was charging Donach for the two drinks Gina and I had given back. Donach was furious and created a mild scene, but the other passengers got their information from the man with the juice, shrugged off Donach's complaints — and that was that.

The scenery was ugly towns initially, then changed to mile after mile of sunflowers. They were nice at first, but after twenty miles, became monotonous. After two or three hours, I was fairly tired of goddamn sunflowers. Better to have been hyacinths. In Greek mythology, Clytie was a nymph in love with Apollo, who wanted nothing to do with her. She died of lovesickness, and was transformed into a sunflower so that her gaze would always be on Apollo. Hyacinthus, son of the king of Sparta, was a beautiful lad who loved all kinds of sports. Apollo and Zephyrus (god of the west wind) both fell madly in love with him, but Hyacinthus cared only for Apollo. One day when Apollo and Hyacinthus were playing quoits, jealous Zephyrus got his revenge by altering the course of a quoit thrown by Apollo until it struck Hyacinthus in the head, killing him. Apollo took the boy in his arms and promised him eternal life, in the form of the hyacinth flower.

The town of Gallipoli seemed to be owned by one man — Tom. We took a room in one of the two hotels he owned (he also had bungalows on the beach), ate at one of his two restaurants, booked a tour of the peninsula the next day from his tour company, and purchased our bus tickets on to Izmir from the same company. He also owned the local taxi service.

We booked a tour because the sights of interest on the peninsula were too spread out to see on foot.

Hopefully, readers have seen Peter Weir's incomparable film, *Gallipoli*. If not, you should. For those who haven't, I should mention the importance of Gallipoli.

In World War I, an English officer by the name of Winston Churchill devised a plan to knock Turkey out of the war. English reinforcements were to land at Suvla Bay on the Gallipoli Peninsula, then move overland to take Constantinople. To divert the Turks' attention while the English forces landed, he proposed that Australian and New Zealand forces land farther down the peninsula and keep the Turks occupied. A strong current caused the lifeboats carrying the Aussies and Kiwis to land at the wrong place — it's now known as Anzac Cove, in their honor — but Ian Hamilton, the British general in command of the operation, insisted the mission continue. The Aussies and Kiwis were stuck on a small beach below a steep hill. The Turks were waiting with machine guns in trenches at the top. During the English landing at Suvla Bay, Hamilton ordered wave after wave of Australian and New Zealand soldiers to charge the impenetrable Turkish lines. It was so futile that eventually the soldiers were ordered to unload their guns before charging, so they wouldn't waste the ammunition — only their lives.

It was the last time Australia and New Zealand allowed their men to be commanded by British officers.

Total Allied casualties at Gallipoli numbered one-quarter of a million. Besides the fighting, a winter blizzard froze some soldiers to death and drowned 280 men in the trenches where they stood.

General William Robertson called the campaign "a wonderful example of gallantry and endurance by men and a calamitous display of mismanagement by authority." The campaign ruined the reputation of Churchill for the next twenty-five years.

One English junior officer who was on his way to the Gallipoli campaign but never made it was the poet Rupert Brooke, who died of blood poisoning before the fight and was buried on the Greek island of Skyros. Alan Moorehead remarked that "Rupert Brooke, with his romanticism, his eagerness and his extreme physical beauty, is the symbolic figure in the Gallipoli campaign." Old soldiers do die — I've seen them; but young soldiers die much quicker.

Peter Weir used a similar character in his film, which besides documenting the tragedy that occurred, presents a fine story of friendship between two Australian soldiers, played by Mel Gibson and an astonishingly attractive actor named Mark Lee, whose character reminds one of Brooke, although he is Australian, not English (Lee also starred in the gay-themed Australian film *The Everlasting Secret Family*). It's a gripping film.

Gallipoli is also the point where Alexander the Great crossed the Hellispont on his way to conquering the known world. It is said that he himself was at the helm of his ship, and that halfway across he slaughtered a bull as a sacrifice to Poseidon. You have to stop and think about things like that: This great conqueror, Alexander, apparently thought it would do some good to make this sacrifice. Some people would say that the more humanity learns about the universe, the more interesting things become. But I wonder if the opposite is true. I see Alexander drawing the curtains so the moon and the powers of the night do not harm sleeping Hephaestion.

It is also said that once on the Asian side, Alexander was the first person out of the boat. He would never set foot in Europe again.

By purchasing tickets to Izmir, we had ruled out traveling to Troy (Truva). Everyone we had talked to told us there was not much to see at Troy. Still, I wouldn't have minded going by, just to have been at the spot where the soldier-lovers Achilles and Patroclus pitched their tent. Perhaps the four greatest outpourings of grief history has recorded are those of Achilles when Patroclus was killed at Troy, of Alexander when Hephaestion died, of the world when Alexander died, and of Hadrian when Antinoüs drowned.

Alexander had gone straight to Troy upon entering Asia. Legend says he laid a wreath at the tomb of Achilles, while Hephaestion laid one at the tomb of Patroclus. History also records that he held games in honor of the heroes, stripping naked and running around the ancient city three times to start the event.

In Plato's *Symposium*, Phaedrus says that Patroclus was the "lover" of Achilles and Achilles, being younger, beardless, and fairer, was the "beloved" — meaning, among other things, that Patroclus was the more dominant in their sexual relationship. Phaedrus goes on to say, "And greatly as the gods honor the virtue of love, still the return of love on the part of the beloved to the lover is more admired and valued and rewarded by them, for the beloved is more divine; because he is inspired by God." This is far from the end of the subject in *Symposium*, but I've quoted enough of it for readers to follow me when I conjecture on whether Alex-

– 149 –

ander's similarities with Achilles and Hephaestion's similarities with Patroclus extended to their sexual roles.

Ψ

We took a walk around the town of Gallipoli, stopping along the beach to have tea with a Turkish family. The family had a lot of attractive children who entertained us playing games with their cat. Our tea was served in the usual tiny glasses. I find this hard to understand. Why do the Turks want to drink hot tea in little clear glasses that absorb the heat and are almost impossible to hold? Why don't they use the cups with handles that they use for coffee?

There was an outdoor restaurant next door with a television outside — not an uncommon sight. The Turks seem obsessed with television, and it's cooler to watch outdoors than inside. Still, it was odd seeing the beautiful backdrop of the Dardanelles ignored in favor of a ridiculous television drama. Donach kept looking across the Dardanelles and expressing dismay that the British thought they could get ships through the passage without being sunk. As we watched, a Russian warship quietly made its way toward the Sea of Marmara. The Russians must hate the American-Turkish connection, enabling the U.S. to keep track of every Russian warship that comes and goes between the Mediterranean and the Black Sea.

Back at our hotel, I met a very friendly New Zealander named Steven, and his traveling companion, Kate. We were going to go out for a drink, but Tom invited all of us up to the roof, and sent an employee out for beer. So we sat on the roof drinking beer, listening to the sounds of Gallipoli at night — incredibly loud for such a small place. Steven had a great smile, long blond hair, and a slightly mischievous angel's face. He and Kate had taken the Gallipoli tour that day and told us it reduced them to tears. He said that one hundred thousand New Zealanders lost their lives in the Gallipoli campaign, at a time when the country only had one million inhabitants; thus, virtually every family was affected.

Steven and Kate had just come from Eastern Turkey. They told us of bars in which, when soldiers entered, all customers would stand up to be searched. They told us of soldiers so sex-starved that the sight of a Western woman — Kate — excited them so much that they would whip out their cocks and masturbate on the spot.

Steven had a tassel glued to his hair, which Kate kept toying with, teasing him that it was on the right side, which meant he was gay. Steven looked at me with his mischievous angel's grin and said, "I'm not really gay."

The noise didn't let up all night. I got little sleep, even with a sleeping pill. In particular, the taxi stand outside our window had people yelling back and forth incessantly. We had purchased tickets on the overnight bus to Izmir the next day, but I didn't want to put up with another night of no sleep, so at dawn I told Gina and Donach that I was going my separate way. They could both sleep on buses, and had planned several overnighters to save money on accommodations. It was a good plan — but not for me.

Our tour guide was a nice-looking eighteen-year-old Turk by the name of Hüsayne (pronounced like the king of Jordan) who had lived most of his life in Germany. The tour was, indeed, a moving experience, especially at Anzac Cove. The idea of a landing at such a tiny beach below a steep hill was absolutely insane. Atatürk, who commanded the Turkish forces, erected a large plaque in 1934 that reads, in part: "Those heroes that shed their blood and lost their lives ... You are now lying in the soil of a friendly country ... There is no difference between the Johnnies and the Mehmets to us where they lie side by side here in this country of ours ... After having lost their lives on this land they have become our sons as well."

Some members of our tour group searched the shore for bullets. At the water's edge someone found one, turned green but quite recognizable. I read the inscriptions on the graves. One epitaph was for a seventeen-year-old member of the Australian Light

An unplanned stop in the coastal town of Ayvalik proved serendipitous.

Horse. It read, "He died a man and closed his life's brief day ere it had scarce begun." Another, for a 21-year-old infantryman, read, "Greater love hath no man. He laid down his life for his friends."

Suvla Bay, by contrast, was a wide, open expanse of flat beach, perfect for landing. The bitterness in the eyes of the Australians and New Zealanders in our group was apparent. They stared out over the bay with arms crossed, then looked at each other with glistening eyes, quickly looking away.

At Atatürk's bunker, Hüsayne talked with me a while about politics. He was planning to vote Social Democrat, and expressed optimism that Turkey might finally have a leader the people supported.

The tour took three and a half hours. I was let off with three Australians in Eceabat, where we were to catch our bus. Hüsayne gave me his address and insisted I send him a postcard from Arkansas once I was home. I said good-bye to Gina and Donach, then was alone again in a foreign land.

The bus was pitiful. It was two hours late, then took forever getting anywhere. It was also crowded, and no attention was paid to seat reservations. I at least got a seat, along with the Australian girl from the tour. Her two male friends had to stand. We crossed the Dardanelles by ferry, into Asia. Every stop took forever. At ten-thirty p.m., we had only made it as far as the coastal town of Ayvalik — about halfway. Not wanting to arrive in Izmir in the middle of the night, I got off in Ayvalik with the Australians. It turned out to be the right thing to do.

We were immediately approached by a woman with rooms to let, but had great difficulty communicating with her. A well-dressed, polite young Turk approached us and helped to translate. The Australians thought the room was too expensive, and walked off down the quay. I was left talking to the young Turk, whose name was Sarif. We walked off in the direction the Australians had gone, exchanging information. He was in the army, stationed in Van, currently at home on leave. I liked him. We came upon the Australians, who were trying to communicate with another woman about a room. Sarif again acted as translator, and this time we all four took the room, which was only a few feet away. The woman who ran the house thought Sarif was one of those street hustlers who find places to stay for tourists — for a fee. She tried to pay him, but he laughed and refused. Before leaving, he made a date to meet me the next evening. After he left, the two Australian guys—both of whom I suspect were gay — asked, "Who was *that*?" The woman said, "Someone Keith picked up," and they looked at me jealously, it seemed. "Didn't he look fine?" the woman continued, "I would die for a man like that, and here I am leaving tomorrow."

Ψ

The Australians got up early to see about catching a ferry to Lesvos, and were in and out all morning. I gathered from snippets of their conversation overheard between dreams that there was no ferry on Sunday, thus they would have to stay in Ayvalik another night.

We spent the day on the beach at nearby Sarimsakli. Despite the cold water and the abundance of tourist hotels along the beachfront, it was my favorite of the beaches I tried in Turkey. On the oppressively crowded bus to Sarimsakli, a stunningly beautiful boy had stood in front of me, much of his weight pressed against me because there was a large woman in front of him whom he seemed to not want to touch. Beside him was another boy, younger, who for some delightfully unclear reason, stuck his hand in the pocket of the older boy and left it there. The older boy turned suddenly and saw that I was looking at the hand in his pocket. I smiled. He smiled back. The Australians got off in the shopping area of Sarimsakli to exchange money. I stayed on the bus and got off when the boys did, thinking they would probably know the best part of the beach. I didn't follow them, but hoped I would see them again at the beach. I didn't, but I did see a muscular transsexual who took a spot near me, laid out topless on a towel, passersby pointing and admiring her muscles, breasts, and tattoos.

After about an hour in the water and on the beach, I went back to a restaurant I had seen when I arrived. They had an odd system whereby you had to purchase five thousand lira ($2.50) in tokens, with which you paid for food and drink. The idea was that you could keep the plastic tokens with you in the water, and therefore not have to worry about having money stolen from you on the beach while you were swimming.

A boy at the restaurant kept staring at me and scratching his crotch. I didn't know why. We were both standing, waiting for a table, and once one cleared, we sat at it together. He continued to rub his crotch and stare at me, making eye contact through my sunglasses. He spoke some English and asked fifty thousand questions. His name was Mehmet; he was fifteen. We went for a swim and he challenged me to race. Although not a particularly good swimmer, I easily beat him. He insisted on buying me a Coke. Then, he announced that he had to go. He had, at least, stopped scratching.

Back in Ayvalik I went looking for Sarif, but he found me before I could find him. We talked among ourselves for a while, then he took me to a café in the liveliest part of town, near the pier, introducing me to a 65-year-old woman from California by the name of Jacqueline. She was a painter, had been to Turkey nine times, and adored Ayvalik. She had already been in Ayvalik two months this summer and planned to stay two more. Also at our table were a Norwegian couple and a Finnish couple, both young. The Finns — Kaija and Marti — were especially delightful. We were being "entertained" — or perhaps driven to distraction — by a Gypsy quartet that sometimes sat idly by and at other times went from table to table collecting tips, refusing to leave until someone gave them something. Sarif refused to give them anything, but Jacqueline was rather generous with them. When they broke into a belly dance song, Kaija surprised us by getting up and dancing it better than the natives. She had been taking belly dance classes in Finland. The Turks — practically all men, as usual — eventually stopped dancing and watched her. When the song ended, they applauded enthusiastically. Several men approached her for a kiss, stuffing money in her hand and dress, while Marti watched. Kaija gave all the money to the band, who nevertheless were back at our table in a few minutes wanting another tip.

The Norwegians were nice, too, but got very drunk. The female of the pair was obviously quite taken with Sarif, asking him many questions about Turkish customs. As one might expect, she was especially concerned about the treatment of women in Turkey. Were most of them really virgins when they married? Sarif said they were. Then what of the men? Were they virgins, too? Many were, Sarif said. Then she did the unthinkable. She asked Sarif if he was a virgin. He blushed and said he was. She thought that was too charming, a 24-year-old male who was still a virgin. You could tell she wanted to change that on the spot.

Ψ

The Australians left the next day. When the woman where we were staying tried to move me onto a cot in a small room just off the family's living space, with no door separating us, I said no thanks and took a room in the Sehir Hotel, upstairs from the café of the previous evening. The room was small, but private, and cost only four dollars a night.

Jacqueline, Sarif, the Finns, and I had breakfast together then went back to the beach at Sarimsakli. We agreed to try Jacqueline's favorite spot. It was at the end of the bus line, past the military installation: nice and private. Everyone loved it except Sarif, who in typically Turkish fashion preferred the crowds. If we all had bodies like his, perhaps we would have liked crowds better ourselves. Sarif studied bodybuilding and *tae kwando*, and it showed. He was all muscle, no body fat. On the beach he was laying out on a mat, his arms stretched over his head, and I noticed he had no hair under his arms. I asked why he shaved, thinking perhaps it had something to do with gymnastics. The answer surprised me. He said Islam required that he shave under his arms and his pubic hair, as well.

Jacqueline, for some reason, brought up the treatment of gays in Turkey. Sarif said "normal people" did not like them, which brought protests from Jacqueline. Further conversation revealed that he was under the impression that the Jim Jones cult at Jonestown, Guyana — the one that committed mass suicide — had been a cult of homosexuals.

We stayed on curious topics of conversation for much of the afternoon. Jacqueline thought it interesting that Turkish boys were not circumcised until they were eight or nine years old, and that the event was a cause for celebration in the family. I expressed gratitude that in America, if we had to be circumcised, it was taken care of at birth. Sarif had been circumcised at age five, but said it wasn't so bad because he received many gifts. Marti and Kaija were surprised to hear that we were circumcised at all; they had thought only Jews were circumcised.

We stayed on the beach all day, getting totally roasted — at least the fair-skinned Finns and I. Jacqueline and Sarif swam across to the peninsula housing the military installation, but were met by an armed soldier who told them they were not allowed because it was a private beach. Sarif returned angry, insisting there were no private beaches in Turkey.

The evening was much the same as the previous one, but without the Norwegians. A cute blond boy who looked amazingly like Mark Lester in *Oliver!* delighted everyone with his wonderful, exuberant dancing. Kaija took a turn with him, as did several of the Turkish men.

Sarif had gone home to change clothes and eat. He returned carrying a gun in his pants, which I felt as we sat at the table.

Ψ

The Finns left the following day. Sarif and I walked around the quay, where workers were constructing a stage and mechanical bull. The event was sponsored by Marlboro, whose signs were everywhere. On one of the large boards to the stage, which would be covered up with a curtain later on, someone (Gerald, apparently) had written, "My name is Gerald. I am gay. I love Chris."

I liked that.

I saw Mehmet, the kid at the beach who bought me the Coke, working in his uncle's carpet shop. Sarif and I then got his father's boat ready, for he was taking Jacqueline and me to a nearby island. There was an old Greek church on the island that Jacqueline had begun painting, and would today finish. Sarif rubbed suntan oil on my back, very thoroughly and thoughtfully, not missing a spot. In the boat, he and Jacqueline sat at the broad end, Sarif shirtless, with fatigues and military cap, Jacqueline in a white cotton dress and blue large-brimmed hat. The photo I took of them there is one of my favorites from the trip.

While Jacqueline sat and painted, Sarif and I located the woman with the key to the church. On top of the church was a stork's nest, with three storks standing in it. Inside, the murals had been badly damaged by vandals, but the woman told us whom each had at one time portrayed. While I tried to stare down an owl sitting on a perch near the ceiling, Sarif and the woman talked in Turkish. At one point the woman's voice rose dramatically and she became visibly angry. After I'd tipped her and we were outside, I asked what she had said. Sarif told me that when she discovered he was stationed in Van, she had demanded that if his battalion caught any of the Kurdish terrorists, they must hang them.

We walked around the island, talking of our lives. Sarif had joined the military when he was fifteen, but regretted it. Despite his fierce looks, he said he would feel more in his element as an artist. Unfortunately, there was no getting out of the army for fifteen more years. Still, he was planning for the day as if his life would not begin until then. He was studying English so that he could get a job in the tourist industry. He hoped to marry, but not until he was out of the army. He told me in a low voice that he was very often "too much depressed." I could certainly see why.

We spoke a bit about sex, too. He was curious about my sex life in America, and expressed bitterness that the Norwegian girl had "laughed" at him. I told him I didn't think she was laughing, but that in Scandinavia it was, indeed, rare to find a man his age who was a virgin. She liked the idea of it, I assured him.

Sarif said that Islamic boys in Turkey do masturbate, but never each other. "This we would consider homosexual," he said.

Ψ

Had another shave the next morning, this time from a darkly handsome boy who did a better job than the man in Istanbul for one-third the price (fifty cents). The "Miss November" posters in the shop — placed overhead on the wall at the point where one stares when one's head is tilted back for a shave — obviously predated him. They probably belonged to his father, a friend of Jacqueline's who owned the shop.

Jacqueline, Sarif, and I went to the bazaar. It was July 12, the eve of the Islamic holy day, Kurban Bayrami. Everywhere we saw lambs about to be sacrificed to Allah the next day. Those chosen for sacrifice were often marked with an orange henna dye on their foreheads, and some had a red ribbon tied around their small horns. Their "baa-aa-aa's" sounded particularly sad that day.

From the bazaar, we went to visit a leather shop. The beautiful girl working in the shop was giving Turkish lessons to Jacqueline and seemed interested in Sarif. I took the occasion to look at some of the coats. It was the only time I had actually looked around in a Turkish shop at leisure. In Istanbul, I had heard tourists complain that they had never even got a good look in a Turkish shop window, because of the men and boys who were always at the doorways, trying to get them inside ("You are from America? Where from in America?").

We went to the beach again, where I met two Scots and a Dutch boy who asked if I knew where they could camp. I told them what I knew, suggesting they might want to go into amiable Ayvalik for their evenings, rather than the touristy discos of Sarimsakli. They told me of another Scot they had met who had booked a package holiday, including hotel, only to arrive and find the hotel still under construction. Indeed, there were hotels under construction everywhere just off the beach, and I wondered if Sarimsakli would soon be ruined.

That evening, I found the Scots and Dutch boy at my hotel. Naturally, I invited them to join us for dinner. Also at our table that night, besides Jacqueline, Sarif, and me, were a Turkish woman and her daughter, a man from Tennessee named Paul, and a singer from San Francisco named Sharissa, who was the first black person I had seen in a long time. They had been sitting at another table, but Jacqueline managed to make their acquaintance at some point, then told me that the man was from my part of the world and I needed to talk to them. I went over to their table and asked in a thick Turkish accent, "You are from America? Where from in America?"

I had planned to leave Ayvalik the following morning, but woke up with my first case of the runs. I felt terrible, and it didn't help that from every corner of town came the bleating of lambs being slaughtered. Jacqueline had told me that when it's done properly, the butcher strokes and talks to the frightened lamb until it is relaxed, then cuts its throat in one efficient motion. From the sound of things, a lot of Turks didn't know how to do it properly.

Sarif and I took a ride on his brother's motorbike. His father prepared a chamomile tea with honey for my stomach. Neil, one of the Scots, gave me some Imodium, which was probably more to the point.

Tried to call home, for it was my mother's birthday, but the only possible phone from which to do it was at the post office, which was closed for the holy day.

The Scots are Neil and Ed. The Dutch lad is Mark. All were around nineteen years old. Sarif and Jacqueline were occupied most of the day, so I went with the other three back to the beach. We went late, which was pleasant since it was less crowded. We had planned to go to Jacqueline's spot, which I had told them about, but for some reason the bus driver refused to take us that far. Mark was tall, dark-haired, and somewhat of a nerd, albeit a cute nerd. Neil was sandy-haired and freckled, with an open, outgoing personality. He had natural British sarcasm ready for every occasion, but was quite clever. Ed was tall and looked like Mel Gibson. They were going the next day to Bergama, which was also next on my itinerary, so I decided to go with them.

9

Ephesus

It was difficult saying good-bye to Jacqueline and Sarif. As Sarif said in a letter I received from him recently, "We were a good triple." Jacqueline wanted a hug. Sarif gave me a private demonstration of his skill in using martial arts weaponry, then walked me to the bus. He asked me to come back in fifteen days, when he would return from training in Ankara. He had another week off then, before being sent back to Van.

I wouldn't have minded staying a day or two longer, but it made sense to leave with Ed, Neil, and Mark since they were also going to Bergama. Neil and Ed were Margaret Thatcher supporters and their views on homosexuality were negative, as one might expect from Conservative Party Brits. Mark was no great supporter, either, but typical of the Dutch, maintained that it was one's own business. I know all of this only because we were discussing the different educational systems in the United States and Britain during dinner one evening, so I asked Neil if the homosexuality of English boarding schools that one sees portrayed in English films such as *If* and *Another Country* and books like *Lord, Dismiss Us* (a brilliant novel, by the way) actually took place. He claimed that in all his years at British schools, he never knew a homosexual, nor knew of any homosexual incidents taking place. Someone then brought up the subject of the decline in gay rights under the Thatcher government, and both Neil and Ed made it clear they sided with Thatcher. Other than that, however, I liked Ed and Neil well enough. Mark, on the other hand, was a bit of a pain.

Bergama is the modern city situated amidst the ruins of ancient Pergamum, a thriving Hellenistic literary city from 300 to 100 B.C. (later bequeathed to Rome) that once held the second-largest collection of books in the world. The books were written on parchment, which takes its name from the city. Pergamum was also the home of Earínus, the boy-favorite of the Roman emperor Domitian.

We hired a taxi for the tour of the ancient sites. The fact that the most notable were high atop a hill at the Acropolis while others were in the valley below made walking out of the question. The temperature was hovering around one hundred degrees and rising.

Ed, Neil, and Mark became very annoyed when their C.I.E.E. student cards did not get them any discount at the three sites we visited, while my Y.I.E.E. card got me in free at all three. I couldn't blame them. After all, they were students and I was not — and the admission prices were not cheap.

The Acropolis was the most impressive site, for the view as much as anything. The huge 10,000-capacity amphitheater, ordered constructed by the tyrannical Roman emperor Caracalla after he was healed by a physician in the city, is one of the most majestic you'll find in either Turkey or Greece. Neil climbed to the bottom to test the acoustics (and tested our patience by insulting us for not following him — we were all too damned hot on top of that mountain in the full blaze of the sun), which were remarkable, as one might expect.

At the second site, the Byzantine Basilica, the admission fee kept Neil and Mark waiting in the taxi while Ed and I had a look around. There wasn't much to it.

The Asclepion, the ancient medical center where Caracalla took his cure, was much more impressive, but I was on my own this time (the other three falling victim to the steep admission charge), and the sun had just about done me in. The ruins are extensive, containing portions of the theater, healing rooms, a marble colonnade, the gymnasium, temples, and the House of Attalus.

We caught a bus on to Izmir, Turkey's second largest city, where we planned to catch another bus to Selçuk. Alexander passed through Izmir and erected a fortress on the hill, but that wasn't enough to make me want to spend any time in this foul-smelling, congested metropolis.

While we were waiting for the bus out of Izmir, Mark created a huge scene over three hundred lira — seventeen cents — which he felt he'd been cheated out of by the waiter. That was Mark's biggest problem — he loves to argue and always thinks someone is trying to cheat him. In Turkey, it's very easy to think that, but you must keep your composure if you want to maintain your health. In the case at Izmir, he had not, in fact, been cheated.

Ψ

There are army bases and *jendarme* bases (a type of state police) everywhere in Turkey. I've never seen a place that looked more like an armed camp.

We assumed we would be let off at the bus station in Selçuk, but instead were dropped off outside of town on the road to Kusadasi. Why, I don't know, but it was certainly typical. At my suggestion we decided to go to the beach town of Pamucak. We stuck our thumbs out and immediately got a ride in the back of a pickup truck. The truck took us halfway before turning off, but we immediately got another ride on a very unexpected vehicle — a small tractor. Try to imagine four guys with four large backpacks and a couple of smaller bags trying to find room to ride on a small red tractor with a white canopy and a smiling driver who looked about ninety years old and who was wearing a black fez (Atatürk outlawed them, but Islamic fundamentalists wear them anyway).

We took up every conceivable space, including the hood, and delighted passing cars. From where the man dropped us, we walked the short distance to the beach, but even then a couple in a Volkswagon van stopped to offer a ride.

Our choice at Pamucak was to rent a hotel room for ten dollars each or sleep on the beach. My companions wanted the beach. We did, however, eat at the expensive beachfront restaurant — the only one around. My meal was horrible: stuffed *aubergine* with enough oil to choke China.

At least the beach was lovely. There were many campers, some of whom chose to play radios late into the night. Sleeping became difficult as the night wore on. The temperature dropped and I had only a beach towel. I put my jeans on, along with two shirts, and slept on the sand so I could use the towel for cover.

The next morning, only Ed mentioned the cold. I wasn't surprised; they had sleeping bags. As soon as the sun was in the sky, it began to get intolerably hot again, so we took a morning swim before catching a *dolmus* to Ephesus (Efes).

Ephesus is a tourist-packed place. The Turks flaunt it as the most impressive of the ancient excavations, with the most extensive and best preserved ruins. The North Aegean Coast tourist bus circuit generally includes stops at Kusadasi, Ephesus, Troy, and Çanakkale.

Today, the ancient port city lies seven miles from the coast. Even during its prime, Ephesus had to be moved several times because of the receding harbor waters. Of course, not everything could be moved — the Temple of Artemis prime among them. One of the Seven Wonders of the World, the temple was described by Pausanius as "the most beautiful work ever created by humankind." The temple was constructed entirely of marble, was four times larger than the Parthenon in Athens, was destroyed by an arsonist (who did so because he wanted to be sure his name was recorded in history — he succeeded, but we'll pretend he didn't) on the night of Alexander the Great's birth in 356 B.C., was reconstructed by Alexander, and was later sacked by the Goths and Byzantines (and most recently, says *Let's Go Greece and Turkey*, by the British School of Archeology). Under Roman rule, as capital of the province of Asia, Ephesus was second in population only to Alexandria, and its library was considered third most important in the world, trailing only Alexandria and Pergamum. In the sixth century A.D., the river Caÿster had deposited so much silt in Ephesus's harbor that the city became swampland. An outbreak of malaria killed more than two hundred thousand people and spelled the death of the city.

Outside the entrance, tourist stalls and restaurants line the road. We found a carpet shop willing to stow our packs while we went through the site. There was some difficulty in trying to determine how much the shop owner wanted to charge for this service, but much to our surprise, it turned out the difficulty was created because he didn't want to charge us anything and was insulted by our persistent inquiries. Again, the problem in dealing with Turks. Had we just left the packs there without asking, no doubt we'd have had the bad luck to get a shop owner who wanted twenty dollars each before he would return them.

Again, my Y.I.E.E. card got me in free, while the others' cards got them nothing but an argument. They were plenty pissed off about it by now, and — wrongfully but understandably — I was beginning to bear the brunt of their anger.

There's no sense in giving you a catalogue of the ruins at Ephesus. I will only point out that they include monuments to two bisexual and one homosexual Roman emperors. The remains of Domitian Square are unimpressive, as was the despotic emperor, but the Fountain of Trajan has been partially reconstructed (I don't much care for these reconstructions, but that seems to be a minority view) and the Temple of Hadrian is especially — and fittingly — well preserved.

While walking along a relatively private path shortly after entering the site, we were approached by two men wanting to sell us some "genuine Roman coins." We didn't fall for it, of course, but I have this little episode to thank for meeting a young Dutchman named Jasper (pronounced "Yasper"), with whom I would soon be traveling. He came over to see what the men were showing us, and cautioned that the coins were fake. Mark, naturally enough, was the first to begin a conversation with him. I liked him immediately and picked up the conversation once Mark left off. Neil and Ed got tired of waiting on us and went off on their own. We finished touring Ephesus, which Jasper and I agreed was being ruined by over-restoration (not to mention the fact that some German company was using steel, glass, and concrete to build modern houses on the site), then had a couple of beers. Fortunately, Mark spotted Ed and Neil at another table and went over to join them, leaving me with Jasper. I told him that I suspected Ed and Neil were going to try to dump Mark off on me so they could travel peacefully on their own again, and sure enough, they came over a few minutes later and announced that they had decided to head on. They gave me a time and place in the Cappadocian town of Nevsehir to meet them. I wrote the information down, not expecting to use it. As soon as they left, Jasper gave me a look, then took charge of the situation, telling Mark we were going into Selçuk and perhaps we'd see him later. Mark asked where Jasper was staying, and Jasper provided intentionally vague directions. Jasper then got the two of us a free ride into Selçuk with two Turks in a 1960 Chevrolet Biscayne — the one with the fins.

Jasper was quite a guy. I like practically all the Dutch, anyway. On the average, they have a greater tolerance for differences and a more playful philosophy than any nationality I know, but they can also be serious and are usually thoughtful. The Brazilians, I think, are similar.

It didn't take long to determine that Jasper was broad-minded and that I could tell him I was gay without having to worry about his reaction. That would be a nice change.

Physically, Jasper was tall, of average build, blond, blue-eyed, and dangerous. I especially liked his curly hair, his beautiful shining eyes, his large flat nose, and his smile. He was a bit self-conscious of the gap between his two front teeth, and told me that for years he had thought of himself as ugly — but he certainly wasn't now. I even liked that gap.

We had tea with one of the young men who had given us the ride — served at his leather shop. I was spared the sales pitch, not speaking German, but Jasper was pressed upon to purchase a leather coat. Jasper said he didn't have enough money, but the young man was sure Jasper made enough money in Holland, and told him that he could send the money once he was back home, and after the money was received, he would send the jacket. Sure he would. Jasper later described him to me as a "slimy creature."

Once we extricated ourselves from the carpet shop, we walked to the Berg Pension, where Jasper was staying. It was an attractive place, with a great view and friendly owners. Jasper had been staying in a room with two beds, but wanted to move to the roof, which was both cheaper and cooler. I wanted his room, with or without him in it. The owners, for some reason, only wanted me to have it with him in it. Jasper was negotiating in German, and I couldn't understand what was going on. I only knew that Jasper seemed annoyed. Finally, they agreed on something and Jasper said to me somewhat irritably, "We'll share the room."

Over dinner that evening, we spent a lot of time talking politics. Then, when the evening was down to beer and conversation, the subject changed to sex and relationships. I told him I was gay. Predictably, he didn't care. He told me he'd had a sexual experience with a boy when he was younger, but didn't like it. He said, however, that he was still open to the possibility, although he didn't expect to ever fall in love with a male. Toward the end of the evening he dared to wonder aloud whether I might be interested in him sexually. I admitted I was. "That's nice," he said, but it was

– 167 –

clear that he was merely flattered and sympathetic — not willing. I liked him a lot and hoped that once he got to know me better he might change his mind. If only I had the power to get other people to do what I wanted them to — and *like* it.

I brought up his seeming irritation at having to share a room and asked what had become of his plans to sleep on the roof. He told me he hadn't understood the conversation with the owner himself, but that it was clear she wanted us to share a room, so he had just given in and agreed to it. The misunderstanding was that he had thought *I* wouldn't want to share because I had just got free from Mark and probably wanted to be on my own. So, as it turned out, neither of us minded sharing the room.

The only sour point to the evening was that Mark showed up at our pension. Somehow, he had managed to track us down. When I first saw him walking up the steps, I turned to Jasper in agony and said, "Can't we push him off the balcony?"

Without being too rude, we tried to be vague concerning our plans, or contradictory where his own were concerned. He never seemed to understand that we were trying to be rid of him, but eventually he decided to leave the next morning, then went to buy his ticket.

Jasper and I spent the next day investigating Selçuk. The day began with a pleasant omen: We had just set off down the hill toward town when a very small, laughing boy ran up, grabbed my hand, kissed it, and ran away.

Ψ

We went to the Ephesus Museum, then climbed the hill on which is located the fourteenth-century Isabey Mosque, the colossal Persecution Gate (seventh century), Selçuk Castle, and the Basilica of St. John (constructed in the sixth century by order of Justinian), which is said to contain the tomb of Saint John. I was much happier to see his tomb than I would have been to see that of Paul, who visited Ephesus and later wrote the people living there a rather condescending letter telling wives to submit to their husbands and servants to obey their masters. John, on the other hand, besides being the most poetic of the New Testament writers, refers to himself in his gospel as "the disciple whom Jesus loved." Gay Christians of later ages apparently assumed he meant exactly that. Saint Aelred of the Rievaulx monastery in England, an adviser to Henry II, wrote, "Although all the disciples were blessed with the sweetness of the greatest love of the most holy master, nonetheless he conceded as a privilege to one alone this symbol of a more intimate love, that he should be called the 'disciple whom Jesus loved.'"

John ends his gospel with a scene in which Peter sees "the disciple whom Jesus loved ... who also leaned on his breast at supper" and asks Jesus, "What shall become of this man?" Jesus answers by saying that if he chooses for John to live until he comes again, what is that to Peter? Jesus could be a bitch when he felt like it.

It is ironic that Saint John's monument was ordered built by Justinian. As mentioned earlier, it was Justinian who first codified the laws forbidding homosexuality in the Byzantine Empire.

It is believed that when John came to Ephesus, the Virgin Mary came with him and chose to spend her last years here.

On the hill we explored the ruins thoroughly, climbed atop the ramparts to watch a wedding procession in the valley below, and climbed to the top of the tower inside Selçuk Castle's abandoned church. There was a flagpole on top which you could grab for balance, which was a good thing, for the stiff wind would otherwise have blown you off the mountain. It provided a great view of Selçuk.

The heat got to us, so we returned to the pension for swimsuits and towels, then tried to hitch a ride to Pamucak for a swim. Unfortunately, there was a *jendarme* base on one side of the road and a local police headquarters on the other. Prospective charioteers would point at either and keep driving. I guess it is against the law to stop in front of a base. We took a *dolmus* instead.

Public beaches in Turkey can be amusing. Many of the women plop into the sea fully dressed, with heads covered, looking just like they do out of the water, except wet.

The evening was almost identical to the previous: sitting at one of the many sidewalk cafés in downtown Selçuk for dinner, followed by a few rounds of beer and intriguing conversation. Jasper tells me that at one point in the evening — it must have been late — he remarked that life was pretty good, and I answered that it was except for him being so fucking straight.

It is partially for these conversations that I sometimes travel abroad. A friend of mine, Anderson Simmons, once wrote in a letter to me, "It has been my observation that in the United States the exchange of ideas amongst citizens generates hostility and the exchange of ideas among friends produces bewilderment. Meanwhile, my family just ignores my ideas." In my journal that night, I wrote down two of the things Jasper said to me during the evening. The first was almost funny, containing the compliment inside the oblique insult: "You are the most healthy-minded American I've ever talked to." But the second got me where it hurts: "If you lived in Holland, I think we would become very close friends."

My stomach was acting crazy again, as it would off and on from Ayvalik until I returned to America. Our waiter, who certainly seemed gay, volunteered to go searching through town for some Imodium for me, but came back half an hour later empty-handed. The drugstores had all closed. Back at the pension, Jasper got some for me from a Dutch girl, then he stayed downstairs to drink *raki* late into the night with the owners and some other guests. I went upstairs, mainly because of my stomach, but also because the conversation was in German. I sat on our unused balcony, admiring the view. We had, after all, put up with the disadvantages of our pension on the hill by having to climb the hill three times that day with the temperature at 104 degrees, so I thought it was time to take advantage of the view. A crescent moon, the national emblem, and

Arabic music being broadcast from a megaphone in the distance made the scene complete. You could hear the music all over town, and it, too, went on late into the night. I thought perhaps it was a party connected with the wedding we had seen earlier, but on inquiring the next day I was told it had been in celebration of a circumcision. They sure let everyone know about it.

It was the fourth night in a row in which something prevented me from sleeping until early morning. The night before it had been, of all things, someone sawing wood outside the pension next door. At one a.m., mind you.

Ψ

The following day was not a good one, filled with fraud. It began with Jasper being charged for an extra night when we checked out of the pension. They insisted he had stayed four nights when he had only stayed three. It was especially insulting because Jasper had been on such good terms with them, and had just made them a present of his sleeping bag, which he didn't want to lug around any longer.

Next, the tickets we had purchased for an "air-conditioned big bus" to Pamukkale instead got us seats on a non-air-conditioned minibus crammed full of disgruntled tourists who had been similarly ripped-off. We compared ticket prices and found that some people had paid about four times as much as others for tickets to the same destination. The price Jasper and I had paid was somewhere in the middle of the scale. While we were waiting on this bus to arrive, incidentally, I had found a drugstore, purchased some antidiarrhea medicine — and received aspirin back as change!

Our problems didn't end with the type of bus. Our driver damn near killed us when he narrowly avoided the back of a truck. Then, when we reached Pamukkale, the driver stopped at the entrance and said each person on the bus would have to pay one thousand lira. This impertinent demand caused a near riot. A young German couple at the front of the bus was livid, loudly announcing that they would not pay anything. The other passengers concurred.

The driver got out of the bus, went to the guard station, and came back with a soldier who stepped on board and said we each must pay *two* thousand lira. Obstinate tourists are charged double the official extortion rate, one supposes. Again, led by the militant Germans, we all refused to pay. The driver then said he was taking us back to Selçuk, got in the bus, and turned it around. Everyone began screaming. He stopped. The soldier reappeared and this time asked for one thousand lira each. We paid, but when the Germans presented their money, one of them said, "I hope you choke on it." Someone behind us paid his exaction money with the advice to "stick it up your ass." It was not a pretty scene. After a wait of several minutes, the soldier returned with five receipts — for about thirty passengers.

According to the tariff list the soldier produced, passengers on minibuses were, indeed, supposed to pay one thousand lira to enter Pamukkale, but the same tariff list indicated that passengers on large buses and tour buses were allowed in free. Since we had all bought tickets for a big bus, the blame lay squarely on the shoulders of the bus company, Pamukkale Tourizm. All passengers agreed to spread the word to other tourists to avoid the company.

Pamukkale was crowded with tourists. The bus let us off beside the calcium springs on top of the mountain. The pensions, unfortunately, were in the valley on the other side of the mountain, past another entrance and guard station. We decided to check the prices at motels on the mountain. The clerk produced a brochure showing large, modern rooms and told us fifteen thousand lira ($7.50) each would get us a room with air conditioning and a shower. That was quite reasonable, so we took the room. He wanted a passport to keep, but we refused this request — and it turned out to be a very good thing we did. He didn't give up easily, but eventually accepted Jasper's medical card in lieu of passport.

When we opened the door to our room, we couldn't believe our eyes: two small beds in a seven-foot by seven-foot room with walls that slanted upward into a "V." *Nothing else!* It had about as much

The calcium-laden thermal springs at Pamukkale deposited the calcium in pools, blue and beautiful until disturbed by a wader, then turning an instant chalky white.

room as a pup tent. The shower was a cold-water stall outside (with no door). The toilet was down the way a bit. There was no air conditioning, nor even a window!

We decided to visit the formations on the mountainside and then just leave — Jasper didn't necessarily have to get his medical card back. We walked there in silence, but the formations were so beautiful, I soon got over being angry. They looked incredible, like a blue-and-white glacier on the side of a desert mountain. The calcium-laden thermal springs deposited the calcium in pools, blue and beautiful until disturbed by a wader, then turning an instant chalky white. The view was spectacular, too. The photographs I took here rate second only to those I took in Cappadocia when it comes to producing awe from those who view them. In both places you're astounded that anything like it exists on this planet.

The name *Pamukkale* (pronounced "pah-moo-kah-lee") means "cotton castle." The hill is 330 feet high, with stalactites five to thirty feet long joining the pools. There are also ruins of old Hierapolis at Pamukkale, including a nice amphitheater and a necropolis that is considered one of Turkey's finest, but the formations are so spectacular that no one pays attention.

When we were ready to go, Jasper decided to try to get his medical card back. We took the key to the office and told them the room was *nothing* like what we had been promised and we were not going to stay. The clerk demanded 25,000 lira. We walked away, the guy screaming behind us.

The walk down the hill was pleasant. We joked about how much the guard station would demand from us before allowing us to *leave*. It wasn't really funny, but then again, it was.

A boy in the town below was peddling a pension with toilet and shower in each room, and a swimming pool outside, for 7,500 lira each. It seemed like a good deal, but this time we asked to see the room first. It was nicer than we dared to imagine.

We had a swim in the murky-watered pool, showered, and went to buy bus tickets for Antalya, avoiding Pamukkale Tourizm like the plague. A friendly boy working at the Akdeniz Seyahat bus company — who said he wanted to go into politics and defeat Ozal — got on a CB radio and had someone assure us the bus would be air conditioned. I don't know what good that assurance really was, but it *looked* good.

We ate at a pizzeria on a third-floor roof garden, listening to Cat Stevens. I suppose he was popular in Turkey even before he advocated Khomeini's death contract on author Salman Rushdie. In any case, he's certainly popular there now. After the meal, we couldn't get anyone to come for our money, so we got a menu from another table, added up the bill ourselves, threw in a tip, and left the money on the table. It had been a day of twenty-minute waits for everything we ordered — even hot Cokes. We found another rooftop restaurant in a quieter part of town on which to sit, write, and have a beer. We even lucked into a good waiter — a beautiful, shy boy of perhaps eighteen. Jasper noticed me watching him and teased me. But we didn't talk much on this, our third night together. We mostly caught up on our journal writing. Music sifted in from a dozen restaurants, but our own was pleasantly silent. Arranged on the upstairs terrace's only wall were different sized lights in odd conglomerates. I really liked it. There was also a minaret in the background, as usual. Late in the evening peculiar sounds began coming from it. Jasper and I, who had heard many prayer calls by now, immediately stopped writing and looked up at each other. This one was beautiful and sad — the loveliest prayer call I would hear in Turkey.

O ANKARA

Bursa T U R K E

Nevsehir ● oGöri
oU

Konya

Pamukkale   Isparta   Tarsus.
Denizli   Mersin

dasi   o Termessos

Marmaris   Antalya oAlanya
Gazipasa

Rödhos
(Rhodes)   oKas
RÓDHOS
(RHODES)

CYPRUS

10

The Road East

Before leaving for Antalya, Jasper and I stood outside the local office of Pamukkale Turizm and discouraged would-be customers from buying tickets. Akdeniz Seyahat turned out to be a legitimate company. The bus was big, comfortable, air-conditioned, and on time. They even served peach nectar during the trip. Most buses in Turkey have water either in bottles or plastic pouches, free for the asking (to ask, say, "*Su, lutfen*"). The water isn't always cold, and buses do run out occasionally, but it's usually available. The plastic pouches come with a sharp-ended straw, which you poke through the plastic to drink. Buses also provide you with lemon water, which isn't to drink. It's meant to refresh you and neutralize your sweat. The steward comes around with the bottle and a rag. If you want some, you cup your hands and he pours it in them. You are then supposed to rub your hands together, then rub your face and hair, finishing with a sniff to clear the sinuses.

Not all the customers on the bus were happy, however. A heated argument between the steward and a Turk almost came to blows. Both stood up and drew back their fists to strike, but were restrained by other passengers.

A major highway runs directly from Denizli (near Pamukkale) to Antalya. There is also a minor highway going due east to Dinar, where you can make a right angle and go due south through the rugged Katrancik Mountains to Antalya. Naturally, we traveled the legs of the triangle rather than the hypotenuse. It was scenic, if not especially logical. Our road to Dinar passed through the Aksu River valley, between the Besparmak Mountains to our left and the Sögüt Mountains on our right. We passed a huge salt flat, which Jasper said was the world's saltiest lake. My map identified it as a lake, all right — albeit one with a dotted line around it, as if it were only a part-time lake — by the name of Lake Aci (Acigöl). I haven't been able to confirm if it's the world's saltiest lake, but it's hard to imagine one saltier. Lake Aci is almost totally white, except in the middle where it's the color of beige sugar. If it wasn't for the ripples and small waves, you would think it was solid. Looking across it, you see nothing else but salt — no trees, no rocks, nothing. Imagine a flat desert with absolutely nothing on it, cover it with salt and make that salt slightly liquid, and you have Lake Aci.

Other sights included white stone villages with red tile roofs, backed by hills like white elephants; scrub mountains in the Taurus Mountains chain (especially nice at Dag), and continuous scenes from the past — horse-drawn wagons, women working in the fields in their bright peasant dresses: a land, in short, where humans and beasts of burden still did much of the work that we have long grown accustomed to having machines do for us.

The annual per capita income in Turkey averages $1,160 — still not that much less than blacks in the Mississippi Delta. The disparity between rich and poor in Turkey is enormous, just like in America (although not as much as in the Delta, where the per capita income for whites is a meager $6,000 — about three times that of blacks but far below the national average of $16,444).

The international symbols for the toilets at the Antalya bus station were interesting: a pipe and a high-heeled shoe. If you don't smoke or wear high heels, you have to hold it.

Our view of Antalya approaching the bus station had disheartened us — row after row of ugly unfinished buildings. They all look as if the money ran out halfway through an ambitious building program, but I was told the true reason is that Turks do not have to pay taxes on unfinished buildings, so few people ever finish them.

We easily found a pension in Antalya's old town, which wasn't quite as depressing as the rest of Antalya. While Jasper showered, I took to the balcony for cooler air, and there met a handsome, golden-haired, golden-tanned German by the name of Carsten who was staying in the room next door. He was twenty years old, traveling alone. He looked a bit like a slightly older version of Jan Hempel, the East German Olympic diver who is two years younger. You just can't look any better than that. Hempel diving in the 1988 Summer Games in Seoul came as close to my ideal of perfect male beauty as I ever expect to see. I asked Carsten to join us for dinner.

Jasper and I had the local specialty, *Iskender kebab*, or "skandish." Both names come from the legend of Alexander. Persian legend said that Alexander's mother had improved her breath by chewing *skandix* (chervil), and to honor the plant she named her son Sikandar. The Sikandar legend gradually spread east to Asia Minor, which apparently is why the name of the city Alexander founded on the southern coast of Turkey was changed from Alexandretta to Iskenderun. He was regarded as a hero in Persia, but they adapted his legend to suite their own history. But back to the *kebab*, it's difficult to say exactly what it consists of, but seems to be *kebab* meat on bread covered with a tangy sauce of tomato, sour cream, and (perhaps) feta cheese. Whatever it is, one should be careful not to confuse it with *iskembecilers*, which is tripe. "Skandish" is really nice, and I was greatly pleased that my favorite food in Turkey should be named after Alexander.

We changed restaurants to find a more private place to talk. Jasper and I ordered the usual *iki* (pronounced "icky") *bira* — two beer — but Carsten preferred ice cream. When he got up to get a second ice cream cone, Jasper grinned at me and said, "I can read your mind."

"Then why haven't you slapped me?" I asked.

Jasper ignored the joke. "You think he's good-looking, don't you?"

"He *is* good-looking."

"Yes, he is."

Jasper played devil's advocate for the next few minutes, subtly, skillfully asking the right questions to determine that Carsten was not gay, but had a good attitude on the subject. You would think Jasper was used to drawing such information out of people, he did it so well.

Antalya had not impressed me. The only site I found interesting was Hadrian's Gate — and that only because of the connection with Hadrian (it was built in A.D. 130 to commemorate the emperor's visit). Most of the city consists of prefabricated buildings, many having obviously stood in an unfinished state for several years. The old town is touristy and, for Turkey, expensive. This worried me because *Let's Go* said it was less crowded with tourists and more Turkish than the other Mediterranean cities. We had not come here for the beach, but I did plan on visiting other beaches along the Turquoise Coast later on, and I wanted fewer tourists, not more.

Our pension was nice enough, however, and on a relatively quiet street. Carsten had not yet developed the bargaining skills necessary for travel in Turkey. He was paying twenty thousand lira for a single room smaller than the double Jasper and I had got for seventeen thousand. There's always a moment of dread when you exchange price information with other pension guests or bus passengers, as you wonder whether they will tell you they've paid half as much as you. Still, younger travelers have a near-obsession

The amphitheater at Termessos overlooks a beautiful mountain gorge.

for sharing this information, especially if they're on their own in a country like Turkey. One must learn from one's mistakes.

Ψ

The nights were so hot (and the days even hotter) that we usually woke up sweaty and tired, no matter how late we slept. Jasper said the television in the reception area was going loud and strong at eight a.m., but I somehow slept through that and awoke at ten. We had breakfast on the roof terrace, sending our soft-boiled eggs back twice (they were next to raw the first time, and still inedibly uncooked the second) before getting two solidified enough to not make us sick while eating them.

I had another shave from a Turk while Jasper watched, wishing his beard had grown out enough to try it, then we attempted to find a way of making a day trip to Termessos, which interested me because it was the one place Alexander had been unable to conquer. Termessos's strategic location high atop one of the Bey Mountains made it virtually impenetrable. Since Alexander conquered the world by age thirty-three, I thought it might be nice to do one thing he himself had not accomplished — make it to the top of that mountain.

After several trips back and forth across town, by foot, bus, and taxi, we located a bus going (they said) to Termessos. Tickets were a buck each. The bus actually dropped us off six miles from Termessos, where a taxi driver sitting in the middle of nowhere wanted twenty-five thousand lira ($12.50) to drive us six miles. Ridiculous! We walked the short distance to the park entrance and caught a ride with a family of Parisians to the parking lot almost on top of the mountain. The drive up was on a dirt road — the longest, most serpentine, most precipitous six miles imaginable. At the parking lot we realized we'd made a major mistake: we had not brought water with us. You grow so accustomed to the ruins in Turkey being surrounded by dozens of shops for tourists that you do not expect to find anywhere a site with no shop whatsoever. There had been a restaurant in the park down below; there was nothing at the parking lot, and it didn't seem likely there would be anything on top.

There wasn't. We walked uphill another half hour before coming to the ruins. It was easy to see why Alexander failed to take Termessos — it's impregnable! As Arrian says, the cliffs make a sort of natural gateway "so that quite a small force can, by holding the high ground, prevent an enemy from getting through." Alexander called the city "an eagle's aerie."

We were very thirsty, but Termessos was certainly worth the discomfort. At first we saw only piles of rocks and were disappointed, but arriving at the amphitheater quickly changed that. On the very edge of the cliff, overlooking a facing mountain with a beautiful gorge between, the theater dares you to imagine how astounding it must have been to see an actual performance in such a setting. A more dramatic theater I've never seen. It is remarkably preserved, as opposed to the restorations one generally encounters in Turkey. The Turks have done almost nothing to restore Termessos, Allah be praised.

Jasper and I took a different trail going down, and were rewarded with an amazing necropolis full of sarcophogi, tombs carved into the hillside, and a pair of masks carved into the rock above five tombs enchased with involuting whorls that looked very Egyptian.

We made it back to the parking lot, where two Flemish families in camping vans provided us with much-needed water and lemonade. When the French family returned, we rode back to the restaurant with them and had something else to drink. The French were nice. They proudly told us that they had paid only fifty dollars for a room in Pamukkale — "with swimming pool!" Jasper and I exchanged looks, but we hadn't the heart to tell them we had paid $7.50 for ours. They had been to Yellowstone Park and liked it better than Pamukkale.

While sitting at the restaurant's outside patio, I witnessed one of the funniest spectacles I've ever seen. Imagine, if you can, a family of four sitting at a patio table, shielded from the sun by the umbrella shooting up through the table's center, chatting pleasantly with each other and minding their own business when, without any warning whatsoever, the umbrella collapses in a fit and swallows them. One would have expected screams, but there was only silence as they carefully extracted themselves with as much dignity as they could muster.

A nice change: this restaurant actually had a stereo on its patio instead of a television. Tracy Chapman was playing. I had been hearing her everywhere in Turkey — buses, restaurants, on the beach, everywhere.

We walked back to the main road and were not pleased when a bus and then a *dolmus* failed to stop for us. When the bus from the company that brought us there — Korkuteli — didn't stop, despite our waving and shouting, we were royally pissed. So we flagged down a car, said, "Antalya?" and were motioned inside. The driver was a nice old man whose head was constantly shaking back and forth an unceasing "no." Actually, in Turkey you indicate "no" by lifting your head up and back while raising your eyebrows; you indicate "yes" by nodding forward and down; and shaking your head from side to side means "I don't understand." To the Turks the man must have appeared rather muddled. He immediately pulled off onto a dirt road going in another direction from what we desired, but we remained calm and enjoyed the scenery: fields full of black sheep, many people working the fields, the road full of tractors. He offered us a small strange fruit. I declined. He offered it again. I took it but didn't eat it. Eventually he deposited us in a small village and told the *dolmus* driver waiting at the corner that we wanted to go to Antalya. Then he left. While we waited on other customers, another passenger offered us cigarettes. The fare back to town was twenty cents.

Back in the horrible city, we searched a long time for a good place to eat, finally settling on a crowded courtyard patio surrounded by buildings and filled with smoke from roasting chickens. We felt sorry for the boys whose job it was to turn the skewers — so very, very hot! It wasn't a place we might usually have picked, but we had searched long enough and were too hungry to look further.

After dinner we walked down to the sea, where there was another "Luna Park." I couldn't talk Jasper into riding my first two choices, but he agreed to the third: one of those devices that propels you into the air like a gigantic circular swing. I stared straight up at the gadget twirling around in the colored lights against the night sky and the full moon, and I got very dizzy but loved it. It's probably quite stupid to trust one's life to the mechanical competence of a Turkish amusement park, but I enjoyed it. Jasper, however, began to feel ill — just like he told me he would when I was hounding him to ride something.

Ψ

More bus problems the following day. We had picked a town on the coast at random, trying to find a place with a good beach and few tourists. We chose Gazipasa because it was not mentioned in either *Let's Go* or Jasper's Dutch guide, but was indicated on my map to have a good beach and nearby ruins. All three guides that Jasper and I had at our disposal told us that the beaches east of the Gulf of Antalya were not good for swimming. Gazipasa was near the eastern edge of the gulf. Although there are no agreed-upon boundaries for Turkey's famous Turquoise Coast, it is generally understood to run from Kas to Alanya. We hoped that going east of Alanya would get us away from the tourists. It certainly did.

At the bus station, a Lüks Akdeniz Ekspres agent quickly wrote us out a ticket to Gazipasa for seven dollars each, but put us on a bus marked for Alanya, which is between Antalya and Gazipasa. We had hoped the word *Akdeniz* (it means "white sea") aligned this company with the good one we used before, but knew we'd made a mistake when three passengers bound for nearby Perge were neither taken there nor let off at the road going there. The driver also refused to stop at their second choice, the turnoff to the ruins at Aspendos. They finally got to depart at the turnoff to Side. They had, quite naturally, assumed the bus would not go to Side either. It did — after letting them off at the turnoff.

Side is a monstrosity illustrating how far Turkey can go in destroying the charm of an ancient city's ruins. All three sites — Perge, Aspendos, and Side — were visited by Alexander. The citizens of Perge, who believed their city had been founded by Greek heroes following the Trojan War, sided with Alexander. Aspendos surrendered, then broke the terms of the surrender and was promptly occupied by Alexander until the people agreed to harsher terms. Side was conquered, apparently, although Arrian gives no details of the battle. Most of the ruins at Side as well as the impressive theater at Aspendos date back only to Roman times.

The Taurus Mountains between Antalya and Alanya are home to the mythological Chimera, the fire-breathing part-lion, part-goat, part-dragon slain by Bellerophon on the winged horse Pegasus. Another myth set in this part of the world is that of Daphne, the nymph turned into a bay tree by Zeus in order that she might escape the aggressive advances of love-stricken Apollo (Cupid had shot Daphne with an arrow producing dislike, and had shot Apollo with an arrow exciting love — he plays the same trick on me a lot).

At Alanya we were told to get off the bus and were given our packs. When we asked about our connecting bus to Gazipasa, we were told to walk to the center of town and take a *dolmus*. Obviously, we were meant to pay our own fare. We protested. All of this information was exchanged between people who did not speak each other's language. When Jasper became exasperated with the driver for not understanding English, German, French, or his broken Turkish, he asked the man if he spoke Dutch — something I'd heard him do once before. It was pretty funny, I thought.

An old man who spoke a little German (and could, therefore, talk to Jasper) tried to help us, but the bus driver threatened him with a knife and he walked hurriedly away. We decided we would leave the driver alone, too, and try the office. They also told us to take a *dolmus* and refused to refund any of our money. We went to the bus station manager, who sent someone back to the company office with us. We were told to wait. We waited. And waited. What were we waiting on? we asked. Just wait, they said. It became clear, after a while, that we were waiting on nothing at all. Their simple strategy was to have us wait until we grew tired of waiting, then we would leave.

It worked.

Although it was located on the only road going down the coast, this bus station had no buses going to Gazipasa. At least that's what they told us. We first had to get to the other station across town. We tried a taxi, but the driver asked for a ridiculous amount of money and refused to negotiate, so we walked to a *dolmus* stop. The *dolmus* driver didn't understand where we wanted to go, but we got on the *dolmus* anyway. He also overcharged us. We got off at the last stop and approached another taxi driver, who told us the bus station was only a hundred meters in front of us. We found it hidden behind a nice, chaotic marketplace. It was more like a stall than a station, but we did find a *dolmus* going to Gazipasa. While waiting, we bought Cokes and were again overcharged. We really wanted to get out of this town. The minibus that was going to take us looked inoperable. Leaving town it stopped at every corner, but eventually made it out of Alanya. We cheered.

The *dolmus* went dangerously, and seemingly impossibly, fast. Nevertheless, we were passed by another *dolmus*, a white one, which then stopped in front of us for passengers — a woman and child — that our *dolmus* would otherwise have picked up. Our driver was furious. He pulled in front of the other *dolmus*, got out, and gave the driver a piece of his mind. We continued on our way, the white *dolmus* passing us once more.

Five minutes later we came around a mountain bend and had to slow down because a car full of Turks was blocking the road. Seven or eight people were by the side of the cliff, looking over the edge. We looked, too, and saw to our horror a white *dolmus* smashed onto the rocks below.

Our driver did not stop.

Ψ

Strange to see so many banana trees in Turkey. I always thought they required lots of water (*fresh* water, that is). There are miles and miles of banana plantations and orange groves along the coast between Alanya and Gazipasa. The Turquoise Coast ended, the beaches becoming rocky. As we neared Gazipasa, however, good beaches reappeared. Gazipasa is not exactly on the beach, we discovered, but it's not far from it. It is very poor, very dirty, and far removed from any tourist circuit. We found a hotel — no Western toilets. I used the sink in our room to do laundry. When I had nearly finished, Jasper noticed that water was leaking from the pipes under the sink into the center of the room. The carpet and my pack were both wet.

We walked around town. Near our hotel was a prison, guarded by the fiercest-looking soldier I've ever seen. Three prisoners marched in step back and forth in the yard.

Jasper cashed a check at the post office. The tellers acted as if they'd never seen one before. We found a place to eat and were treated like celebrities. Our waiter, a boy of about fifteen named Ali, was constantly at our table, and finally couldn't resist sitting down with us. The restaurant was dirty and full of flies, but the food was good. I ordered *shish kebab* and french fries, using the French *pommes frite*, which I thought was universally understood, but what I got was *kopoglu* — french fries and *aubergine* smothered in yogurt. It was quite good, at least. The *kebab* followed.

Ali's younger brother and another friend joined him at our table. The friend was a particularly dirty, overweight kid wearing a t-shirt that read, in English, "Impress someone. Be seen with me." I doubt if he knew what it said. Jasper hopped back to the hotel for his Dutch/Turkish dictionary and managed to converse with them, giving me English translations from time to time. Ali left for a moment and returned with flowers for each of us. We took photographs: Ali and me shoulder to shoulder, Jasper and Ali the same. I took the Peruvian friendship bracelet from my wrist and tied it on Ali's arm. His father, who had been watching behind us, laughed delightedly and brought us complimentary tea. Ali also gave us each a photograph of himself, and was very unselfish with his expensive German cigarettes (sent to him by an uncle in Germany, he managed to tell us). His younger brother read and wrote much better than he. I hope that means that education is improving in the Turkish heartland. While we ate, a few chickens strolled through the restaurant, entering through the front door and exiting through the back, seeming to know where they were going.

Later that evening, as we sat in another restaurant to catch up on our journals, we came across two German tourists — the only other tourists we would see in Gazipasa. At Ali's restaurant they had acted as if they'd never seen a tourist before.

The following morning did not begin well. I was awakened at four-thirty a.m. by a persistent rooster, then again at 4:48 by the loudspeaker of the minaret blasting morning prayer call. "Who the fuck wants to pray at 4:48 a.m.?" I asked Jasper, as he groaned and covered his head with his pillow. We laughed, then got angry. Between five and five-thirty the door to our room was opened twice. The second time I looked up to see two dark Turkish eyes peering through the crack in the door at me. We had left it unlocked, but after the second interruption, I got out of bed and locked it. Went back to sleep only to be awakened at six-thirty by another blast from the minaret. Jasper was furious and said he was going to complain. I was mad, too, but had to laugh. "To whom?" I asked. "The imam?"

They were also doing some construction work on the hotel. The jackhammers began around seven-thirty. When we finally crawled out of bed at eleven, we took Jasper's shoe to the shop to be repaired and were invited in for tea by a neighboring barber. After tea, of course, he asked if we wanted a shave. Jasper did, so I agreed to one as well. Jasper got the older barber; I got a nice-looking, serious kid about thirteen or fourteen years old. The man gave Jasper a shampoo and began styling his hair. Jasper looked horrified. I wondered how much we were going to be charged for this. As I was wondering, the kid nicked me badly on the chin. His first look was not at me but at the older barber. I guessed it was probably his father, and could tell from the look that the kid was afraid of him. Although I wasn't too happy about being cut on the chin, I decided to say nothing. The kid quickly patched it up, but it was a bad cut. After the shave, he applied — what else? — after-shave, followed by cream and powder. He then went over my face with a small blow torch. That was different. I tried to recall the last time I'd entrusted my face to an adolescent with a blow torch. The massage he then gave me felt good on the arms, but he wasn't strong enough to do much for my shoulders, which needed a good massage after the burden of my pack. I thought the massage would be the end of it, but he motioned for me to lean over the sink, and gave me a pointless shampoo; I had just given myself one at the hotel, and we were headed for the beach, besides. The nicest touch of all was his carefully removing the soap from inside my ears with his finger. I hope he enjoyed it. He then spent a great deal of time frying my hair with a blow dryer while attempting to curl it into positions to which it was greatly unaccustomed. I looked at Jasper and almost laughed out loud: The barber had managed to transform my handsome friend into a Dutch Liberace. In other words, his hair looked ludicrous. The man then charged us twice the going rate.

Jasper was furious, as I expected he would be.

"He's *ruined* my hair!" he kept saying. "He *combed* it! I'll never get it looking the way it was."

I told him the salt water would probably bring it back to its old form. He wouldn't be cheered. I showed him the cut on my chin. He stopped in his tracks, wide eyes opening wider.

"You're going to have that for some time," he said.

I hoped he was mistaken, but as I put the final touches on this manuscript eight months later, the scar remains.

We had to take a taxi to the beach, for the *dolmus* only ran mornings and late afternoons. The beach was great, if outrageously dangerous. With its literally overwhelming undertow, it reminded me of Cape Hatteras, North Carolina. Jasper was singing a line from the Stranglers, "Walking on the beaches looking at the peaches," while a line from Joni Mitchell, "Breaking like the waves at Malibu," played over and over in my head. There were ruins along the hill overlooking the bay: walls up and down the hillside, with the remains of a castle on top. The beach was pebble, but uncrowded. It was the undertow, however, that made it special. We were pushed and shoved and twisted and pulled about like toys, thrown on the sand and carried out to sea by the waves and undercurrents, thrown into each other, thrashing arms and legs underwater and trying to come up for air, only to be thrown headfirst onto the shore, then pulled back out to sea before we could stand up.

Gazipasa is apparently a stronghold for one of the socialist parties in Turkey. One of the two restaurants at the beach had been reserved for a party meeting. We saw the candidate get in his car, driven off amongst much good will and optimism.

We caught a *dolmus* back to Gazipasa. For some reason the driver refused to let us pay, insisting the ride was "*gratis*."

We found Jasper's shoe in a good state of repair, but the rug in our room had mildewed from the water it had absorbed and stunk badly. We carried it into the hall and left it.

Back outside, we thought the whole town was on fire. Thick smoke was billowing up from the street a block in front of us. We walked over to see what was going on and were confronted with a pickup truck of sorts, on the back of which was a machine-gun-looking thing shooting chemicals into the air. Mosquito control. Now, I've seen insecticide sprayed from trucks before football games to keep mosquitoes away, and I've seen crop dusters drop their payload on fields of cotton and soybeans, but I've never seen anything like the all-out blitz against nature that took place that night in Gazipasa.

We quickly fled.

Had dinner, later, at Ali's place. He again went out and brought flowers for us. The meal wasn't very good this time — tough meat and *aubergine* in too much grease. We walked to the main highway, found an Akdeniz depot, and sat and watched buses come and go to Alanya. Why had they told us we couldn't get here by regular bus? It made no sense. There was at least a bus every ten minutes with a destination marked Alanya. Surely they went the other direction as well.

Many of the men in Gazipasa wear baggy pants — the kind where the crotch hangs down below the knee, almost to the ankle. They're keen on game rooms, too. They sit and play all day while the women and children work. The children are sweet enough to eat, and beautiful. Those dark eyes, in a child, are particularly striking. The town is full of funny-looking chickens walking around like they own the place. I never saw a Western-style toilet in town. Motorcycles carrying families of four are not an uncommon sight. Neither are street sweepers. There is also the usual military presence in town. I doubt if there exist too many Turkish towns without it.

This was my final night with Jasper. We had agreed at the beginning that a week traveling together would be about right, then we both wanted to be alone again. You get to know a person pretty well after a week on the road with them. Any longer and the natural differences between people begin to rub. I was anxious to get on to Cappadocia.

We had a final beer at Ali's place. Jasper needed a toilet so Ali grabbed his hand and led him down the street to one. He again gave us flowers. And Turkish-style kisses. In return I gave him a big hug, which he obviously liked. Jasper and I also went by a restaurant run by four young boys, all quite cute. They were almost certainly brothers. When they weren't busy, they sat at a table together, the youngest feeding the oldest by hand. The looks of pleasure they gave each other was something I don't see often between brothers. It was moving.

There was no water to be had in our hotel that night, nor the next morning. Thus, we began the next day still salty and sandy from the beach. Ali went with us to the bus station, walking hand in hand with Jasper, and stayed until the bus came. He tried to buy us Cokes and corn (the Turks and Greeks love roasted ears of corn — they're sold everywhere), but we wouldn't let him. It was a sad farewell.

The Kâmil Koç bus was half an hour late, but air conditioned. More one-lane hairpin turns than I care to recall graced the wild and crazy coastal road to Anamur. It was a beautiful journey, if dizzying.

Jasper was staying in Anamur for a day or two. I had not been able to change money in Gazipasa because the banks were closed. The first two I tried in Anamur were closed, also, and I was getting worried. Finally, we found a bank that, although closed, had someone inside who agreed to change my money. It looked suspiciously unofficial, but I got the correct amount of lira, so I was thankful. Jasper and I got something to eat but forgot to ask the price in advance. Stupid, stupid, stupid — and we paid for it.

I bought a ticket on the legitimate Akdeniz bus company for Mersin. Jasper presented me with a nice going-away present: three kisses good-bye (American heterosexual friends take note). It was depressing to part from him, even though I knew it was time. As the bus pulled out of the station I saw that he had waited behind a corner to wave farewell.

It would not be the last time I saw Jasper. Six months later he showed up at my home in Arkansas — an unexpected, delightful surprise.

Ψ

It was another hair-raising roller coaster ride from Anamur to Mersin. The coastal mountain curves were again breathtaking. We passed a truck loaded with timber and hanging precariously off the road on two wheels. Going around another curve and meeting a truck in our lane, we ourselves went too close to the edge, the right rear tire of the bus going off the road and almost giving us all a stroke. The road, for a bus or large truck, was basically one-lane, so our driver sounded his horn when rounding the curves. It's more than I've seen them do on similar roads in West Virginia.

East of Silifke, we passed two miles of impressive ruins. The landscape is strewn with the fallen columns of the old Roman cities of Kanytelis and Pompeiopolis. Since Ayvalik, I had noticed an ever-increasing number of storks in this country. They like to build their nests atop tall buildings, then stand in them like squat, white flamingos.

The first hotel I tried in Mersin was very nice, with a Western toilet and shower in the room, for only five dollars. I took a room and immediately hopped in the shower. Spent the evening in the downtown area. Mersin was surprisingly modern, with few tourists other than native Turks. As I ate dinner, I was joined by a polite, well-dressed man who said he was an Armenian tour bus driver living in Ankara. We spent most of the evening talking. Despite being rather well off for a Turk, he, too, hated Ozal and planned to vote socialist. This was encouraging for the lower classes, I thought. The man bought fruit and beer for me. I walked around some, at one point stopping to buy an ice cream and noticing a small boy sitting beside a scale and staring at the cone as if he could kill for it. I bought him one, but, alas, he refused to take it. I suppose some Turkish children, like Americans, are told not to accept candy from strangers. His reaction made me feel as if I'd done something wrong. I ate both ice creams myself and caught a taxi back to my hotel. The driver wanted too much money. As the days had passed I had reached the point that I could tell when these people were lying in an attempt to cheat me. I find it embarrassing to be lied to. Rather than confront them, I would laugh. Then they would laugh, knowing they had been caught, and after that it was not so bad. When the taxi driver asked for twice the going rate, I laughed and quoted the correct price. He laughed, too, and motioned me inside. Then, when we arrived, he refused to give me change. So it goes...

My luck: a wedding party going loud and strong across the street from my hotel. I sat outside talking to the hotel manager. Since I'd been in Turkey, I'd watched the moon go from their national emblem, the crescent, to a full moon, and now down to a half. I think one needs to mark one's time in this land by the phases of the moon — the passing of one cycle is more than enough.

The toilet in my room was the biggest challenge I faced in Turkey to my goal of leaving no toilet unflushed. The key to this one: Lift entire lid six inches in the air.

11

O ANKARA

R   K   E   Y

Nevsehir ● o Göreme
        o Ürgüp

● Konya

Tarsus ●
Mersin ●

Cappadocia

A ll over Turkey you see boys selling round flat bread, usually from a tray balanced on top of their heads. At the bus station in Mersin there must have been more than forty of them. Just outside of Mersin, we passed what well could be a symbol for this part of the world — an old mosque sitting in a field of oil refineries.

Another bus lie: The air-conditioned bus to Nevsehir wasn't. I boiled in my own sweat for two hours until the earth rotated sufficiently to place the sun on the other side of the bus.

We went first to Tarsus, where Alexander caught a bad chill after jumping in the river Cyndus for a swim (he was sweating so badly from the heat that he couldn't resist). I completely understood. He had been seized with fever and convulsions afterward and Arrian says all doctors save one thought he would die. But Philip, a soldier as well as a doctor, wanted to give him a purgative and Alexander agreed to take it. Just as he was about to swallow the potion, he was handed a note from Parmenio, one of his generals, which read, "Beware of Philip. I am informed that he has

– 194 –

been bribed by Darius to poison you." Alexander read the letter, then handed it to Philip. As Philip read it, Alexander swallowed the medicine. Arrian tells us that from that moment on, Philip knew that Alexander was his faithful friend.

When Alexander recovered, he defeated Darius at a site near Tarsus on the Plain of Issos, now known as the Çukurova Plain. To celebrate his victory he founded the port city of Alexandretta, now called Iskenderun.

Tarsus is also supposedly where the Apostle Paul was born and where Cleopatra had her first meeting with Marc Antony (they also married in Turkey and he gave her a large stretch of the Mediterranean coast as a wedding present).

South and east of Tarsus, the Çukurova Plain is known for growing that strangest of fruit, cotton. We passed some of the fields before turning north, following, more or less, the route Alexander had taken to Tarsus, going south. The scenery from Tarsus to Kemerhisar was mountainous and interesting. I saw my first camels in Turkey.

Then, at Derinkuyu, things got especially interesting. We passed two underground cities, but the villages above ground weren't without interest themselves — especially Göre. All the houses were made of white stone, were perched along a hillside, and were small, rounded — and haunting.

At Nevsehir, everyone wanted to be my tour guide. I went to the tourist office to see what they recommended, and discovered that Mark had left a note there for Neil and Ed, telling where he was staying. The office suggested I hire a guide, and said thirty thousand lira was a good price. A strange-looking student travel agency called Tulip Travel was asking twenty-five thousand lira for a tour, but I found a teacher on summer vacation (or, rather, he found me) who made ends meet by taking groups of three or four people on tours at twenty thousand lira each. That seemed like the best deal, especially since he also claimed to know a good place in Göreme to stay, and offered to drive me there. I had seen enough

The troglodyte city of Üçisar is like a huge rock condominium, pitted with cave dwellings.

of Nevsehir to know I didn't want to stay there, so I accepted. Just a few miles out of Nevsehir, I was absolutely staggered by the strangest sight I'd ever seen in my life: the troglodyte city of Üçisar. Sure, I'd seen the photographs in the tourist brochures, but the photographs do not prepare you for the shock of actually seeing Üçisar with your own eyes.

I asked, no, begged, for the man to stop. He was quite happy to. Outside the car, I tried to take it all in, but was at a loss. Besides the troglodyte city immediately in front of me, there was also a spectacular, not to mention peculiar, landscape in the distance, which looked like a continuous wave of pink sand nipples.

The name of this region is Cappadocia, although this name does not appear on most maps. Within the triangle bounded by the towns of Nevsehir, Avanos, and Ürgüp lies some of the most remarkable rock formations in the world, and sights you will see in no other land but your dreams. There are hundreds, or perhaps thousands, of homes carved out of inverted stone cones. There are more than three hundred churches, some covered with frescoes, carved out of solid rock. There are entire cities built underground. There are cliff dwellings. There are strangely eroded rock pillars that narrow almost to a point, with large black rocks sitting on top, known as "fairy chimneys" because earlier inhabitants thought only fairies could have balanced the black rocks on top.

Cappadocia was formed three million years ago, according to geologists, by violent eruptions of the volcanos Erciyes Dagi and Hasan Dagi. The formations occurred as wind and rain eroded the brittle tuff into dadaistic pinnacles, ravines, and cones in an assortment of earth tones such as beige, violet, cream, rust, cool green, sandy gray, gold, and other colors. Any bright color, however — such as the Turkish flag — stands out as if it is the only color in the panorama. Üçisar, this first troglodyte town I had come to, is like a huge rock condominium, pitted with cave dwellings. At the very top there was, in fact, a Turkish flag.

Cappadocia is also where the legends of Alexander and Hadrian came together in the form of Flavius Arrianus, better known as Arrian, the biographer of Alexander who was appointed governor of Cappadocia by Hadrian in the second century A.D. At one time Cappadocia was in the same Roman colony as Bithynion, to the northwest, where Hadrian met Antinoüs, who was born there. Antinoüs was born of Greek parents from a town called Mantineia in the Arcadia region of the Peloponnesus. When Hadrian first met Antinoüs, Hadrian was just over fifty years old and Antinoüs was about sixteen. He was probably a slave. Of all the Roman colonies, Hadrian loved Greece most dearly, and he was no doubt delighted to meet a Greek who was everything he desired in a young man. Pausanias wrote that Hadrian "invaded him [Antinoüs] with a kind of impassioned attention." Hadrian is quoted as saying that Antinoüs had "the mind of a grown man, though only a youth."

In Sulamith Ish-Kishor's book *Magnificent Hadrian*, which despite its painfully ridiculous Freudian psychoanalysis was probably the most complete account of their relationship until the publication of Royston Lambert's *Beloved and God* in 1984, it is written of Antinoüs: "By the very nature of the period in which he lived, with its slave economy and its high mercantile valuation of the beauty of boys, Antinoüs had been conditioned from early years to attract his own sex and to regard men's love as natural. From all that is known of him, he was amiable and yielding, anxious to please, eager to be liked."

Portraits of Antinoüs reveal a strikingly handsome face in which can clearly be seen a passive melancholy, like a dreamy angel, seeming to underscore the descriptions of him in several sources as beautiful without being vain. He is almost always sculpted with his head tilting downward, curly locks sometimes concealing parts of his face.

Lorentz Dietrichson lists 562 renderings of Antinoüs in art in his book *Antinoüs: Eine Kuntstarchäologische Untersuchung* (1884), and observes that "the droop of his head resembles a flower as it bends when full of rain," and that "with him, melancholy entered antique art."

One rather comic segment of Ish-Kishor's psychoanalytical book reads, "The beauty of his mouth had no doubt intensified its erotic importance to himself; there would besides be an instinctive association with the mother's breast, and whatever is instinctive is undiscriminating." Reading between the lines, one gathers that this is Ish-Kishor's explanation for the possibility that Antinoüs performed oral sex on the emperor.

Hadrian took Antinoüs with him to Athens, where Hadrian restored the city, physically and financially, and made some sense of its tangled legal system. They stayed the winter, receiving artists, scientists, and philosophers as their guests. Antinoüs served Hadrian during this period as cup-bearer, and Lucian wrote that Hadrian "always turns the cup Antinoüs hands him so as to put his lips upon the very place from which Antinoüs drank, as if rather to kiss his favorite than to drink." Later, Antinoüs became Hadrian's hunting companion.

The Greeks loved Hadrian and erected more statues in his honor than for any other Roman in history.

Athens was not the only city restored by Hadrian. Coins described him as *"Restitutor Orbi"* — Renewer of the World. During his reign, he traveled to all parts of his empire, erecting temples, libraries, theaters, baths, aquaducts, statues, not to mention the Pantheon, as he went. He built the library at Alexandria. On his visit to Troy, he restored the grave of Ajax and sat a new stone on the grave of Epaminodas.

Hadrian not only encouraged art and literature, but wrote books including *History of Rome*, and *Alien Graftings* (it's probably more than just coincidence that practically nothing he wrote survived, but more on that in a moment). He developed a public postal system. He gave certain legal rights to slaves (masters could no longer kill them and go unpunished, for instance). Hadrian banned the sale of young slaves and forbid the mutilation of boys. He abolished slave prisons.

Like Alexander, Hadrian was worshipped by his soldiers. He once said that he never saw an unhappy face without being touched by it. He increased the state dole for poor children, and he hated graft with a passion. It is safe to say that his rule did not favor the Roman aristocracy.

Antinoüs died in A.D. 130 during a trip to Egypt with Hadrian. All that is known is that he was swimming in the Nile, sent the boatman across to meet him on the other side, then drowned.

In Göreme's strange valley of cones, people live in houses of cones.

Many historians record it as a suicide, but this is by no means certain. Hadrian said it was an accident.

Hadrian constructed Antinoopolis, or Antinoe, on the Nile opposite the place where Antinoüs drowned. In a decree resembling that of Alexander following the death of Hephaestion, Hadrian ordered that Antinoüs be worshipped as a god. Much to Hadrian's pleasure, many of his peoples were quite happy to oblige. Antinoüs became a beautiful, tragic symbol. He was worshipped as the god of the sick and desperate. Temples of Antinoüs appeared in Athens, Olympia, Eleusis, Mantineia, Bithynion, Smyrna (which also issued a coin with Hadrian's likeness on one side and that of Antinoüs on the other), Ephesus, Delphi, Naples, and Lanuvium. There were many reports of miracles, even by Christian detractors, who attributed them to demons.

Unfortunately for Hadrian's reputation in history, this cult of Antinoüs developed at the same time as Christianity was beginning its spread across Europe. For three hundred years, the devotees of Antinoüs worshipped him, and he was seen as a rival to Christ. The official Church began a smear campaign, spreading lies such as the one that Antinoüs had died while being castrated under Hadrian's order, that his youth might be longer preserved. The fact that Antinoüs continued to be worshipped for at least two centuries following Christian control of Rome whipped up anti-Hadrian fervent. All of his good deeds were disregarded, replaced with invented evils. Statues built in his honor, or in the honor of Antinoüs, were sold by various popes as material for lime-kilns.

For his part, Hadrian had tolerated the Christians in his empire, much as he tried to tolerate the Jews, who nevertheless ended up hating him, for it was he who forcibly exiled them from Palestine. In Hadrian's defense, it should be pointed out that he had earlier sided with the Jews when they came under attack from the Greeks, and that he had twice undertaken trips to Jerusalem to mediate disputes and attempt to quell the Jewish revolt.

Nevertheless, with both the Christians and Jews at odds with him, it is understandable that Hadrian has never received the respect he deserves, and that much of his glory and virtually all of his writing was destroyed. Strangely, there was a resurgence of attacks upon Antinoüs by many Christian writers of the eighteenth century, who portrayed him as a personification of homosexual evil.

Hadrian, by the way, spent the eight years following Antinoüs's death at a private villa, mourning his loss and growing increasingly ill. Finally, in A.D. 138, he apparently used his knowledge of medicine to request the correct foods to poison a man in his condition.

Ψ

Göreme, if anything, is even more spectacular than Üçisar. It was an excellent place to stay. My pension was nice enough for four dollars a night, although my door was a pain to lock and unlock. Looking out of my window at the Tur Pension over the town, I thought: *People live here.* What jolts one, especially, besides the landscape of cones, is the people going on about their business as if it was the most normal thing in the world to live in a cone in a valley of cones. I walked around the village cones for several hours, amazed how the villagers went about their daily chores without seeming to notice me. I felt invisible. Except for the cones, however, I suppose life here wasn't much different from what I had seen in the rest of rural Turkey. Cows and goats stood in the yards. Chickens roamed the streets. The women worked, kept their heads covered, and gathered in doorways to talk. The men sat and played with beads, a nervous habit shared by Turks and Greeks alike. The Turks will tell you they're prayer beads; the Greeks smile bashfully and admit they just like to mess with them.

The houses of cones have strange little windows and low door-ways hollowed out of them. Some have mats of grass along the roof. For some reason, the windows often have small stones covering up the lower half. Some roofs were flat and were used for any number of things, from weaving areas to livestock pens. One house had a camel in front. Many cones contain more than one level of dwellings inside them. Even more intriguing than the houses are the mountainsides with doorways in the bottom and boxes of tiny windows in combinations of nine or six on top and smooth stone on bottom, looking like blank-six and blank-nine dominoes, high above. It makes you wonder if there are passages inside the mountain leading up to the windows. There must be. I expect they are a type of necropolis.

For the first time in several weeks, I was not hot. Summer evenings in Cappadocia are windy and cool. After dinner, I went back to my pension to change into warmer clothes, but I didn't really have anything with me warm enough for the chilly nights. Baris, the fourteen-year-old son of the pension owner, had to come lock my door for me after I gave up, and asked if I had a jacket. I said I didn't, and he removed his Lee Cooper denim jacket and insisted I wear it. I refused at first, but he absolutely insisted. The jacket was made in Morocco. I loved it.

"When will you be in?" he asked.

"Maybe late," I said.

"It doesn't matter," he said. "You can give it back to me tomorrow."

His name, by the way, means "peace" in Turkish.

I wandered into a combination hotel-disco. There were no customers, but the proprietor wanted me to stay so badly that he offered me free wine. I knew what he was doing. If he could get a few customers to stay, then others, upon entering, wouldn't turn around and walk out. He turned out to be a nice guy. I also met three of his four brothers, then we were joined by two Australian girls, one of whom was an avid Hunters and Collectors fan. They're an Australian band that I like enough to have followed them across Texas on one of their tours. The proprietor, Memduh, said he was a teacher but wasn't teaching because the pay was too low. Later, after he had a couple of drinks and learned a little about me and my political sentiments, he admitted that the reason he wasn't teaching was because the government wouldn't give him his certificate. While he was a student, he said, soldiers had come into his room, examined the books on his shelf, handcuffed him, blindfolded him, and taken him to an unknown place. There he was refused water, food, sleep, and toilet. He said they tortured and interrogated him for seven days, demanding that he give them information on "communist" student organizations (which he said he knew nothing about). When they let him go, he burned many of his books — he said he had a library of more than sixteen hundred volumes — because it had become too dangerous to possess them. When he graduated and went to pick up his teaching certificate, the government refused to issue it, saying he had been a political agitator.

So, now Memduh and his brothers run two hotels, which they lease from the government. He was playing Tracy Chapman over the disco speakers. I asked why everywhere I went in Turkey I heard Tracy Chapman. "Because she's socialist," he told me. "Oh," I replied.

Narrowing almost to a point, and topped with large black rocks, these strangely eroded rock pillars near Zelve, Turkey, are known as "fairy chimneys," because earlier inhabitants thought only fairies could have balanced the rocks on top.

I went back toward my pension, but stopped next door at the Kristal Bar to see what was happening inside. It was a rather sixties-looking scene, with boys and girls lounging around on large pillows on the floor listening to Arabic music. I talked to a highly attractive Turk who was half Japanese. When I left, the bartender refused to take payment for my beer.

There is absolutely nothing on the radio in Göreme. On the AM dial, stations are jammed all across.

Ψ

Continuing problems locking and unlocking my door, plus the fact that it was very cold the next morning and there was no hot water, led me to change pensions the next day. I returned Baris's jacket, and also gave him the pair of outgrown Levi's I had in my pack. There was no water at all at the first two pensions I tried — I insisted on checking the water before I would take a room — but

I finally found one with its own reservoir on the roof, the Köse Pension — and they promised all the hot water I wanted. Unfortunately, I was so concerned about the water that I totally forgot about my usual first requirement in a pension, Western toilets. There wasn't one. Nor was my room particularly clean.

The teacher who was to be my guide never showed up. Baris told me later that the others he had booked on the tour backed out. I decided I could do it on my own if I tried hard enough, so I got a map and planned an itinerary. The guide books made a great deal out of the Göreme Open Air Museum, so I walked there first, but wasn't particularly impressed. For one thing, there were too many tourists — the timid kind who would go to the museum because there were other tourists there, but who wouldn't have considered taking a walk through Göreme itself because there were natives about. There were a lot of frescoes, but I'm not particularly keen on frescoes, either. I didn't think it was worth the $3.50 admission, so was glad I had gotten in free with the student card.

There was no *dolmus* to Zelve, so I walked back to the main highway and tried to catch a ride. Got one as far as the turnoff to Zelve, from where it was a peaceful and extremely scenic two-mile walk. I was totally alone in the middle of a vast colored desert until I reached the fairy chimneys. *Beautiful!* They look impossible.

Zelve is not for the feeble. The steps are steep and slippery, especially in the troglodyte caves. I walked around and up the back, then just sat a while and tried to imagine growing up there. All things considered, I believe Zelve is the most beautiful place in Cappadocia. It has it all — the cones, the fairy chimneys, the scenery. There's even an ancient cemetery nearby. The cones themselves are not much different from those at Göreme, but whereas Göreme still has people living in the cones, those at Zelve have been abandoned and turned into an "outdoor museum," which allows you to walk through them. One further difference is that there are many cones at Zelve that are still in their natural state, having never been carved out, whereas practically every cone at Göreme has someone living in it.

I eventually walked back to the highway, where I caught a ride with a pleasant couple in a rental car who were from Grand Rapids, Michigan, the hometown of former president and perennial bimbo Gerald Ford. I scrapped my itinerary when I learned they were on their way to the underground city of Derinkuyu. It was the deepest of the two underground cities — nine stories underground — and this was a golden opportunity to see it. They seemed happy to have me along, trading travel stories along the way. They had spent a lot of time in Yugoslavia, looking up relatives they had never seen. It had been a very emotional experience for them, and judging from what they said, even more emotional for their Montenegrin relatives. I mentioned this couple earlier in connection with the horrible transportation system of Yugoslavia — they had rented a car there, too. Turkish buses had frightened and maddened them into renting a car again. They had been let off in the middle of nowhere at one point, which apparently had been the last straw. They had also had a rough experience crossing Bulgaria by train. An official extorted money from them at the border, even though they had a valid transit visa, and wanted them to give up their seats because they were American and he didn't think Americans should be sitting on a Bulgarian train when Bulgarians had to stand. They told me that a Yugoslav sitting opposite them had motioned for them to keep their seats, which they did, and the man eventually went away.

I had heard there were unexplored caves at Derinkuyu, but everything was sealed off except for the caves with lights. These were extensive, however, and we spent quite a lot of time and energy exploring them all. The stooping over and climbing must be very hard on older people, for it was hard enough on me. If one descends to the ninth level down, one must then climb nine levels up. Although thousands of Byzantine Christians are believed to have inhabited the city as a shelter from Arab raiders, it's hard to imagine anyone actually living there. The lowest level smells as if it had been their toilet. At every level we could only conjecture on what had taken place in those rooms, for there wasn't much information on the city to be had.

Back in Göreme, I ran into Baris, who told me the jeans I'd given him "were good for me," which must have meant they fit. I ate dinner at the Kristal Restaurant and had quite an interesting conversation with my waiter, a sultry, sexy James Dean–type sixteen-year-old named Sevket. He began the conversation by asking if I liked the music being played. I said I did, which was true, and he told me it was "Turkish socialist music" and that he liked it very much. Immediately I knew he was "different," because most Turks will not volunteer such political information to strangers. The conversation was political for a while — he hated Ozal and wasn't crazy about America, either — but he also told me incredible stories of his school life. He plans to attend a university and sees no problem being accepted because he and his friends steal tests and get good grades. He and his friends had also killed two people recently by running over them in a car. The driver of the car is now in prison, but Sevket wasn't charged. I asked how that made him feel. He shrugged and said it was very bad, but it was accidental — his friend was going very fast and the man and woman in the street had hesitated, unsure whether to run on across the street or go back.

There was a bizarre honesty about this kid that I liked, even if the tales it produced appalled me at times. I mentioned the James Dean comparison to him. He liked that, but said others compared him to Humphrey Bogart. A brief catalog of what it was to be Sevket: He could tell me exactly how many seats in the parliament were controlled by Ozal's party (over two hundred) and how many were held by the opposition parties; he enjoys causing fights ("It's wrong, but I enjoy"); he enjoys writing "People younger than eighteen not allowed" on the doors of mosques at night when no one is around; he loves porno movies; his friends call him "Holmes," after the porn star John Holmes. The name "Holmes" was, in fact, written on the leg of his jeans. While he was off waiting on other customers, I quickly dug out my journal and wrote down much of our conversation, so I wouldn't forget. I recorded the information about John Holmes with the note "Big cock, I guess." It was because of those words, and the fact that I'd described him as sexy, that I hesitated when he came back to my table and asked to see what I'd written. I showed it to him, anyway. He read it, smiled, and said, "Thank you. Very nice." He was sitting across the table from me, his chair turned around backward so that his legs straddled it and his elbows rested on the low back. He was wearing a red-and-white striped shirt with a white muscle shirt underneath. His hair was charcoal black, cut short on the sides and long on top. Dark, brooding eyes. Perfect lips, over which a light, adolescent moustache had formed. He was staring at me, as if he expected something. I took a chance, and asked him if he knew that John Holmes had sex with men as well as women. Although the information didn't seem to phase him, he answered, "Then I'm not Holmes." His look didn't change, but I didn't try to read any more into it. I think he just naturally looked that way, like he was waiting to go to bed with someone. Like he knew he was attractive but didn't know what he wanted and didn't think being attractive was going to make him happy. Like he found life an absurd affair and had given up on happiness, content with thrills instead.

Here's looking at you, kid.

Before I left, he asked me to go with him to Özkonak the next day. Later that night, Memduh invited me to go with him the next evening to see the sunset at Kizilcukur, which is supposed to be spectacular. The day seemed set, but the next morning Sevket dejectedly told me that his relief help had not shown up, so he had to work. Deciding I had seen enough cones, anyway, I made plans to leave Cappadocia. It was nearing the end of July, and I still had Greece to see. I looked farther to the east across the thirsty expanse of Anatolia and realized the bird had flown as far east as he would fly this summer. It was time to look homeward. *O lost.*

12

Kas and Bodrum

I had never considered eating French toast without syrup, but when I ordered it next morning for breakfast, that's how it came. When I asked for syrup, I received a blank stare, so I asked for honey, which I got — but they charged me extra.

Kamikaze flies had dive-bombed into my face all night, a donkey in heat tied to a tree across the street had repeatedly broken the still of the night with the most ungodly sounds I've ever heard an animal make, and roosters had been crowing from four a.m. on, so I wasn't in the best of moods. When Holmes couldn't spend his day with me, I was more relieved than disappointed.

The *dolmus* going to Nevsehir sat in the parking lot packed full of people for forty-five minutes before leaving, don't ask me why. Actually, I think the last fifteen minutes we were waiting on someone's wife to finish shopping. Still, I eventually got there, but had missed the bus I hoped to catch, and had a two-hour wait before the next bus going west. I didn't particularly care at this point where the bus was going, as long as it was in the direction of the southwest coast, where I planned to make my final stops in Turkey before hopping over to one of the Greek islands.

While I waited in Nevsehir, I had another shave from another handsome barber. This one was about eighteen, had extremely smooth features except for one nasty pimple under his nose, and hair as black as a raven. He spent a long time rubbing the lather across my face, shaved it twice, gave a wonderful, sensuous face and shoulder massage, did the lotion-cream-powder routine, then spent eight or nine minutes combing my hair. About midway through all this, I wisely commented that he was a good barber, which brought a big smile, a cup of orange tea, and possibly accounted for the perfect massage. By the time he was through combing my hair, I wanted to spend the rest of my life with him.

I'd left my pack sitting in the bus terminal with a lot of other packs. As I was pondering how to kill another hour, it dawned on me that this was the day Neil and Ed had told me to meet them at the tourism office at eleven o'clock. It was 10:50. I decided to see if they would actually be there. They weren't, but Mark's note was, still. The office provided me with another cup of tea while I waited, and I got still another cup back at the bus station, from an old man wearing a fez. At least I think it was from him. He spoke no English, but came and sat by me and talked nonstop, regardless — and the tea appeared.

My bus was going to Konya, one of the world's oldest continuously inhabited towns, and home of the whirling dervishes. The Mawlawiyya (or Mevlevi) order of dervishes was founded by the Persian mystical poet Jalalu'ddin Rumi (Celaleddin), also known as Djalal al-Din Rumi, or his full title of B. Baha Al-Din Sultan Al-'Ulama' Walad B. Hüsayn B. Ahmad Khatibi, or, most often, by the sobriquet Mevlana (or "Mawlana," meaning "our master").

Mevlana had the help of a friend in establishing the order named after him. The story goes that when Mevlana, already regarded as a great teacher of Sufi, met another great Sufi teacher, Shamsi Tabrizi (also known as Shams al-Din Muhammad B.'Ali B.

Malikdad-I Tabrizi, or just Shams), in 1244, the two immediately embraced, then retired to a retreat cell, where they remained undisturbed for one hundred and one days. Mevlana wrote later, "When Shams comes to me and speaks, the fire of mystic love shoots a flame into my heart."

It is also said that Mevlana's students, unable or unwilling to understand what Mevlana and Shams could have done in that room for three months, became very jealous of Shams and twice succeeded in driving him away. Both times, he came back — the second after Mevlana became distraught, retired to the room in which he and Shams had spent their three months, wept often, and finally sent his son to Damascus to find Shams and beg him to return.

After Shams returned the second time, Mevlana's students became crazy with jealousy and plotted to kill Shams. They eventually stabbed him to death, but as they fell upon him with their knives, Shams is said to have cried out, "There is no God but Me," then to have disappeared except for a few drops of blood. Mevlana refused to believe Shams was dead. He remained in his house, refusing to see anyone, and sometimes whirled around the poles in his garden. On the fortieth day following Shams's murder, Mevlana ordered robes, a white shirt open at the chest, and a honey-colored fez. After these things were brought, he put them on and began wailing and uttering verse, which was the beginning of his *Mathnawi*:

> Hearken to this Reed forlorn,
> Breathing, even since 'twas torn
> From its rushy bed, a strain
> Of impassioned love and pain.
>
> The secret of my song, though near,
> None can see and none can hear.
> Oh, for a friend to know the sign
> And mingle all his soul with mine!

'Tis the flame of Love that fired me,
'Tis the wine of Love inspired me.
Wouldst thou learn how lovers bleed,
Hearken, hearken to the Reed!"

Eventually, the *sema*, or whirling dance, was established, with the dancers dressing much like Mevlana had that day. Mevlana, describing this dance, said, "It is ... to know the vibration of meeting Joseph and the smell of his shirt."

Before Atatürk outlawed the Mevlevi practices in 1925, the dervishes maintained five schools, or *tekkes*, in which boys were initiated. The initiates had the choice of attending a retreat or living at home and coming to the school each day (one who chose living at home was known as a *muhip*, or "lover"). After completing the initiation, in which they were taught the *Mathnawi*, the boys could either live in the city or remain in the *tekke*. Those living in the tekkes were forbidden to marry.

Today, the dervishes only perform their whirling dance in December. Officially, it is only meant to be a tourist attraction, with no religious overtones permitted. In reality, the Mevlevis still approach it as a real sema. Their *tekke* in Konya is now the Mevlana Museum. It is considered "correct" by the Mevlevis to first visit the tomb of Shamsi Tabriz — a simple mosque in one of Konya's backstreets — then visit the Mevlana Museum. The Yenikapi *tekke* burned in 1961.

Aside from these dervish memorials, Konya doesn't have much to recommend it. It is industrial, dusty, and controlled by conservative Muslims — not even the bus station cafés served beer, the first time I'd seen that in Turkey. On the bus I'd met a nice woman from New Jersey who said she'd met a Turk from Ankara who had been stationed in Konya and hated it for that very reason — no beer.

There was daylight left, so I bought another bus ticket, picking a spot on the map at which a bus could arrive before midnight. The spot I picked was Isparta. There was more suspicious activity regarding the bus company, although this time it did me no real harm. I had paid ten thousand lira for the ticket, which is rather steep, but once I got on the bus the steward told me his ticket log did not show my seat being purchased. I gave him my ticket, which he kept, writing me out another one that said I had paid nine thousand lira. Naturally, I did not get the other thousand lira back.

"If you don't mind having to deal with Fagin, it's a fine life!"

There was an honest man in Isparta — my taxi driver, who spoke no English but took me to a clean, inexpensive "good hotel," which wasn't luxurious, but did have double beds — the first I'd slept in since Yugoslavia — as well as a Western toilet in the room and a shower with something that I had forgotten existed — water pressure! The hot water wasn't warm, but it wasn't cold, either — sort of like the "cold" tap water in Arizona in the summer. I also experienced another first in toilet flushing: a lever that went from side to side.

The drive to Isparta had been very scenic. The late afternoon sun cast long shadows on the rolling fields and the surrounding Sultan Mountains, which became a showcase of field pictures: a dozen brightly dressed women in one, a child with a donkey in the next. We passed an open wagon with about thirty women in it, all covered from head to toe. We reached the big, beautiful lake, Egridir Gölü, just as the sun began descending behind the Barla Mountains on the far side. The town of Egridir was a pleasant-looking place on the southern tip of the lake. The only other tourists on my bus got off there.

Isparta wasn't a bad-looking place, either. There was a place to eat upstairs next to my hotel. The bread was moldy and the french fries arrived not only late but cold — otherwise it was a nice enough meal. People who've spent less than three weeks in Turkey, or who have arrived on an overnight train from Romania, might tell you the food is wonderful. It isn't. It's almost always the same choices, and all of them are always too oily. Basically, you can have *kebab*, potatoes, rice, tomato, cucumber, olives, beans, yogurt, and goddamn *aubergine*. If you're lucky, you might get a shot at chicken or fish (with the head attached) or the stingiest portion of beef you can imagine (Banquet TV dinners give you more). There was not a single woman in the restaurant this time of night. The men were sitting around watching Turkish music videos, some with wicked belly dancers, on a television monitor. One video began with a couple of guys who at first reminded me of Homer and Jethro, then of Mojo Nixon and Skid Roper, then — when the singing started — more of *La Cage Aux Folles*. The vocals were obviously coming from a woman, but one of the men in the video mouthed the words to the other man, who smoked cigarettes and looked unconcerned, as they drove down a road. That was all. I sure wish I could have understood the words. Another video featured a woman in a department store trying on clothes. Exciting stuff. Another had a man and child praying amidst a field of sheep. My favorite showed masses of Muslims praying at Mecca, when one man begins to sing a chillingly beautiful song — the best Turkish song I'd heard — and the restaurant manager changed video cassettes in the middle of it, replacing it with a semi-erotic belly dancing tape. Women are only farm animals and sex objects in Turkey, I fear. It's not hard to understand why there seem to be so few gays. Even I was getting tired of constantly spending my time in the company of only men.

I took a walk around town and was surprised and delighted at how many people were still on the streets around midnight, and at how clean the town was. It seems to be a popular tourist town for Turks. I didn't see any recognizable foreigners, but the number of hotels suggests the strollers were not all native to Isparta.

My hotel also contained the first elevator I had seen since Istanbul. Some people got stuck in it during the night, which was unfortunate for me as well as them, as my "window" opened into the shaft.

Ψ

Was awakened the next day earlier than I would have liked, thanks to some loud Turks talking incessantly outside my door. My bus to Antalya wasn't bad — the Gürman company. It possessed something similar to air conditioning, the price was fixed, and the attractive steward kept me company from time to time.

To get to Kas on the Turquoise Coast meant going through Antalya again, but I had no intention of spending a night there. Instead, I used the hour-and-a-half layover for the one thing Antalya was good for — *Iskender kebabs*. It was the first "skandish" I had eaten since the last time I was in Antalya.

The journey to Kas was long and hot, with the bus descending hairpin turns on one-lane dirt roads — the map fools you into thinking it's a major highway. But the scenery was nice, with a lot of mountain goats and blue, blue sea, turning turquoise along the shore. Look up the etymology of the word *turquoise* and you will see that it comes from the Old French word *Turc*, which of course meant "Turk." Specifically, the word derived its meaning from the color of the water along this coast.

The young man sitting next to me on the bus to Kas looked something like, wore the same type of shirt as, and had the same chest carpet as Brad Davis in *Querelle*. He kept falling asleep on my shoulder, which I didn't particularly mind. I was listening to Western music on my portable cassette for the first time, being sick to death of the pathetic droning of the Turkish singers on the bus speakers. Besides the Turk asleep on my shoulder, another Turk across the aisle and one seat forward contorted himself around so that he could stare at me — Turks do not think staring at someone is rude — and literally fell asleep looking me up and down. Another man on the bus was talking so loudly that even with my headphones attached it sounded is if he was yelling in my ear — pretty damn loud.

At the next stop the steward asked me to change seats since Brad Davis was getting off and a couple was getting on. I was ushered next to an extraordinarily dressed, well-built young man who looked like a cross between Jimi Hendrix and John Travolta. He was wearing an earring, headband, armband, bracelet, and a tank top cut off above the navel. I thought he was perhaps a tourist from Germany (there are thousands of Turks living in Germany, working the jobs that the Germans themselves do not want to do—much the same as Mexican immigrants in the U.S. — and these Turks frequently take their vacations in their home country to visit relatives), and he told me later that because of my dark tan and hair color he had thought I was a Turk—and we both were wrong. His name was Oguz and he was going to Kas for only one night to see his brother sing and play the guitar at a club. Oguz was himself a musician, as well as a ski instructor, at a club in Antalya. Following the established pattern, he considered himself a socialist, hated Ozal, and hoped to leave Turkey soon. He told me more stories of the Turkish police beating up students. At Kas, he helped me locate a pension, then left to hunt down his brother, asking me if I would meet him at a seaside café in an hour. I ended up going with him to see his brother perform folk songs in English and Turkish with another male singer. Some of the English lyrics were close approximations, particularly on Simon and Garfunkel's "Mrs. Robinson." The result was sometimes humorous — "puttitinchur panties witchur cupcakes" — but I was careful not to laugh. I enjoyed the show. Between sets we heard Tracy Chapman music and Oguz's brother joined us, as well as a friend about whom Oguz told me, "We call him AIDS-man." The friend was skinny. I used this opening to ask about gays in Turkey. Oguz said most of them were Italians, and that he worked with a gay man from Italy who was always telling him to smile for the customers. He did not like smiling for Germans. I didn't blame him. He told me he preferred British, American, and Australian tourists. He also mentioned that he thought there were too many gays in Italy. Nevertheless, I liked Oguz. He insisted on paying for all my food and drink during the evening, claiming I was his guest. I gave him a hug when we parted.

I had hoped to have a leisurely breakfast the next morning, then take a boat to the ruins of the sunken Lycian city of Kekova, but I checked the schedules and discovered all the boats left at ten a.m. I ended up hopping on one at 10:08. It was already pulling out to sea, but I jumped on the boat beside it, ran the length of it, and jumped across from the stationary boat to the one going to Kekova, the captain helping pull me aboard. This wasn't especially dangerous; had I not made the jump, it was an easy swim back to shore.

I had been told at the boat's office that I could get breakfast and a towel on board. Neither was available, but a sympathetic crew gave me bread and cheese and a Coke for a dollar — about what it was worth. Cruises tend to bore me, and this was no exception. The most enjoyable moments were the three times when the boat anchored offshore for swimming. You could dive from both the lower and upper decks. Our first stop was being visited by four other boats at the time; thus, the water smelled of boat fuel. But the other two stops were wonderful — beautiful, clear, turquoise water, with only the boat's passengers around. The highlight of the trip was supposed to be the ruins of Kekova, but the government forbids boats to stop at the site — so what was there to see except a few ancient rock steps disappearing into the turquoise water? We saw some other Byzantine ruins from the boat, then made a stop at an island fishing village containing Lycian tombs and a castle on its hill. Our large boat apparently couldn't dock at the island's port, so a smaller boat shuttled us back and forth. The people of the island, besides fishing, appeared to earn their living by making and selling colored handkerchiefs.

There was a boy on the boat who I thought might be gay. We kept noticing each other looking at the other, so I finally asked if he spoke English. He did, his name was Ergun, and he was eighteen. He was Turkish, but had lived in Germany all his life. We climbed up to the castle together, then sat on the hillside and talked for a while, but he ignored my questions designed to get him to speak his mind. Walking back to the dock, however, he did make a stop to buy me a beer. Back on our boat, the music was Tracy Chapman.

That evening I walked to the bus station to buy a ticket for somewhere farther west along the coast, knowing only that I was gradually making my way to Bodrum, and then to Greece. Two ticket peddlers besieged me outside the station, each demanding I go to his bus office first. When I saw that one was employed by Pamukkale Turizm, I told him I wasn't going to take a Pamukkale bus anywhere. He called me a "fucking" something. I wanted to hit him, but didn't think that was the wisest thing to do in this country. Sadly, the other bus company turned out to be just as rotten as Pamukkale.

Ate dinner at the restaurant attached to the Nirvana Disco Bar (imagine that), then went to a club where I had heard Janis Joplin music playing the evening before. It was what I expected it to be, a sixties-throwback place with music by the Stones, the Doors, Hot Tuna, etc., and decor of posters and pipes from the drug culture. I hadn't seen anything like it since Austin, Texas, in the early seventies, when Austin contained such colorful places as Nothing Strikes Back, Mother Earth, The Garden, and Armadillo World Headquarters.

From three English tourists I learned that my favorite drummer on earth, Peter de Freitas of Echo and the Bunnymen, had been killed in a motorcycle accident. This thoroughly depressed me. The three Brits shared my tastes in music and politics. They even liked English gay political musicians such as Tom Robinson and the Communards — and they hated Margaret Thatcher, which was good enough for me. They could tell that the news they had passed along about Peter de Freitas had put me in a funk, so they kept buying rounds of beer to cheer me up, until we were all almost too drunk to walk. Somehow I managed to find my pension, stumble up the stairs, and climb into bed.

Ψ

Now, about that bus ticket I bought. The ticket "to Bodrum" cost eighteen thousand lira, outrageous by Turkish standards, and was supposed to be an "express bus" not stopping at small towns. It stopped *everywhere* — even places where there was no town — and took its time about leaving again. The radio wasn't grounded, but the driver played it anyway; thus we had to endure a high-pitched whine that increased in pitch each time the bus accelerated, posing the question: Which did we want — to get there faster and be deaf once we did, or get there sometime next week, but only partially deaf? I knew I would probably not actually be taken to Bodrum when, at Fethiye, passengers bound for Marmaris were told, much to their dismay, to get off and take a *dolmus*. We'd bought our tickets from Kas Turizm. The bus was Fethiye Turizm. The *dolmus* belonged to dear old Pamukkale Turizm. It was a conspiracy of Turizms.

Also at Fethiye, a passenger got on with a ticket for my seat. I checked my ticket, saw that they had sold the same seat twice, and refused to give it up. It turned out they had sold about seven seats twice. The new arrivals stood.

The road was incredibly bad at times, although the scenery often made up for it. I charted our progress carefully on my map, and at Yatagan, the turn-off point for Bodrum, inquired where the bus was going next. The same steward who had checked my bags "to Bodrum" and had three times that day checked my ticket and written down "Bodrum" on his seating chart, now acted quite surprised that I was going to Bodrum and told me I would have to take a *dolmus*. I don't know where I would have ended up had I not charted the course and inquired at the correct town.

The *dolmus* did not leave for one hour. I passed the time watching the cutest barber I had ever seen in my life. He was about fourteen, I imagine, with beautiful brown face and arms, black hair hanging over huge brown eyes, unbuttoned white shirt, and the freshest smile you will ever see. He offered me *Turska kava*. I took his photograph. His fellow barber looked to be about ten.

I had left Kas at ten a.m. and didn't make it to Bodrum until eight p.m. The town was packed with tourists, forcing me to look for an hour before I could find a pension or hotel that wasn't full. Amazingly, the one I finally found — Hotel Nur — was the nicest I'd seen. I expect the thirty thousand lira they charged was what sent many tourists elsewhere. That was more than double what one usually pays for a room in Turkey, but if you stop and think, it's only fifteen dollars for a much nicer room than you're likely to find anywhere else. For those who can afford them, there are some first-class hotels in Bodrum that charge around eighty dollars a night.

Bodrum stands where once stood the ancient city of Halicarnussus, the birthplace of Herodotus (the "Father of History" who wrote that the Persians "learned" homosexual behavior from the Greeks) and capital of Caria that contained the tomb of Mausolus (from whence comes the name *mausoleum*), one of the Seven Wonders of the World.

I was pleased to find a restaurant serving spaghetti, just to get away from the awful Turkish cuisine, but the spaghetti was even worse. If you can imagine a sauce composed of tomato juice and Spam, you'll get the idea. It was then time to search for that terrific Bodrum gay scene I'd been hearing so much about. *Spartacus* listed two cafés and a beach. The cafés were listed as being on Atatürk Caddessi, so I tried to hunt down the street. The tourist information office, which didn't have maps, and seven cabbies told me they had never heard of it. The beach was identified as Gümbet. I had seen a *dolmus* at the bus station with a Gümbet sign in its window, so I tracked it down and rode across the bay to Gümbet. The *dolmus* let me off on the hill containing the tourist village of Gümbet. I walked through every street but saw nothing that looked like a gay bar, nor any sign of Atatürk Caddessi. There were, however, lights below on the beach, so I descended the hill and found ... two straight bars. By this time I had spent three hours in two towns doing nothing but looking for a gay bar. I'd had enough. I will only go so far trying to find a bar that I most likely will not enjoy once I do. I walked back up the hill to catch the *dolmus*, but while waiting for it, heard music of the Communards coming from a club higher up the hill. I think the Communards are popular in Turkey without regard to their sexual identity, but it was worth a try. At the club I found two boys dancing together — nothing unusual in that — and other boys with short hair, smartly dressed, being waited on by a small effeminate waiter. This must be the place, I thought — but I was wrong. As I sat and watched the customers come and go, it became apparent that this was yet another straight bar. Sometimes it's so damn hard to tell. The waiter told me he was quite positive there was no Atatürk Caddessi in either Bodrum or Gümbet, which is strange, for I found it the next day in Bodrum, accidentally, and it turned out to be a major street only half a block from where I'd asked the cabbies the previous evening. Still, I found neither bar listed by *Spartacus*, though I walked up and down the length of the street three times.

Bodrum is a horrible tourist trap, very Western and full of English tourists. I hated it. Nothing was what it is in Turkish Turkey, from the food to the people to the prices.

Although I had planned to stay longer in Bodrum, I'd had enough by the second day and bought my ferry ticket to Greece. I tried to escape the crowds by walking along the pier at sunset. It was pleasant — the first moments in Bodrum I had enjoyed. There was a boat quite a distance from shore playing Enya loudly enough to be faintly heard — "sail away, sail away..." I sat at the edge of the pier for quite a long time, eventually noticing several men who were very possibly cruising. When the boat playing Enya switched to Tracy Chapman, I decided to leave. Sorry, Tracy, but enough is enough. Just as I was about to leave the pier, a handsome Turk, strongly built, came walking up the steps staring at me. I met his gaze; we passed. His look had gone straight to my heart. I considered a moment, then glanced over my shoulder. He was looking back at me, over his. He stopped walking. I walked as far as the wall at the base of the pier and stopped also. He walked toward me, breaking into a smile about ten feet from me, then asked where I was from. He seemed to like the idea of talking to an American and asked if I would walk around with him. Okay, I said. The Istanbul experience came back to me in a flash. I would be careful where I went with him.

We walked to one of the many outdoor cafés along the water's edge and sat down. I had established by this time that he had come to Bodrum from Istanbul hoping to land a job as a waiter, but had no luck. He also mentioned that he had been arrested a month before after getting in a fight with a drunken English tourist, and had only been out of jail for two days. He said the police had beat him every day for a week, but then had left him alone. He wanted very badly to emigrate from Turkey.

He said his name was Muhammad Ali, and he asked me to help him remember Ali's old theme. I told him I thought it went, "I float like a butterfly and sting like a bee. I am the greatest, Muhammad Ali." The words seemed to please him a great deal. I determined later that his name wasn't Muhammad Ali, but his first name *was*, at least, Ali. He was twenty-three.

Ali offered me a cigarette. I ordered a beer, but he said he didn't want anything. I expected this was because he had no money, so I offered to buy him one. He said he didn't like beer but would drink one "for you." I tried to talk him out of it, but he ordered one, took a sip or two, then sat it aside with a look of disgust on his face.

He brought up the subject of AIDS in the United States. I felt like this was probably an attempt to bring up the subject of gays, and I was right. He was especially interested in how one kept from getting AIDS — information I was happy to pass along. He looked worried and told me he had slept with male tourists for money, because he was broke. He asked if I was gay. I said I was. He said he wasn't, but that he wanted to have sex with me.

An interesting dilemma. On the one hand, I had no reason whatsoever to trust him, didn't like the idea of his having just gotten out of jail and having slept with tourists for money, and liked even less his worried look when we were discussing AIDS. On the other hand, safe sex does exist, he was one of the most handsome men who had ever come right out and said to me, "I want to have sex with you," and I had never had sex with a Turk before.

We had left the café and were walking along a street. He put his arm around me and pressed his weight against me, making it harder to refuse. I asked if he was expecting money. He said he wasn't and added, "But we must have safe sex, that is the only condition." This made me trust him a great deal more, so I agreed. First, I asked him to show me where the gay bars were in Bodrum. He took me to a little side street off one of the main tourist pedestrian streets. There was a sign in front advertising a transvestite show. A glance inside told me I wanted nothing to do with the place. Ali said he did not like the bar.

We resumed walking, heading in the direction of my hotel. "I love you," Ali said. I reminded him that he wasn't gay. He said nothing at first, then repeated, "I love you."

The hotel manager gave me a strange look when I walked in with Ali behind me, but said nothing. We went to my room and took a shower. In bed, he wanted the light left on. I'm sorry, Ali, but I don't think it is possible to love a man so exuberantly, to get so rapturously involved, and not be gay.

Afterwards, he was moody and depressed. I felt sorry for him — he reminded me of myself when I was fifteen. We sat and talked about life. He asked a lot of questions about my life in America, and told me a great deal about his life, as well. His father had been killed by his uncle in a small town in Eastern Turkey where they lived. Ali, three at the time, was sent to an orphanage in Malatya and lived there until he was fifteen, then was forced to join the military, which he hated. He had been stationed in Istanbul, following the usual Turkish pattern of stationing soldiers from the East in the West and soldiers from the West in the East. He said he knew no one in Istanbul and had not been able to get a job. He had sex with one of the transvestite prostitutes licensed by the government, then robbed him afterward. He told me that before tonight he had engaged in sex with exactly ten men, but until now it had always been for the money, and he had beaten up a couple of men who wouldn't pay. With a married American doctor at the Istanbul Sheraton, he had walked into the hall buck naked and said he was going to report the man to the hotel management if he didn't pay. The man paid.

I felt sorry for the prostitute and the American doctor. What lonely lives we lead. But I felt sorry for Ali, too. What chance had he had? What would I do in the same situation?

His telling me that he had lived in an orphanage at Malatya filled me with sadness, for it was in Malatya that fifteen hundred Armenian orphans were placed in 1914 after their parents were executed. Most of the orphans died of hunger, abuse, or disease. The three hundred who somehow survived the orphanage for two years were reportedly massacred by the Turks in 1916.

Ali also said that he hated English men because "they act like the baby," and added that he thought they were racist.

As we dressed, Ali told me he had only enjoyed sex with two men — an Australian and me. I gave him a supply of condoms and checked my pockets for money. There was twenty-five thousand lira. I kept five thousand and gave him the rest. Ten dollars. He hugged me warmly, gratefully. In Budapest with Adam, no money had changed hands, yet he was definitely acting in the role of a prostitute; in Bodrum with Ali, money did change hands, but there was no prostitution involved. Life is strange.

Before going downstairs I picked up a couple of books, which the man at the desk didn't fail to notice, giving us a very warm smile as we made our way out. We walked around town some more, eventually sitting down at another café near the harbor where I gave Ali an English lesson. Then he walked me back to my hotel.

"Will I see you tomorrow?" he asked at the hotel door.

"I have a boat ticket to Kos, leaving at nine-thirty," I said.

"Then I won't see you," he said, and offered his hand. We shook.

It was tempting to change my plans, although the ticket was nonrefundable. But deep inside I knew that one perfect evening in Bodrum should be kept just that — *one* perfect evening.

It was time to see Greece.

13

The Dodecanese

So many poets and novelists have sung the praises of Greece and reported on the bisexual nature of the ancient Greeks that I can do little to improve on them. What I will do instead is attempt to tie together some of the historical references regarding homosexuality here, and provide a few observations regarding the sexual nature of the modern Greeks, which might be more to the point.

To begin with, I will cite opinion polls indicating that anywhere from fifty-five to seventy-five percent of modern Greeks disapprove of homosexuality. There is also the case of the 1981 bill that says that gays should have themselves regularly examined to protect against VD. This law replaced an earlier, much harsher bill that was withdrawn in 1978 after demonstrations sponsored by the International Lesbian and Gay Association in front of Greek embassies.

The situation for gays in Greece is steadily improving. Melina Mercouri and other celebrities have publicly stated their support of gay rights. A gay liberation group is active in Athens (A.K.O.E.,

P.O. Box 26022, Athens, 10022), and two gay magazines are published there. *Spartacus* lists twenty-six gay bars in Athens, and gay bars or beaches in eleven other Greek towns. And then there's the "gay mecca," Mykonos, with many bars catering to a gay-straight mix, several hotels catering primarily to gays, and gay beaches known as Elia, Panorama, and Super Paradise (the last one nude). If you're going to Mykonos, it's a good idea to arrange everything in advance through a travel agent, preferably one belonging to the International Gay Travel Association (IGTA, P.O. Box 18466, Denver, Colorado 80218; 303-467-7117).

Ψ

There are classicists who despise the present-day inhabitants of Greece, feeling that they have supplanted a far superior species, the Greeks of ancient history. Some of the remarks I've read are so unnecessarily cruel that I suspect racism has crept into the criticism — the modern Greeks' lack of blond hair seems to upset some classicists, for instance.

Their history weighs heavily upon the modern Greeks, I think: It is a lot to live up to, both in the eyes of the world, and in their own. To their credit, they don't seem particularly ashamed of the bisexuality that played such a large part in their history, but they don't go out of their way to honor it, either. In a place such as Thívai, for instance, on the site of ancient Thebes, one might expect the local inhabitants to have *some* knowledge of the Sacred Band, the army of lovers who once defended their city. One might expect a statue or an available book. One won't find them. The modern Greeks are apparently more interested in honoring twentieth-century heroes — those who helped the modern nation gain its independence after centuries of Turkish domination. Of these heroes, the one of most interest to gays is perhaps Lord Byron, who, of course, wasn't Greek at all. More on him later.

Other writers, instead of shaming the modern Greeks, appear to adopt Panglossian perspectives and describe Greece as if it were Shangri-la. They tell us the water tastes better here than anywhere else in the world. They tell us that "it lies bathed in a light such as the eye has never yet beheld" (Hugo Von Hofmannsthal), that "in every Greek landscape ... the light is the protagonist-hero" (Nikos Kazantzakis), and that visiting Greece for the first time "was as if I had always been conscious of a haze; a refraction caused by the air standing between me and the world. Now that haze was gone" (Nicholas Gage). They tell us it is a nation of Renaissance men (Gage, again) or a nation of poets.

I didn't find the water any better than that in the Rockies, or the light any better than that of New Mexico, nor did I find the people any better or worse, generally speaking, than the inhabitants of other lands. True, they love to talk — about politics, the weather, whatever. True, Greece has one of the lowest violent-crime rates in Europe. But a nation of poets? I rather think not. What it all comes down to is that Greece is a country like many other countries, with the same pollution and economic problems plaguing much of the world, inhabited by people who are both good and evil, rude and friendly, brilliant and silly, just like any other of the world's nations.

Having said that, I might add that young Greek men get my vote for the sexiest in Europe.

I'm not sure why they strike me as sexier than, say, Italians or Spaniards or Latin Americans, who look similar and are just as physically attractive. I think it has something to do with their general attitudes toward sexuality. While the others tend to maintain a tough *machismo* that generally puts me off, the Greek boys possess all the fire and vitality of the *machismo*, but without the toughness and the predisposition toward heterosexuality. Their "live and let live" attitude makes them appear both more vulnerable and more available, which, I guess, makes them sexier in my eyes.

Greece is probably the hardest country in the world in which to figure out which men are gay or bisexual and which are straight. It's especially hard at clubs, where many of the good-looking boys dance with each other, drape their arms over each other's shoulders, sometimes appear to be trying to pick each other up or having a lover's quarrel, and then, suddenly, put the make on some girl. A month of observing them led me to believe that many are indeed, just like the ancients, bisexual — but I would not swear to it.

I got my first taste of this confusion on the island of Kos, in the Dodecanese chain running up and down the coast of Turkey. The Dodecanese were the last of the Greek islands to become part of Greece, not able to join with their fellow Greeks until the German surrender in 1945. The Germans had taken control from the Italians, who had taken over from the Turks, who had taken over from the Crusader Knights of the Order of St. John of Jerusalem, who had taken over after being evicted from that city, and who built stalwart fortresses over many of the islands. Despite the close proximity with, and long occupation by Turkey, the Dodecanese bear no resemblance to that country. They're convincingly Greek.

The name *Dodecanese* means nothing more than "twelve islands." Unless you have your own boat at your disposal or quite a lot of time on your hands, erratic ferry schedules make it difficult to see more than two or three of them on one trip. This wasn't a problem for me because I only wanted to see Kos. However, I ended up visiting Rhodes (Ródhos) as well because that seemed the easiest way of getting out of the Dodecanese. Island hopping in Greece is not as easy as one might think. You cannot, for instance, go from Kos to Santoríni (Thíra), which is what I really wanted to do; nor can you go from Kos to Mykonos, my second choice. You *can* get to Athens from Kos, but it will cost you either a fortune for the plane fare or more than a day on a boat. If you want somewhere to sleep on the boat, that will end up costing quite a lot, as well. Perhaps the strangest inconvenience is that the travel agents on any particular island have information only for the boats to and from that island. It's the same as if my travel agent in Little Rock (bless you, Philip) could get me to Memphis, Dallas, or New Orleans, but had no idea how and when I could then get to Tucson or Seattle.

I chose Kos as my first stop mainly because it was easily accessible from Bodrum — that's where the ferry goes. But I also knew that Kos had been occupied by Alexander, which appealed to me, and *Let's Go* claimed it was something of a paradise. *Let's Go* also said it is one of the most expensive islands in Greece and that it is packed with tourists in July and August, which frightened me a great deal.

Let me say now that visiting Greece, and especially the Greek islands, in August is about the dumbest thing a tourist can do. I did it, so I speak from experience. I expect that any other time of the year I would have found Greece much to my liking. The water and whitewashed seaside villages are beautiful, Greeks share my favorite color — blue, and they seem to possess a toleration for differences. But in August I experienced one disappointment after another: islands with no available rooms, waiters who had seen too many tourists to care, all manner of transportation booked weeks in advance for many destinations, Greeks who did not especially want to talk to one more tourist, and fellow tourists who had become so soured by their own trials and tribulations that they were no joy to talk to, either.

Let's Go warns, "If you are allergic to the tourist scene, go elsewhere and leave Kos for the off-season." When I first arrived on the island, I was quite sure this warning was true. I'm still sure that Kos is best visited in the off-season, but as for going elsewhere, hindsight tells me that Kos was the island least crowded with tourists of the several I visited. Or at least it was the island most able to accommodate them. I had some trouble finding a room, but far less than anywhere else. It was also the easiest island to leave (I thought I would *never* get off Rhodes).

Actually, I walked around Kos Town for an hour to decide if I wanted to stay, and once I saw how beautiful it was, knew I did. The decision made, I found a room at the second hotel I tried, which was remarkable, I would come to find.

The room at the Hotel Milva was sixteen dollars a night — which was about what I had expected to pay in Greece, at least on the islands. What makes the island special is its incredible variety of flowering plants (including a large rock gate covered with a mass of brilliant purple flowers) and different types of architecture (including Archaic, Classical, Hellenistic, and Roman ruins). Palms line several streets and appear at random in many yards. I loved the harbor with its assortment of brightly painted boats — most of them blue — backed by the sea on one side and the impressive walls of the fifteenth-century Castle of the Knights of St. John on another. I was also pleased to find that there were far fewer English tourists than at Bodrum. I know my aversion to English and German tourists is just as bad as the aversion some foreigners feel toward American tourists, but I think both aversions are grounded in a somewhat truthful generalization: All three nationalities tend to want the world on a plate.

There were also laundromats on Kos — a nice surprise. My clothes had been washed by nothing but my hands for well over a month. My main disappointment with Kos Town was that the beach wasn't so great. There were many people swimming, but I had been so spoilt by the Turquoise Coast that I didn't care to swim at any beach looking so filthy.

Other than the beach, Kos Town was a striking contrast to tacky, bustling Bodrum. The tourists were spread out over larger areas and seemed much more relaxed. The buildings were painted and well maintained. There were not as many peddlers and hawkers. Also, the cool sea breeze made it not as hot.

Food was expensive, but I found one place where I could buy a *pita* sandwich, a beer, and a Coke (one gets thirsty) for two dollars. I used it often, for I think it was the *only* cheap place to eat in Kos Town other than two fast-food hamburger joints. (Not McDonald's, I might add. The Greeks seem proud that there is not a McDonald's anywhere in their country, but all this means is that it's impossible to get a decent hamburger in the whole of Greece.)

Kos has some of the best nightlife you will find in Greece. There didn't seem to be a club exclusively for gays, but many clubs appeared to have an indiscernible mix of gay, straight, and bisexual customers peacefully coexisting. As I've said, it's damned near impossible to tell in a Greek club who is gay and who isn't. I'm not sure they know themselves. What's certain is that it's no big deal to them one way or the other. Personally, I like places like this, for I often get bored in ghettos.

I settled on the White Angel for the evening because it had the best sound system I've heard in my life, played good music, and had a lot of good-looking boys inside dancing with each other. There is a four-block area of Kos Town near the agora on Nafkliron Street in which there are nothing but clubs. At night the streets are full of revellers going from one club to the next. Around the tables outside the White Angel were couples, mostly — but you could see inside from the street with no problem, and so I saw the boys, some of whom were dancing in let-loose, free-style fashions that I found exciting.

The clientele at the White Angel was about as interesting to look at as you'll find anywhere. There were too-cute boys dancing together, too-chic girls dancing together, a long-haired boy wearing a Motorhead t-shirt dancing with a guy whose shirt read, "AIDS kills. Don't be silly, put that condom on your willy." Most of the boys in the club had short hair and were sharply dressed. I would learn later that most of them were Greek soldiers stationed at a base on the island. All I can say is they don't make soldiers like that in America. I have been to bars frequented by American soldiers and I have never seen them dancing together or leaning against the wall with their arms around each other's waist.

The staff of the White Angel was interesting, too. One bartender had beautiful, long, curly hair, was very tall, and danced about wildly behind his bar. Beside him were two barmaids who looked like the sexy women in Robert Palmer and Golden Earring videos. The other bartender twice performed a sexy striptease, dancing on top of his bar and stripping down to his bikini briefs. The crowds on the street stopped to stare; the boys in the bar loved it. The disc jockey had energy plus, sometimes bursting onto the dance floor and out into the street in a dancing frenzy. He played great music — the Waterboys, Talk Talk, U2, Depeche Mode, and even Deep Purple's "Smoke on the Water," plus some songs that I tend to think of as gay bar nostalgia, such as Spandau Ballet's "Enola Gay," Human League's "Don't You Want Me," Men Without Hats' "Safety Dance," and Bryan Ferry's "Let's Stick Together." I had never heard any of these songs sound as good as they did on the White Angel's sound system. I decided I would have to spend another night in Kos Town just for the music.

The deejay looked like the drummer of the Australian band INXS and winked at me a lot, but that's the closest I came all evening to social contact. There was a cute and seemingly gay soldier from Athens whom I tried to talk to, but he wasn't interested. Still, it was a good evening and I was sorry when the place closed at midnight. The nightlife scene in Kos Town abandons this four-block area at midnight, moving far down the beach — about a mile to the north — to the late-night discos. The exodus and pilgrimage are something to see. I didn't see all of it until my second night, for all I wanted to see my first night was my bed, only three blocks away. It was the quietest room I had slept in for weeks.

Ψ

The next morning I went across the street for a cream croissant and coffee at the Croissanterie Philippe. The woman wanted to know how I wanted my coffee. "Hot? Warm? Cold? Ice?"

I said, "Hot."

"Ice?" she asked.

"Hot," I repeated.

"Hot?" she asked.

"Yes."

So she brings me an ice coffee blended with ice and cream and tasting rather like a White Russian, which I love.

– 233 –

I saw a marching band composed of police officers, male and female. You would never see that in Turkey.

Aside from a brief swim — I backed down on my opposition to using the beach, but I did keep my shoes on — I wasted the afternoon doing laundry and trying to telephone St. Louis to confirm my charter ticket back to America. I will never use a charter again. I waited two hours at the telephone company office for the call to be placed, then was told to return to my hotel and they would connect me there. An hour later, they did, but I was on the line a solid twenty minutes and never got through to St. Louis. At one point I was talking to three different Greek operators, two of whom knew my name and what I wanted. Between operators I was treated to a wild assortment of electronic noises, which Brian Eno or David Byrne might have enjoyed recording. One operator got on the line and said, "The last name is spelled C-A-R-L-I-S-L-E." No, it wasn't. The first operator kept coming back on to say, "Hello, Mr. Keith, speak up please," but then would leave the line before I could say a word. It was like being caught in a tape loop of the Beatles' "Revolution 9." My room grew dark. Finally, the first operator came back on and said, "Hello, close the telephone and we call you again, please." This was too much. I had spent almost six hours of my day doing laundry and trying to make one lousy phone call. I left. The desk clerk at my hotel volunteered to take a message if they called back, but they never did. The experience brought it home to me that I was indeed on an island and that society was somewhere *out there*, no longer quite within my grasp.

The White Angel cheered me up. There were people on the street wearing togas and people too drunk to walk being carried by their friends. One young woman, who looked Scandinavian, sat down in the middle of the street and began to cry. Both Kos and Rhodes were full of Scandinavians, whom I suppose are my favorite tourists to encounter, next to the Dutch, Kiwis, and Australians, because they tend to get drunk every night and make absolute fools of themselves.

Inside the club, it was the same as the night before, although I managed a good deal more social interaction, first with four guys who thought I was Greek and began talking away to me before I interrupted and asked if they knew English, then with a guy I had been watching all night just because he was so damn cute and interesting. He seemed to know a lot of the boys in the club and seemed to be rather intimately attached to one of them, who held him around the waist a lot and often tried to kiss him. He didn't appear to want to be kissed, but was good-natured in his rejections. He also seemed to be trying to pick up a very attractive young woman. I watched him play back and forth between apparent lover and possible pick-up. Eventually he noticed I was watching him and laughed blushingly. He was from Crete and said "yes" when I asked if he was on holiday, but later said he was in the military. I wanted to talk to him in a quieter environment, but didn't especially want to leave the club, so I asked what he was doing the next day. He had military obligations, but said he would like to meet me the day after. I told him I would be gone, having already purchased a ticket for Rhodes. Sometimes it just doesn't pay to plan ahead.

Most of the short-haired sexy boys in the club were apparently in the military. I don't think they were all gay. Probably about half were and the other half were their straight friends who had come for the girls. But a good many could also have been bisexual. Greek bisexuality seems to be alive and well in the modern democracy. It's quite nice, at least, how the soldiers can be so free with their affections for one another in the middle of the town where they are stationed, with no one seeming to care. I laugh to think of soldiers from Fort Hood acting the same way at the bars in Killeen, Texas. You would never see it in the U.S. — and certainly not in Turkey. Having been to both countries, there is no question where my sympathies lie in the Greek–Turk dispute. I'll pick the country where human rights are respected every time.

Some day, I want to visit Crete. I couldn't fit it into this trip, but I kept meeting outrageously sexy soldiers from Crete all over Greece, many of them seemingly bisexual. Perhaps no part of Greece has a stronger bisexual history than Crete. Karl Otfried Müller, in his *History and Antiquities of the Doric Race* (1840), wrote, "It was disgraceful for a well-educated youth to be without a lover" and describes a ritual in which a younger boy was forcefully carried away by an older boy, who had previously stated his intention to the younger boy's family. They remained together for two months in the mountains or on the older boy's estate, after which the older boy dismissed the younger, who was then free to decide whether to break off the relationship or continue it. If he chose to continue, he was called a companion in arms and fought in battle next to his lover (doubly inspired in valor by the gods of war and love, the Cretans believed). The two months together was apparently a sort of "trial marriage" much like the *sirvinacuy* practiced in the Andes (by heterosexuals, alas). John Boswell adds that "males not married to other males in Crete were socially disadvantaged." Similar customs existed in Thebes and Sparta, but Crete seems to take the cake for revering homosexual relationships.

As the White Angel closed down at midnight, a strange fight broke out between the deejay and a drunk customer. The deejay ended up right beside me, sweating and practically hyperventilating. I asked what had happened, to which he replied, "I don't know." The drunk was tossed out by other customers, hurling insults at everyone within reach of his voice.

When the Greeks get mad, I had read, their curses are usually blasphemous. Some of their favorite curses are: "I fuck your All-Holy-One," "I fuck your Christ," "I fuck your Cross," "I fuck your faith," and the weirdest of all, "I fuck your Easter."

And Americans think "God damn" is blasphemous.

I remember once when I was working on the copy desk of the *Arkansas Gazette* one of my fellow editors, Mark, had spent several minutes trying to come up with a headline for a major page one story, and finally cried out in despair, "Goddamnit to hell! [pause] It won't fit!"

"Try just 'Damnit to hell,'" I suggested.

"What are you, some kind of atheist?" Mark asked. "You would take the *God* out of *Goddamnit*?"

"How about 'X-damnit to hell'? See if that fits."

I suppose he could have tried, "I fuck your Easter" — *that* would have shaken them up in Dogpatch.

Ψ

I followed the crowds the mile across the beach to the discos. Some of the bars along the way were desperately trying to keep their customers and lure new ones in, but I think the White Angel and the bars around it did the honorable thing by simply giving way to the inevitable and closing up shop. The two major discos, situated side by side, were called Heaven and Calva. The more interesting crowd was going into the Calva. Unfortunately, I hadn't thought to exchange more money after purchasing my boat ticket earlier, and someone had given me back as change a five-hundred Turkish lira note instead of a five-hundred drachma note, which I hadn't noticed until now, so I didn't have enough drachma left to cover the seven-dollar admission. Ah, well...

Spent the next day exploring the ruins on Kos, which are pervasive, but not especially interesting after having seen Ephesus and Termessos. The ancient Plane Tree of Hippocrates, split into fragments but still living, was interesting. The tourist literature insists that it is the oldest tree in Europe, but it also says that Hippocrates, the great physician, wrote many of his books under this tree — highly unlikely, since Hippocrates lived twenty-five thousand years ago and trees of this type live several hundred years, tops. It's a nice tree, though.

The small Archaeological Museum had some good statues, including the statue of Hippocrates that is often used to illustrate the man's features in encyclopedias. Another interesting building was the Synagogue of Kos, abandoned after virtually the entire

– 237 –

Jewish population of the island was murdered during the German occupation of Kos in the Second World War.

At an expensive café where I had stopped for a decent lunch, I instead had to witness the indecent dressing-down of a young boy of thirteen or fourteen, who was being yelled at by my waiter. I don't know what the boy's job was, but he apparently lost it on the spot, for he began to cry and was then sent off, without ever having said a word in his own defense. It was a horrible thing to watch, the power of words in a language I could not understand reducing the boy to tears. I was reminded of Richard Wright's "Words as Weapons," and the child inside me shuddered again to recognize the cruelty of man. I don't know what the boy had done or not done, but I think he and the customers might have been spared the public execution.

It is perhaps worth mentioning that the Greeks do many things on the streets that North Americans are not accustomed to viewing in public. Heated domestic disputes are not an uncommon sight. It is not my intention, however, to offer this as an excuse for the waiter's behavior. I did not leave a tip.

In Turkey, I had become used to seeing families of three and four people riding together on a motorcycle. While walking to catch my boat on Kos, I saw a man and a very large dog ride by on a motorcycle.

I went to a drug store to restock my supply of toothpaste and shampoo. They carried American brands, but I decided to give the Greek products a try. Neither stayed in my pack for long. The toothpaste was foul-tasting (perhaps I'd picked up antifungal ointment by mistake?) and the shampoo cap wouldn't stay on snugly once it had been opened. I replaced it the next day with an American product that announced on the bottle, in lettering implying that I should be excited about it, that it was giving me twenty-five percent more, free!

Ψ

The boat to Rhodes was a big one. I arrived early and went to the upper level to listen to the radio and catch up in my journal. While

I was up there, and before the other passengers came on, they roped off the stairs. No one could come up, and I could not go down. Gradually, the lower level filled to overflowing, but they kept the upper deck roped off. I suppose those people wondered who the hell I was, that the crew had roped off an entire deck for me while they shuffled for space below. The crew paid me no attention, so I stayed where I was. Curiously, it was only windy while departing Kos and entering Rhodes. On the high sea, the wind was calm and I quietly enjoyed my perch.

Trying to find a place to stay in the town of Rhodes was a nightmare. I walked through the Old Town checking pension after pension — all full. Gave up and decided to go back to the harbor, hoping someone would be hawking a pension in the New Town. Couldn't find the harbor! Got very lost, wearing fresh blisters on my feet. Eventually found myself back at another entrance to the Old Town and decided I would try one more pension. It was full, too, but a man inside had a room in the New Town for twenty dollars a night. I took it, of course, although it was on a hill far, far away. The Themis Hotel Stoudios, at Papanastasiou 20, was for me a new experience in lodging — furnished studio apartments in a very residential neighborhood. It felt strange. Following a shower, I took the map the owner had provided and found my way back to the Old Town, which seemed much nicer without a pack on my back.

There are two gay bars and a gay nude beach on Rhodes. The beach is called Faliraki. It's part of a much larger beach that is packed with tourists in the summer. To get to the gay section, get off at the bus stop, walk to the beach, then walk north to the third cove. The gay bars are both in Rhodes City. *Spartacus* lists four, but the Trianon Café near the Teachers College is not a good bet, and one glance at Player's Café Bar on Diacou Street is enough to tell you that it is anything but gay — at least during tourist season. The Berlin Bar, Orfanidou Street 47, is a short walk through interesting streets from the Old Town. It is a typical gay bar, playing typical

– 239 –

gay bar disco music, serving a typical gay bar clientele. It could be anywhere.

I didn't stay long. While making my way to the other bar, I was stopped in the street by an old man probably in his eighties, who talked to me a few minutes and then invited me inside for an *ouzo* — that licorice-tasting drink the Greeks love. He was a painter by the name of Marco. His wife's name was Cleopatra. I looked at some of his paintings, which weren't bad. One was of a small boy. While I looked at it he began telling me a story of a Norwegian man who had sat and masturbated in front of the painting, he'd been so turned on by it. Noticing that Cleopatra had disappeared, I thanked him for the *ouzo* and left.

Valentino's is pretty damn difficult to find. It is in the Old Town, down an alley off Parodos Socretous. "House of the Rising Sun" was playing as I walked in. This seemed promising. But the six customers and two bartenders I found inside all looked rather comic. The older bartender looked amazingly like My Favorite Martian, and the younger one, who looked like Morrissey, was full of camp and led the customers in sing-a-longs with songs like Herman's Hermits' "Something Tells Me I'm Into Something Good."

The bartenders, Ian and Will, were the owners. They had come from Cambridge, England, and had purchased Valentino's in December because they were "pissed off with England."

One customer was a delightful woman who sounded exactly like a character in a Monty Python sketch. Valentino's was decorated with photographs of old movie stars, mostly actresses — Garbo, Crawford, Monroe, Hepburn. There was a photo of James Dean, too, and quite large photos of Dietrich, Davis, and, of course, Valentino.

Ian and I had a nice chat, then he walked me to the place where I could catch a taxi back to my hill. Walking through the Old Town late at night, after the tourists have gone, is pleasant.

In Turkey, I was mistaken for a Turk. In Greece, I was mistaken for a Greek, which I considered a compliment. I was darker than I had been in years. My hair had grown long and become about as manageable as seaweed, but I liked it.

The next day I walked through the back alleys of the walled city, which is interesting but not beautiful, then tried to buy a ticket to Mykonos. No way. Boats were impossible and planes were booked solid "until December." Mykonos would have been an even more horrible hell, anyway. I spoke to others who had been there and who told me hundreds of people were sleeping on the beaches because they couldn't get a room and couldn't get off the island, and that there was no water to be had anywhere.

I got a standby ticket to Athens instead, hoping I could get on the plane. Rhodes is hell to get off of. They get you there, then you can't leave. I'm at a loss to understand its popularity. Although I was there only a very short time, I saw none of the charm I had seen on Kos. It seemed to possess all the disadvantages of a tourist trap, with few of the advantages.

I did get on the plane to Athens, but only because they swapped the scheduled aircraft for an Airbus A300. It was the first Airbus I had flown on, but I was still a bit disappointed that I couldn't fly on one of those Olympic Airways planes that look like flying fish. You get the feeling that if one of those fell in the water it could just take a dip and jump right out again.

Greek airport security isn't very secure. The woman in front of me set the beeper off, but showed the guard her watch and was motioned on through. She was carrying Amelia Earhart luggage. How can they call it that? I set the beeper off, too. The guard, who must have either been on drugs or possessed extremely low-beam intelligence, asked if I was carrying any metal objects. I showed him the binder of my notebook and he motioned me forward. Had it not been a cause for arrest, I would like to have yelled back at him, "Oh, I forgot to mention the gun."

Met a decent Swiss guy on the plane. We decided to get a room together in Athens, settling for one near dirty Omonia Square. The hotel manager at first showed us a room with one small double bed and seemed disappointed when we declined it.

My Swiss friend wasn't feeling well, so he stayed in the room while I went out to eat. My first impression of Athens came from the newsstands displaying porno magazines, both gay and straight, in public view. One stand had about twenty issues of the magazine GAY clipped to its banners.

The waiter at my restaurant became involved in an argument with another customer — in English, although it was obviously the first language of neither. After five or ten minutes of bickering back and forth, the customer delivered the devastating line, "Well I lived in San Francisco for seven years. You make my day!"

To which the waiter replied, "Well I lived in Brooklyn five years!"

I could not determine if they were bragging or trading horror stories, so I can't say who won this argument.

Back at my hotel, however, I heard one even stranger, coming from the three Ivy League–type young men — Americans all — in the room next door. They were obviously drunk and were talking very loudly, so that we could hear almost everything they said quite plainly. One said, "Kiss my ass." A second voice said, "He'll do it!" This was followed by the only line we couldn't make out, after which the second voice said, "I never said you had a large asshole. You shouldn't be so sensitive!"

Amazing conversation.

14

Byron's Greece

I have heard good things about the Peloponnesus — the large peninsula making up the lower portion of what is generally thought of as "mainland" Greece — from many tourists who have been there, but I didn't have time to see it and still be able to visit Epirus and Thessaly in north-central Greece, and the Sporades Islands, all of which I instinctively wanted to see more. I did see the north coast of the Peloponnesus while traveling from Athens to Mesolóngion (Missolonghi), but that was all.

Mesolóngion, thankfully, is far removed from any tourist circuit. The only visitors one is likely to encounter there are Greeks from nearby towns who have decided to spend their vacation by the sea. I had chosen the town for two reasons, one of which was that it promised to be tourist-free. The second was that Mesolóngion is where Lord Byron spent much of his time in Greece. He also died there.

Although remembered primarily as the handsome, romantic, clubfooted Englishman who wrote beautiful verse, was a social philosopher, took up the Greek cause against Turkey, and had a penchant for falling in love with very young girls, George Gordon, Lord Byron also had a habit of falling in love with adolescent boys, and wrote several of his poems for or about these young men. We would know a great deal more about Byron's private life had not his wife and publisher decided to burn his memoirs shortly after he died (he had entrusted them to the poet Tom Moore, who apparently didn't exactly guard them with his life). There seems first to have been "a cottage boy near Newstead," followed by an attachment that would last him throughout his short life. Byron's poem "The Cornelian" concerns the reddish quartz which had been given to him during his years at Cambridge by the choirboy John Eddlestone, two years his junior. About the gift, Byron wrote:

> Some, who can sneer at friendship's ties,
>   Have, for my weakness, oft reprov'd me;
> Yet still the simple gift I prize,
>   For I am sure, the giver lov'd me.

When Byron died in Mesolóngion at the age of thirty-six, he was still in possession of the stone. He seemed to be writing about it again in "The Adieu," especially the lines:

> And thou, my friend, whose gentle love
>   Yet thrills my bosom's chords,
> How much thy friendship was above
>   Description's power of words!
> Still near my breast thy gift I wear
> Which sparkled one with Feeling's tear,
>   Of Love, the pure, the sacred gem;
> Our souls were equal, and our lot
> In that dear moment quite forgot;
>   Let pride alone condemn.

While at Cambridge, on July 5, 1807, Byron wrote a letter to an acquaintance in which he said of Eddlestone, "His voice first attracted my attention, his countenance fixed it, and his manners attached me to him for ever ... I certainly love him more than any human being, and neither time nor distance have had the least effect on my (in general) changeable disposition ... He certainly is more attached to me than even I am in return." Byron also dedicated a portion of *Childe Harold's Pilgrimage* to Eddlestone, who had died suddenly:

> Thou too art gone, thou loved and lovely one!
>   Whom Youth and Youth's affections bound to me;
>   Who did for me what none beside have done,
>   Nor shrank from one albeit unworthy thee.
>   What is my Being! thou hast ceased to be!
>   Nor staid to welcome here thy wanderer home,
>   Who mourns o'er hours which we no more shall see—
>   Would they had never been, or were to come!
> Would he had ne'er returned to find fresh cause to roam!
>
> Oh! ever loving, lovely and beloved!
>   How selfish Sorrow ponders on the past,
>   And clings to thoughts now better far removed!
>   But Time shall tear thy shadow from me last.
>   All thou couldst have of mine, stern Death! thou hast;
>   The Parent, Friend, and now the more than Friend:
>   Ne'er yet for one thine arrows flew so fast,
>   And grief with grief continuing still to blend,
> Hath snatched the little joy that Life had yet to lend.

"On This Day I Complete My Thirty-Sixth Year," written in Mesolóngion a few weeks before Byron's death, was not his final poem. The last poem was written to Lukas Chalandritsanos, Byron's handsome young page and the object of his apparently unrequited love. Just north of Mesolóngion, at the town of Anatolico (Etoliko), trying to get ashore in the midst of Turkish frigates, Byron had feared for the life of Lukas:

> I watched thee on the breakers, when the rock
>   Received our prow and all was storm and fear,
> And bade thee cling to me through every shock;
>   This arm would be thy barque or breast thy bier.

Whether the love was requited or not, the desire for Lukas caused Byron much pain. It is apparently to Lukas that the verse from "On This Day I Complete My Thirty-Sixth Year" was written:

> The hope, the fear, the jealous care,
>   The exalted portion of the pain
> And power of love, I cannot share,
>   But wear the chain.

And, of Lukas's illness with fever, Byron wrote:

> I watched thee when the fever glazed thine eyes,
>   Yielding my couch and stretched me on the ground,
> When overworn with watching, ne'er to rise
>   From thence if thou an early grave hadst found.

Byron says that he would rather die with Lukas than live without him, but it was Byron who was to die, not Lukas. The last verse of the last poem Byron ever wrote, fittingly, was written to Lukas, his last love:

> Thus much and more; and yet thou lov'st me not,
>   And never wilt! Love dwells not in our will.
> Nor can I blame thee, though it be my lot
>   To strongly, wrongly, vainly love thee still.

Another nearby town, Vostitza, on the northern coast of the Peloponnesus, is where Byron met the Greek boy Eustathius Georgiou, with whom he had a five-day romance before deciding the boy was too silly to be worth his while. Of the affair, Byron wrote, "I think I never in my life took so much pains to please anyone, or succeeded so ill."

That affair was followed, in Athens, with fifteen-year-old Nicolo Giraud, who taught Byron Italian while Byron was living at the Capuchin convent. This was probably his most successful romance with a male — at least in Greece. The monument of Lysikrates is all that remains of the convent today (Byron Street leads up to the monument).

"If I am a poet," Byron once said, "it is the air of Greece which has made me one." His love affair with the Greeks was mutual; when he died the government proclaimed twenty-two days of mourning.

Ψ

I wandered through Mesolóngion thinking of Byron and looking for a pension. I found none, and had soon left the town and come to the shore of the Gulf of Patra. There I found Hotel Theoxenia, of tourist class, in which I took a room. After a quick swim at the disappointing beach, I wandered through town once more, enjoying myself if only because I had finally found a corner of Greece not overrun with non-Greeks.

There were many political signs on the buildings and in the shop windows. Greece was currently undergoing a crisis of sorts because none of the three strongest parties — the Panhellenic Socialist Movement (Pasoc), the Communists, and the conservative New Democracy Party — could win enough of the vote to govern alone, and no two of the three wanted to form a coalition. An unlikely coalition of the Communists and Conservatives *had* been formed, but only to clear out the Pasoc officials left over from Andreas Papandreou's scandal-ridden government. Judging from the posters, the Communists had a lot of support in Mesolóngion, but I stopped at a café with a poster for Constantine Mitsotakis, the New Democracy candidate, in its window. I was immediately summoned to another table to join four men — two of them truck drivers, the third a mechanic, and the fourth I'm not sure — who wanted to talk politics, as Greeks often do. I was surprised to find their views very similar to my own, and wondered if in Greece I would be considered a conservative. They were certainly more knowledgeable about world affairs than any American truck drivers I've ever met. One insisted on buying me a beer, and before I left they showed me a good place to eat, where I had the best *souvlaki* I found anywhere in Greece.

After the meal I noticed groups of young men all walking in the same direction. Deciding they must be headed to a very popular night spot, I followed for about a mile and a half, until they disappeared behind the gates of a military base! Retraced my steps back into town center, at first finding no signs of life and wondering if there could really exist a town in Greece that closes down with the sun. Shortly, however, I came across a street crowded with people and leading to a bustling town square. The whole town must have been there, sitting in the café chairs along the sides of the square or strolling around up and down the one busy street. I had a *frappé* — an iced coffee — for which I had developed quite an addiction, while I watched the crowd. I noticed a good many youths heading toward a darker street, followed them, and found a little bar playing the Smiths, Talking Heads, New Order, Was (Not Was), and other music I like. Only the bartender talked to me, but I don't think many people in Mesolóngion speak English (only one of the men at the café had). The bartender, probably alone among the Greeks I met, was delighted to meet an American. He told me that the rare English-speaking tourist who shows up in Mesolóngion is generally British, coming to see the Byron exhibit in the Mesolóngion Museum of Art and History.

Around midnight the younger kids headed off to another disco that played acid house music, according to the bartender. They were replaced by a slightly older group, and the music got even better — mostly Smiths and some vintage David Bowie songs such as "Lady Grinning Soul." The bartender seemed very pleased when I complimented him on the music.

Ψ

I went first thing the next day to the Byron exhibit at the museum. They don't have a lot, a large marble statue of Byron being the centerpiece of the exhibit, the rest of which is mostly paintings and documents. What they do have is nicely displayed, and the curator is eager to provide information. He told me how to get to the site where Byron's house once stood. I left my pack in his care and set off to find it. Two adolescents who spoke a few words of English eventually showed me the way. I took their photograph with the monument, which seemed to impress them.

Most of the museum's space is given to remembering the Greek resistance fighters who died in their war for independence. The Ottoman Turks burned Mesolóngion to the ground shortly after Byron's death, and many paintings in the museum portray this event, including one of a woman who has just taken the lives of her children and is about to take her own rather than allow her family and herself to fall into the hands of the Ottomans.

There was little reason to spend another day in Mesolóngion. My bus took me first to Etoliko, where Byron was so worried over Lukas, then on to Ioannina (pronounced *EE-WAN-ya* or *Yo-AWN-ee*, or even *YAWN-ee-na* from the old name, *Yannina*). The ride from Agrinio to Ioannina was wonderful, especially once we passed into the region of Epirus. I wouldn't have minded getting off the bus in Amfilohia, a beautiful town at the back of a bay. From Filipiada to Kalentzi, the mountains were spectacular. Somewhere in their midst were the theater and ruins of the oracle of Dodoni, one place I was determined to visit on a day trip from Ioannina.

Epirus has its place in the stories of Achilles, Alexander, and Lord Byron. Achilles' band of warriors, the Myrmidons, were from Epirus, and Alexander's mother, Olympias, was born here. Some inhabitants of the Thesprotia region, which includes Ioannina, have blond hair and blue eyes. "They are, perhaps," wrote Byron, "the most beautiful race ... in the world." Aristotle claimed the Greek race began here. The Slavic invasions didn't reach into these mountainous regions; thus, the dark-haired peoples did not entirely supplant the blonds.

It's interesting, from a scientific standpoint, that Mediterranean and equatorial peoples have dark hair, while Scandinavians tend to be blond. If the Scandinavians were dark-haired and south Europeans were blond, our scientists would tell us the sun had caused the blond hair, which is useful in reflecting heat, and that the Scandinavians had black hair because black absorbs heat, which they need. We would believe them because it seems logical. I understand that polar bears are white because it helps them blend in with their environment, thus serving as a camouflage, but I don't think the same explanation is plausible for the Swedes and Finns.

The mountains have kept Epirus apart in ways other than the color of hair and eyes. In some villages natives still put coins on the eyes of the dead to buy them entry into Charon. Survivors still dig up the remains after several years to wash the bones with wine (wine stains were also found on the bones in the royal tombs at Vergina believed to have been Philip's — possibly washed by Olympias in the Epirian tradition).

About half of Epirus is now in Albania. It is in one of those towns — Tepelene — that Byron met Ali Pasha, the ruthless Ottoman governor of Yannina, a region that included most of Albania and Epirus. Among the crimes committed by Ali Pasha was his taking the most beautiful from amongst the children of Epirus for his sexual pleasure. Girls who did not please him were stuffed in a sack and thrown into the lake that surrounds Ioannina on three sides. Boys who did not please him were impaled. Byron had been summoned to meet him because Ali Pasha was a great admirer of Byron's poetry and had heard that Byron was in the area. Ali Pasha complimented Byron on his "small ears and curling hair" and invited him to visit often, and at night when he had more spare time — an invitation which Byron did not accept. Byron did, however, refer to Ali Pasha's grandsons, both about twelve, as "the prettiest little animals I ever saw."

Another backpacker, Ollie from Germany, got off the bus with me in Ioannina. He was a schoolteacher who had just spent a week at one of the Club Med resorts in the Peloponnesus, which he had enjoyed very much (his descriptions of the experience did not appeal to me, however). We inquired after each other's plans and decided to share a room. Locating the center of town was more difficult than we expected, so we stopped at a sidewalk café to ask. The proprietor, who spoke German, invited us to sit for a drink while he called a friend who ran a hotel. After making the call he came to join us, along with his son, who was studying gymnastics in Bucharest. With Ollie translating, I asked the son what it was like to live in Romania. He said that the gymnastics program was first-rate, but complained about the food. Both father and son asked several questions about American politics, particularly why Michael Dukakis — understandably popular in Greece — had lost the last presidential election. They appreciated the fact that I had voted for Dukakis, although I told them my first choice had been Jesse Jackson.

The man drew us a map showing the way to the hotel, then put his name on it and told us it was the ticket to a good price. The hotel was on the main street of Ioannina, and we did seem to get a good rate on the room.

Ali Pasha's castle on the lake was interesting, as well as Ioannina's old town. There were signs pointing the way to the castle which said, "This way to the Popular Museum." Better than the unpopular museum, one supposes. The lake is beautiful, especially at sunset. There were hundreds of people on the lake front, including the usual women dressed completely in black selling roasted ears of corn. One man was selling music cassettes and was playing a pleasant, mystical-sounding tape. But as soon as we approached, he switched the tape for an awful tape of *bouzouki* music, for us tourists, I suppose. Ollie returned to the hotel about ten-thirty, but I stayed out a while to watch the Greeks. There were a handful of blonds, but not many. Those I saw appeared to be enormously popular.

On the way back to the hotel at midnight, I tried to stop for a *souvlaki*, but the owner of the place was drunk and was only interested in showing me photographs of himself in the military. I never did get the *souvlaki*.

Mosquitoes, which had been pesky every night I had stayed in Greece, were especially bad in Ioannina. Ollie had mosquito coils, which we burned, and I had spray-on repellent.

The next day we took a ferry to Ali Pasha's island in the middle of the lake. We walked the circumference of the island, seeing many lizards, flowers, a few strange-looking plants unknown to either of us, sheep, and baby chickens. There were a few grown chickens, too, and I was amused to find Ollie very afraid of them. It seems that as a child he had been attacked by a cock.

The island restaurants had tanks full of trout, frogs, turtles, eels, and crayfish. You could select your meal, but we didn't want to. The Ali Pasha Museum on the island wasn't much, although you could see the spot on which he died, if that interested you (Ali Pasha had tried to proclaim his independence from Constantinople, but the Ottomans successfully put an end to his pretensions).

I had planned to take a day trip to Konitsa, near the Albanian border, but couldn't coordinate a bus schedule to make it feasible. Instead, Ollie and I made plans to undertake the other day trip I had planned, to Dodoni — but in the form of a night trip. There was a performance of Aristophanes' *Plutus* in Dodoni's restored theater that evening. I would rather have seen the work of just about any ancient Greek playwright other than Aristophanes, but one can't always be choosy, and I definitely wanted to see Dodoni.

There were only a handful of non-Greek tourists in Ioannina, but Ollie managed to meet up with two other Germans, and the four of us split the cost of a taxi to Dodoni. It was a wonderful fifteen-mile drive through the Pindus Mountains.

Dodoni is beautifully situated. One can easily see why it was considered sacred and chosen for the oracle. In Alexander's time, it was ruled by his uncle, and it is where he took his mother before crossing the mountains north into his Illyrian exile.

We walked through the ruins and found a good seat in the theater. Looking at the crowd of Epirians, I again noticed the strain of blond on several heads. I expect that when Byron wrote about them there were a good many more blonds in the region. One guesses they are fast disappearing, now that Epirus can no longer remain an island unto itself (well, those in Albania can, perhaps). A small blond boy sitting in front of us turned around and stared into my eyes, seeming to look at me from another time, not of this world. I thought of a poem by Miller Williams titled "The Last Person To Speak His Language Is Dying." In North America, it's happened more than a few times.

I wasn't expecting to follow the play — a comedy involving the blind god of Wealth having his sight restored, after which he does the right thing and enriches the good while condemning the bad to poverty — but I had expected it to at least be staged authentically. Instead, high in the mountains at the sacred site full of the glory of ancient Greece, we got a disco number and boxes of Pampers disposable diapers at the end. We all agreed that the play was dreadful but sitting in the theater under the stars had been wonderful.

Following the performance, the winding mountain road with its string of cars was something to see. There were no taxis but we managed a free ride on a crammed bus, which wasn't the place for such twisting and descending. A couple of passengers got sick, the steward providing bags in the nick of time.

Ψ

It was back in the Pindus Mountains the next day for a glorious ride to Métsovon, a town situated on a mountainside. The streets of Métsovon are crowded with some of the last of the oddly dressed Vlachs. There are also a few Sarakatsáns. The sealing off of Albania must have been particularly troublesome to the Sarakatsáns, a nomadic people who roamed northern Greece, Serbia, Montenegro, Bosnia-Herzegovina, Anatolia, Albania, and Bulgaria. You still see a few of them in Greece, where they are more or less confined to now. Unlike the semi-nomadic Koutzovlachs and Karagounis, the Sarakatsáns are completely nomadic. They dress in black pillbox hats, black goat-hair coats, black tights or long white stockings, black skirts, and black shoes that curl up and over at the tip, ending with a black pom-pom. Most carry walking sticks and many have long, bushy moustaches. They make their living as shepherds. Although sparsely scattered all over Greece, their dress, speech, and habits are the same in all areas. They probably remained about the same for nearly three thousand years, but the last sixty years, introducing border closures and compulsory military service, have changed them. The Vlachs, of which there are many more in Métsovon, also wear black, but their dress is neither as elaborate nor as inveterate as that of the Sarakatsáns. The Vlach women dress in black from head to toe and wear scarves that are formed into two tunnels in back, through which their hair pours out on either side like pigtails. The young, however, do not wear the native dress; thus, I fear in thirty or forty years there will be none of these black-draped figures to see in Métsovon or anywhere else in Greece.

The people of the village obviously take pride in it, adorning their balconies with an array of flowers. The Vlachs' primary architectural style makes use of beautiful wood paneling. Some of the roofs are gray slate, but most are red shingle. The walls are usually white, trimmed in heavy paneled wood. The evening promenade is very similar to those elsewhere in Greece and Yugoslavia, except perhaps more interesting because of the varied native costumes. There was a monument outside my hotel, the Athens — a very old, creaky place furnished with pieces that would be enormously valuable in American antique shops — honoring the Métsovonians killed by the Germans in World War

II. The relief on the monument shows the Métsovonians lined up in front of a firing squad, holding their walking sticks. The Vlach inhabitants of Métsovon, by the way, had been especially useful to the Allies during the war because their language is so similar to Italian that they could serve as translators when dealing with the Italian forces.

The following day I enjoyed yet another awesome bus trip, from Métsovon to Kalambáka. It took forever, with miles of zig-zagging turns. I saw Meteora in the distance, but we got close enough to see only one of the many monasteries on the tops of the sheer rock monoliths. It's amazing that they took the trouble to build them up there (for protection), not to mention the trouble of having to haul food, water, and people up and down by rope. I couldn't imagine how the first people got up there, without a rope.

During a two-hour layover in Trikala I noticed that the young Greeks in the area liked to dress in black, too, although their clothes were entirely modern, very unlike the Vlach and Sarakat-sán clothing. Black looks good on Greeks. I was now in Thessaly, home of Achilles (and Jason, of Argonauts fame, as well). History records at least one touching scene to have taken place in this region: the death of Cleomachus. The Thessalians were fighting the Eretrians and had called upon Cleomachus for help. When he arrived, they begged him to be the first to charge the Eretrian cavalry. Plutarch says that Cleomachus

"asked the youth he loved, who was by, if he would be a spectator of the fight, and he saying he would, and affectionately kissing him and putting his helmet on his head, Cleomachus, with a proud joy, put himself at the head of the bravest of the Thessalians and charged the enemy's cavalry ... the Chalcidians [who included the Thessalians] won a splendid victory. However, Cleomachus got killed, and they show his tomb in the market place at Chalcis..."

Chalcis is where Aristotle chose to retire (and where he died) after leaving Pella following the death of Alexander.

An indication that homosexuality was common in Thessaly can be implied from a letter Philostratus wrote to a young man disinterested in the subject, in which Philostratus tells the youth that he could not have come from Sparta, Thessaly, Athens, Ionia, or Crete.

I spent the night in Vólos, one of the hottest and noisiest places I encountered in Greece, then left the next afternoon for another island adventure. I had thought the Sporades would be less crowded than the Dodecanese, but spent much of my time the next few days singing to myself a song by the Dream Syndicate: "It Just Goes to Show How Wrong You Can Be."

15

Skyros

*L*et's Go assured me that at least two of the Sporades — Alonissos and Skyros — "remain far enough off the beaten track to provide you with a peaceful vacation and some of the best beaches in Greece." Perhaps thousands of others read the same information and, seeking that same peaceful vacation, decided to visit the islands at the same time I did. Every island of the Sporades chain was overflowing with tourists, making it impossible for me to find accommodations on all but one.

I made only a brief stop at Skiathos, not regretting my decision to skip it, even if it did contain two gay bars and a gay nude beach (the Banana Beach, of all things). Had planned to stay a while on Skópelos, but I should have skipped that one, too. It looks like a very pleasant island, and I'm sure it would be fine in the off-season, but I searched from one end of Skópelos Town to the other and could find no place to stay. The hotels were booked solid for the next three weeks.

Originally inhabited by voyagers from Crete, Skópelos was invaded in 1538 by the infamous Ottoman admiral Red Beard (Khay El-Din Barbarossa was his real name), who slaughtered the entire population of the island. I had thought an island with such a tragic past would surely possess some melancholy appeal. I think it does, but it's hard to detect among the tourists and the pricey restaurants and shops. I did buy a vase in one of those pricey shops, which wasn't the most logical thing to be lugging around, but it was the prettiest and most original pottery I'd come across in Greece and I had to have it.

My only choice, aside from sleeping on the beach, was to buy a ticket for the last boat to the next island in the chain, Alonissos, hoping *Let's Go* was correct this time. The boat was supposed to leave at 10:45 p.m., which wasn't promising. It also showed up one hour late.

In the meantime, I sat at a restaurant and had an unusual conversation with a Catholic priest connected somehow with the University of Notre Dame, although in what way I can't remember. He was a nice-looking man, probably in his late thirties, and the keen interest he took in talking to me made me wonder if he was gay. He was politically involved, having spent several years in Guatemala and El Salvador. He was intelligent, funny, wide-eyed, and believed in things he couldn't see.

Eventually he asked about my religion. Seeing me hesitate, he changed the question to a simple, "Do you believe in God?" We had been talking almost an hour at this point and I felt enough at ease with the man to be candid. I told him that I wondered how a god could be so fucked up that he would make this mess of a world, unless we were just the forgotten science project of some baby god. He laughed out loud.

"And what about Jesus?" he asked. "There is great historical evidence that he lived, so you must have some thoughts about who he was."

I told him that there was historical evidence that Achilles lived, too, but that I didn't think he was really invulnerable except for his heel. Besides, I said, John quotes Jesus several times in *Revelations* as saying, "Behold, I come soon," and "Surely I come soon." So what happened to him?

"*Soon* is relative," he said.

"Well, two thousand years is hardly soon," I rejoined.

He didn't say anything for a minute, then asked what I expected would happen to us when we died.

"I want some god to take me in his arms and tell me that it's all right now, that it was all a joke."

"So you do have some concept of there being a god," he said.

"I only said that's what I *wanted* to happen. Having seen what I've seen on this planet, if I have any idea of God at all, it's such that I feel that these people who murder someone and say God told them to do it could very well be telling the truth."

He looked at me and said, "You're a good man."

The remark was so unexpected that I didn't know what to say. I resorted to a cliché and said, "Life is strange."

The priest looked me in the eye and, smiling slightly, asked, "Compared with what?"

Our conversation ended on that cryptic note, for my boat was finally approaching the harbor.

Ψ

The late-night journey was rather nice, watching the lights of Skópelos fade into the distance, then become a mirage, then flicker out. Blackness all around, except for the occasional ships passing in the night. Then the lights of Alonissos appeared. There weren't very many of them, which was both encouraging, from the isolation standpoint, and discouraging, from the standpoint of looking for hotels. When we docked, there was no one at the pier hawking rooms, but it was late, so I had not expected a welcoming party. I walked up one street and down another, trying every place that had a sign for rooms. No luck. Everything was full. On a hill were many hotels built specifically for package tours — not what I would call "off the beaten path." Yuck. The hotels were ugly, as was the town. *Let's Go* claimed the island had only fifteen hundred inhabitants. There were at least that many hotel rooms, all full.

Alonissos has its melancholy past, as well. The island's primary crop, its vineyards, was entirely destroyed by blight in 1950, forcing most of the island's male population to take construction jobs in Athens. An earthquake further devastated the island in 1965, and the government chose to undertake a massive housing development at the port of Patitiri rather than repair the existing structures in the old town of Alonissos. Eventually all but nine residents of the old city were forced to move to Patitiri.

As for my own plight, there was little to be done. At the harbor was a concrete circle where about fifteen other tourists were passing the night, either in sleeping bags or sitting up talking — very loudly, in some cases. Some were there because they couldn't find a room. Others were waiting for either of two ferries that call at Alonissos in the early morning (5:15 to Athens and 6:00 to Skópelos).

I stretched out on my towel and lay down a while. The cool sea air on my sunburned skin made me shiver. Bats squeaked overhead. Cats howled in nearby alleys. No rats, at least. I hope when I die and my life flashes before me that I can skip this part.

As I lay there, a large dog walked up and slavered in my face, then lay down beside me. He only stayed a minute, loping off to lead his doggy life somewhere else. Sleep was impossible. Eventually I got up and climbed the hill to watch the sun rise over the sea. I debated whether to wait until people got up and try again to find a room, or buy a ticket on the hydrofoil to Skyros at eleven a.m. I would have liked to have stayed a day, but there were only two boats per week to Skyros, so if I stayed one day, I had to stay three. I bought a ticket to Skyros as soon as the hydrofoil office opened.

Dazed from lack of sleep, I walked around the island a bit trying to pass the hours until my ferry left. Sitting on a hillside terrace, I noticed the leaves above me rustling and looked up to find a *very* old woman, probably in her eighties or nineties, out on a limb picking pears. She wore bloomers and was barefoot, and she walked farther out on that limb than I would ever have dared, then hopped to another!

The hydrofoil voyage had its moment of excitement, too. Although the passengers were supposed to remain inside at all times, someone managed to fall overboard, so the hydrofoil had to stop while a lifeboat was sent out. Inside, our only entertainment was a television that seemed to be showing one Greek cigarette commercial after another.

Skyros was my last hope for a "Sporadic" vacation. Unfortunately, I had company. The hydrofoil was packed with other tourists who had not been able to find accommodations on Skiathos, Skópelos, or Alonissos and were determined to find them on Skyros. We arrived at the port town of Linaria and looked around for the buses that all the guide books said would be waiting to take us across the island to Skyros Town, known locally as "The Village," but they weren't there. They arrived about forty-five minutes later — after we'd all made a panicky run on maps of the island at a local store — but waited until the Lykomides ferry from Kimi arrived before leaving Linaria.

The Lykomides is named for King Lykomides, under whose sovereignty the history of Skyros begins. Achilles lived on the island prior to the Trojan War. Theseus was killed here, according to the legend.

The drive across the island revealed it to be one of the most beautiful I've seen. The populated areas are all in the north because the southern half — where Rupert Brooke is buried — is dominated by Kochylas Mountain. There were plenty of secluded beaches, hills, goats, and Skyrian ponies — little mule-like creatures that are supposedly related to Shetland ponies.

One thing was clear — Rupert Brooke had been buried in a beautiful place.

At the Village everyone rushed out of the bus in a frantic dash, looking for a room. I saw two couples have success, but in both cases they snatched up the last available room. The tourist bureau had nothing for eight days. Twice, old Greek women took pity on me and telephoned their friends, trying to find something. No luck. They already had people sleeping on their floors, so they couldn't offer me anything, either. Skyros Town is situated rather spectacularly on the sides of a hill. Carrying my pack up and down the steep streets in the middle of the day after a night with no sleep, I was drenched with sweat and about as miserable as you can get. The thought of another night without a room was almost too much to bear, and the last ferry to Kimi had departed at two p.m.

On Java, it's the custom to change your name if you have a run of bad luck.

I walked down a goat path out of town to try farmhouses and a couple of pensions I had seen from the hill, but had no luck there, either. While I was trying to catch a ride back into the Village, to avoid climbing up the hill, an unmarked bus stopped in front of me. I was suspicious because, although the young men inside were not in uniform, it appeared to be a military vehicle. However, since it stopped where I was standing and opened its door, I assumed they were offering me a ride. But as soon as I made a motion to board, the driver wagged his finger at me, began laughing, and said, "No, no, no!" The soldiers were all laughing, too, and the door was shut in my face. As Thomas Wolfe wrote in *Look Homeward, Angel*, "I hate him that would upon the rack of this tough world stretch me out longer."

Standing in the dust kicked up by the bus, I yelled to the wind, "I want to go home!"

Back in the Village (via taxi), I found a place to stop for a beer. My waiter was blond-haired, blue-eyed, and arrogant as hell. He made me come to him to pay.

My one hope was to go back to the sleepy village of Linaria and see if there was a room to be had there. I found four other backpackers who were interested in going to Linaria, so we crammed into a taxi for the eight-mile ride. Buses make the journey back and forth from the Village to Linaria only when ferries arrive and depart.

The only hotel in Linaria was closed and I saw no signs for rooms to let. I stopped a boy, who told me to "try Sophia" and showed me where she lived. Sophia thought about it for a while and decided to let me have a room. It was a fairly comfortable room. The toilet in the hall had no seat, but hey, who's complaining?

I can't say they make you feel very welcome on Skyros. Every restaurant or bar I visited had awful service, with waiters who never approached you unless you flagged them down, then seemed highly insulted that you had bothered them. Too, when I went to bed that night, a girl knocked on the door and asked for the mattress from the other bed in my room.

"Are you leaving tomorrow?" she asked.

"No," I said.

"We shall see," she said, and left.

I've never liked people who were cats in their previous lives. What crime had I committed? The only explanation was that this woman didn't like the fact that Sophia had let a room with two beds — which is all that was available — be taken by one person. It was in keeping with the general character of Skyros, however, that the girl chose to handle the situation with no tact whatsoever.

It was the same the next day, when the same girl, who was apparently the cleaning woman, told me I had slept too late to have a shower, that she had already cleaned it.

"I beg your fucking pardon?" I said, and had a shower anyway. I didn't leave it dirty.

A *frappé* and yogurt with honey is a popular breakfast on the island, but when I went for mine the waiter ignored me. I called to him; he still ignored me. I tapped on his arm as he came by; he

– 263 –

In Skyros's Rupert Brooke Square, in a white rock circle at the edge of a hill overlooking a dreamy blue ocean, stands a striking statue of the nude Rupert, engraved in English, "To Rupert Brooke, 1887–1915, and immortal poetry."

ignored me still. I went to another café, where the service wasn't with a smile, but at least they served you. Skyros.

The Village is a charming place, if you can ignore the people. The town map shows a maze of lines with no names, but I managed to find Rupert Brooke Square, with the fine statue of the nude Rupert, engraved in English with the words, "To Rupert Brooke, 1887–1915, and immortal poetry." One wonders if his English dignity would have been offended by the sight of his genitals in public. Since every account of him makes note of his startling handsomeness, it's no wonder that the statue is striking, too, even if its 1931 creator made little attempt to create a likeness. It is, nonetheless, quite remarkable, standing in a white rock circle at the edge of the hill, with the beautiful blue ocean behind it. As I looked down from the hill, the sea was dreamy. The water, interrupted only occasionally by a boat or swimmer, was so clear I could see the bottom for several yards beyond shore.

This is a good point in which to mention a few things of interest regarding Brooke's life. The first is that he met Virginia Woolf (Virginia Stephens at the time) when he was thirteen and they remained friends until his death.

At age thirteen, Rupert's autograph album listed his favorite amusements as cricket, tennis, football, reading, and cards, and his favorite qualities in "man" and "woman" as fidelity and wit, respectively. His "idea of misery" was "ignorance, poverty, and *obscurity*" (he had emphasized the last word).

At age seventeen Rupert became friends with the poet St. John Welles Lucas-Lucas, who introduced him to the work of Oscar Wilde (whose famous trial had taken place only nine years prior). The first lesson Rupert read in Chapel was David's lament over Jonathan. Early on, his favorite poet was Housman.

All of this apparently made quite an impression on the boy. Despite his ironic reputation in history as the great patriotic poet of England, he was, in fact, quite a radical, an agnostic — and counted several gays among his closest friends. He called himself "a rabid Socialist," edited a newsletter with scathing criticisms of Conservative Party candidates, defended the working class, tried to convert everyone in his life to socialism, and, in 1910 (the same year that he and Virginia Woolfe swam nude on the beach one night), declared, "I HATE the upper classes."

Rupert once wrote to a friend that one should read Housman's *A Shropshire Lad* "on an autumn morning when there is a brave nip of frost in the air and the year is sliding quietly toward death."

He became keen on Marlowe, as well, and helped to form the Marlowe Dramatic Society. He loved *Peter Pan*. He made it a point to meet André Gide and D. H. Lawrence, and also met Siegfried Sassoon, who described his favorable impressions in *The Weald of Youth* (1942).

Brooke instructed a cousin who asked to be shown culture to digest "one third of Swinburne, all Oscar Wilde, and the drawings of Beardsley," and he wrote to Lucas, "I want, for instance, to complete my set of the three great decadent writers — Oscar Wilde, St. John Lucas, and Rupert Brooke."

At age eighteen Rupert heard that a boy in another house of his school had asked the school photographer for Brooke's photograph. Rupert wrote to a friend that he took "a huge delight in the whole mad situation." He began a correspondence with the boy, and described the letters he wrote as resembling

> the Song of Solomon — indeed they are often in imitation of that wonderful purple ecstasy. I usually address him as Hyacinth, Apollo, or Antinoüs [!], and end with a quotation from Swinburne or Catullus. I bring in odorous and jewelled phrases ... 'the fragrance of your face is myrrh and incense before the pale altar of Beauty'... I don't know what he thinks of such communications; but if he has any literary sense, they must do him a lot of good.

The letters certainly show that Brooke himself had literary sense.

By the age of nineteen, Rupert had grown incredibly handsome. He was just under six feet tall, had small ears, a long neck, a mix of auburn, blond, and golden brown hair (which was very thick and worn long — he is described as tossing it back off his forehead quite often), deep-sunken eyes, and extremely sensuous lips.

Brooke possessed more than ordinary good looks. There was something about him that made practically everyone, male or female, gay or straight, take note of his beauty.

Yeats once said, "He is the handsomest man in England."

Arthur Stringer, in *Red Wine of Youth* (1948), wrote, "He seemed like a Norse myth in modern clothes. Yet there was no vanity in the man."

Atlantic Monthly's Ellery Sedgwick, in his book *The Happy Profession*, wrote of meeting Brooke: "A young man more beautiful than he I had never seen ... Man's beauty is much more rare than woman's. I went home under the spell of it and at the foot of the stairs cried aloud to my wife, 'I have seen Shelley plain!'"

Charles Sayle wrote in his diary, "I did a little shopping, and came home. Standing in my hall in the dark, thinking of other things, I looked towards my dining-room, and there, seated in my chair, in a strong light, he sat, with his head turned towards me, radiant. It was another unforgettable moment. A dramatic touch. A Rembrandt picture. Life."

The photographer Scherril Schell, who coaxed him into a photograph without his shirt on, wrote, "He stripped to the waist, revealing a torso that recalled the young Hermes." His friends sarcastically suggested that a totally nude photograph "would doubtless find a large sale."

Even the British general, Sir Ian Hamilton, after offering Brooke a staff position that was refused, wrote in his diary, "He looked extraordinarily handsome, quite a knightly presence, stretched out there on the sand with the only world that counts at his feet."

Henry James said simply, "I think of him quite inordinately."

Much of Brooke's personality can be gleaned from his own words and what is recorded of his deeds. When his friend Justin Brooke was stung by a wasp, for instance, Rupert sucked out the poison.

Brooke once said to his friend Jacques Raverat that he had once observed a peasant woman in the arms of her lover, her face shining with the aura of love, and he had felt "sick with envy."

Brooke made it clear exactly how important his friends were to him in another letter to Raverat:

And there is no man who has had such friends as I, so many, so fine, so various, so multiform, so prone to laughter, so strong in affection and so permanent, so trustworthy, so courteous, so stern with vices, and so blind to faults or folly, of such swiftness of mind and strength of body, so polypist and yet benevolent, and so apt both to make jokes and to understand them. Also, their faces are beautiful, and I love them. I repeat a very long list of their names, every night before I sleep. Friendship is always exciting and yet always safe. There is no lust in it, and therefore no poison. It is cleaner than love, and older; for children and very old people have friends, but they do not love. It gives more and takes less, it is fine in the enjoying, and without pain when absent, and it leaves only good memories. In love all laughter ends with an ache, but laughter is the very garland on the head of friendship. I will not love, and I will not be loved. But I will have friends round me continually, all the days of my life, and in whatever lands I may be. So we shall laugh and eat and sing and go great journeys in boats and on foot and write plays and perform them and pass innumerable laws taking their money from the rich.

In a letter prior to going to war, Brooke wrote, "Occasionally I'm faintly shaken by a suspicion that I might find incredible beauty in the washing place, with rows of naked, superb men, bathing in a September sun..."

On his twentieth birthday, Brooke wrote to Lucas, "I am now in the depths of despondency because of my age. I am filled with a hysterical despair to think of fifty dull years more."

A little later, he wrote to another friend, "What I chiefly loathe and try to escape is not Cambridge nor Rugby nor London, but — Rupert Brooke. And I can only do this by rushing suddenly to places for a few days. He soon overtakes me."

Rupert joined up for the war not so much because of his patriotism as his sickness over living. He remarked that some men of England apparently did not want to die, "and this I cannot understand." The war gave him a purpose, a needed excitement.

He was buried under twelve olive trees in a spot called Mesadhi, on Skyros. Later, his mother had the rocks and wooden cross which his fellow soldiers had placed on his grave removed in favor of a memorial slab.

When D. H. Lawrence learned of Brooke's death, he wrote, "I first heard of him as a Greek god under a Japanese sunshade, reading poetry in his pyjamas at Grantchester ... O God, O God, it is all too much of a piece: it is like madness."

Henry James, upon hearing the news, said simply, "Of course, of course," then lowered his head and began to weep.

Ψ

I found a little piece of paradise off the road from the Village to Linaria, just before it departs the coast. The beach was absolutely isolated, and spectacular. I had passed a nude beach closer to town, but kept walking until I was entirely alone. Spent most of my time there sifting through the wonderful colored stones, choosing a few small ones to take with me.

Skyros, like Bodrum, is not really the place for the single traveler. Most other tourists are in groups, or at least pairs. Checking out the nightlife in the Village that evening, I saw only one other solo traveler among thousands. The difficulty with meeting people in Greece continued. The Greeks simply see too many tourists this time of year to be interested — and, unlike the other island groups, most of the tourists in the Sporades are Greeks. They tolerate you, but just barely.

There is quite a bit of nightlife both in the Village and at nearby Molos Beach. I was sitting at a café on the beach when my day became complete: A small bug flew in my ear and refused to exit. Well, what does one do if sitting at a crowded café with a bug buzzing and scratching around one's eardrum? I had an idea, and discreetly as was possible carried my Coke around a corner, poured it in my ear, and drowned the sucker.

At the Renaissance Pub back in the Village, I encountered the only friendly waitron I saw on the entire island — and she was English.

The next morning the cleaning woman told me, "I must know when you are leaving because I need your room." I told her I would leave the next day. One more day on the beach was all I needed, in any case.

Actually, about an hour on the beach was all I needed before realizing I was tired of beaches. Instead, I bought a bottle of water and set out walking through the hinterland, with fuzzy plans of somehow making it to the far tip of the island to see Rupert Brooke's grave. I had a map and knew it was too far to walk, but was hoping someone on a horse or motorbike might stop and give me a lift. As it happened, however, I saw absolutely no one during the four or five hours I walked. It was a relief, though, to get totally away from civilization for a few hours. Practically all of Skyros's 2,750 residents, and the thousands of tourists, stick to the Village or Molos Beach, except for the 200 residents and handful of tourists in Linaria.

Skyros is a beautiful place, but I can't say I was sorry to be going.

16

Athínai

Before returning to Athens (Athínai), I wanted to stop in Thívai, the modern city on the site of ancient Thebes. I expected there to be monuments to the Sacred Band, but as I've already stated, there were none to be found.

According to legend, Thebes was founded by Cadmus after he consulted the oracle of Apollo. This legend is referred to several times in Sophocles' "Theban Plays" — *King Oedipus*, *Oedipus at Colonus*, and *Antigone*.

The Sacred Band of Thebes was an elite fighting corps of three hundred men composed entirely of pairs of lovers. The philosophy behind the formation of such a battalion was simple, according to Plutarch: "For men of the same tribe or family little value one another when dangers press; but a band cemented together by friendship grounded upon love is never to be broken, and invincible; since the lovers, ashamed to be base in sight of their beloved, and the beloved before their lovers, willingly rush into danger for the relief of one another."

The theory apparently worked, for the Sacred Band never met defeat until they went up against Philip II at the battle of Chaeronea. Plutarch says that when the battle was over and Philip surveyed the field, he "came to the place where the three hundred that fought his phalanx lay dead together, he wondered, and understanding that it was the band of lovers, he shed tears and said, 'Perish any man who suspects that these men either did or suffered anything that was base.'"

Thebes was also home to Epaminondas and Pelopidas, statesmen and generals whose close friendship was recorded by Plutarch in his "Life of Pelopidas" (which also contains a wealth of information on the Sacred Band).

Further, the ancient citizens of Thebes believed that Ioläus, the charioteer of Hercules, had been Hercules' favorite lover. The Thebans worshipped Ioläus alongside Hercules and named their gymnasium after him. In *Eroticus*, Plutarch says, "As to the loves of Hercules, it is difficult to record them because of their number; but those who think that Ioläus was one of them do to this day worship and honor him, and make their loved ones swear fidelity at his tomb."

The Sacred Band made their vows of love and loyalty at the shrine of Ioläus, and Alexander camped by the enclosure of Ioläus on his way to defeating Thebes a final time. He asked for surrender, but the Thebans insulted him instead. What followed was probably Alexander's most brutal act. Over six thousand Thebans were killed, thirty thousand more were taken captive, and Alexander ordered the town razed.

Arrian, armed with a long list of Theban treacheries, said the Greeks believed the gods destroyed the town as punishment. He himself put the blame for the massacre on the Phocians, the Plataeans, and other Boeotian towns that had taken part in these "treacheries." Renault blamed the Athenian statesman Demosthenes. Plutarch said that Alexander was often remorseful over Thebes and never failed to grant a favor to any Theban survivor who asked.

One house in Thebes was left standing on specific orders from Alexander. That was the house of the poet Pindar, whom Alexander greatly admired. One of Pindar's poems, "Ode on Theoxenos," ends with the lines:

> But I, apart from this disease,
> Wasting away like wax of holy bees,
>
> Which the sun's splendour wounds, do pine,
> Whene'er I see the young-limbed bloom divine
> Of boys. Lo! look you well; for here in Tenedos,
> Grace and Persuasion dwell in young Theoxenos.

Pindar died at the theater in the arms of Theoxenos. The German poet August Von Platen wrote a poem about Pindar's death. In it, he asks for a death as pleasing as that of Pindar. The poem ends with these words:

> Long at the play, hearing sweet Harmony,
> He sat; and wearied out at last, had lain
> His cheek upon his dear one's comely knee;
> Then when it died away — the choral strain —
> He who thus cushioned him said: Wake and come!
> But to the Gods above he had gone home.

Ψ

On the bus crossing the large island of Euboea from Kími to Halkida, a tall, muscular young Greek slept on my shoulder. I didn't mind, although he smelled strongly Greek (what produces that smell? the olive oil?).

Thívai was a difficult town to get to. I had to change buses twice. Once there, the first thing I noticed was that it was absolutely overrun with nineteen-year-old males. This could only mean one thing, and sure enough it did: Thívai is home to a major Greek military base. As I walked the streets I wondered absentmindedly if the young soldiers were told about the Sacred Band.

I don't want to belabor this point, but I think it bears repeating that Greek soldiers are not at all similar to American G.I.'s. They are neatly dressed, feigning aloofness (I think all Greeks love company too much to actually *be* aloof), and they hold their liquor well. Their hair is longer, too. They do pick their noses a lot in public, however. Quite a few of them were carrying duffel bags around, apparently having returned from a weekend pass.

My first night in Thívai, I spent with the soldiers. As the night wore on, it became clear that two rooftop bars were the places to be. One had for its clientele about fifty percent girls and fifty percent local town boys (you could tell they weren't military by the length of their hair). The other had about ninety-five percent soldiers and a handful of young women who were mostly left to themselves (don't ask me why, they were certainly attractive). I landed on a bar stool near the balcony and next to a table of four nice-looking guys. One of them seemed interested in me, and another, who looked very young and East Indian (gorgeous, I might add), had his eyes on the tallest of the group, who was blond. The fourth was actually my favorite, perhaps because he didn't seem particularly interested in anyone, but possessed, it appeared, the most winning personality of the lot. A lot of eye contact went on between us all night, and it got a bit strange. They were messing around with their candle and accidentally put it out, and at the critical moment when you want to catch someone's immediate reaction, all four looked at me at once, and somehow, in the split second, I managed to briefly catch all four pair of eyes. The East Indian–looking one eventually put both arms around the neck of his favorite, and the other got up and left with him. I had never become sufficiently interested in the boy showing the interest in me, so I eventually left myself.

The next day was frustrating, for I wanted to find information on the Sacred Band, or find out how to get to Chaeronea to see if the lion Alexander the Great had erected to honor the Sacred Band was still there, but there was no tourist information office, no information books in English at the bookstores, no maps of Thívai, no maps of Greece that made mention of Chaeronea, and the taxi drivers and soldiers I asked had never heard of it. I eventually walked into a church, thinking I might find someone with an education inside. I was disappointed here, too. Whoever it was that I talked to knew that there was a battle site from ancient Thebes nearby, but he had never seen it and didn't know how to get there.

I began walking around the hills outside of town, looking for ruins. I found some, but they didn't seem to be significant. I kept walking, and kept asking, but finally had to give it up. It's too bad the Sacred Band wasn't Dutch; I think they would be better remembered. But they died for each other, not for the inhabitants of modern Thívai, whose monuments commemorate Greek independence, with history prior to 1821 ignored.

The excavations in the center of Thívai — the only reminder (aside from the archaeological museum) of an ancient past — are filled with litter.

I met two more cute soldiers from Crete. They didn't speak English, but made it clear enough that they hated Thívai and wished they were back in Crete. One indicated he was in the military by pointing to himself and saluting; the other, by holding up his hair and pretending to cut it with scissor-fingers. Several men sitting across the street from us were taunting a hunchbacked man, who looked impoverished, by throwing coins on the sidewalk, laughing with delight as he scurried after them. I had noticed before that the Greeks do not seem very sympathetic to the underprivileged, having heard them laughing and hurling insults at the patients on the lawn of a mental institution near Athens.

That evening when I went out to dinner I was confronted with the worst marching band I've ever seen in my life (and I've been to too many high school football games) followed by the local heads of the Greek Orthodox Church, followed by four soldiers carrying an ornately framed "portrait" of Jesus, followed by children carrying incense burners, followed by practically the whole town, minus soldiers. It was mostly women and children, actually. The priests happened to stop directly in front of me to perform some silly ceremony, then the procession continued on down the street, downhill and back to the church. It struck me how little things change in history — the Greeks are still performing rituals for the gods.

The Archaeological Museum contains a few decent pieces, mostly from the Mycenaen period. The objects from the graves moved me — the hand-carved little birds they'd sent off with their loved ones. There was no mention of the Sacred Band in the museum. By now I was becoming almost enraged by their neglect. There were huge marble lions in the museum's courtyard, one much larger than the others — but it was in a reclining position, so it could not have been the lion honoring the Sacred Band, which sits upright.

There didn't seem much point in staying in Thívai. I caught a bus to Athens.

Ψ

My first visit to Athens, following the flight from Rhodes, had produced a couple of interesting moments. I had been sitting at a café in Syntagma Square minding my own business, when a well-dressed man came up and asked if he could take me on a cruise to three nearby islands the next day. I thanked him but indicated I had just come from Kos and Rhodes and didn't want to see another crowded island for a while. He then asked if I would have dinner with him the next evening.

The only lead-in to these invitations was, "Are you married?"

"No."

"Good."

When I declined the dinner invitation, he sat quietly for a few moments, stood up, said "good-bye," and left. As soon as he left, another man came up, asked if I had the time, then asked if I would come with him to his bar for a drink on the house. I again declined. Another man, who didn't look Greek, had been sitting at a nearby table watching the proceedings. When I caught his eye he laughed and exclaimed, "Hustlers!" He asked where I was from, then asked several other questions of introduction. His friendly manner made me trust him, so I didn't mind when he picked up his drink and joined me at my table. He was an unlikely refugee — a Ghurka, from northeastern India. We spoke at great length about India, a country I was considering visiting some year in the middle future. It was fairly clear that his intentions were innocent, so I also accepted an offer to go with him to his apartment to look at his photographs of India. We sat in his sparsely furnished living room drinking Darjeeling tea. I looked at the photographs while he leaned back with his hands behind his head, dreaming of a Ghurka homeland.

There will be no Ghurka homeland.

I had visited the Archaeological Museum in Athens, as well. It's an incredible experience — the one thing in Athens you don't want to miss. I spent two hours inside on the first visit, and another two hours during my second stay in the city. The great bronze statues of Poseidon and the young jockey will stay with you for a while. My favorite statue was one that had no English name on it and was badly damaged, but showed a nude youth bending on one knee with legs spread apart, reaching forward in wild enthusiasm, incredibly capturing an emotion I had never before seen in marble. Looking at it, an inspiriting flame passed through me and I shuddered involuntarily.

The *kouros* are excellent, as well. These are marble statues of nude youths, standing static, left leg slightly in front of the right, thighs and calves bulging, arms to the side of the body, fists clenched tight. The hair, body lines, and facial composition show strong Egyptian influence. There are a considerable number of them, most dating from the fifth and sixth centuries B.C. There are also vases, mosaics, coins, and other objects, but the statues were my main interest. A special exhibit, "The Spirit of the Athlete: Mind and Body," was, considering the theme, disappointing.

I also took care of the mandatory climb to the Acropolis during my first visit, but repeated it on the second stop because they were selling posters at the top that I could find nowhere else in Greece. Just the fact that the Acropolis is still there is something. The view of Athens from the top is inspiring, but it's impossible to concentrate on the awe of it all with so many tourists surrounding you. I looked longingly across at the more isolated Mars Hill, then descended into the forests of the Agora.

An evening in George's Pub had also been interesting, although not something I'd care to repeat. There were four attractive young men in the pub when I entered — two Austrian tourists and two Greeks. Of the several other customers, two immediately became interested in me and it was clear I would have to deal with them before I could size up other prospects. This is largely the story of my life, and perhaps yours, too — re-enacting these scenes from Jean Paul Sartre's *No Exit* in which Garcin wants Inez who wants Estelle who wants Garcin. One of my suitors told me he was an actor whose name "is known by everyone in Greece." I asked around later and found he was telling the truth. Like many actors, he was full of himself, and therefore easy to disengage. This was not the case with the other guy, a whining young man who spent the entire evening trying to find a way to get me to go home with him, even after I'd made it clear I wasn't interested ("You won't have to do anything ... Just being in bed with you would be enough..."). What can one say? What can one do? Meanwhile, the bartender had seen me watching the four boys at the far end of the bar and informed me, "If you want to meet a boy, tell me, no problem." I wasn't sure what he meant, but had a pretty good idea. The boy I most wanted to meet was quite obviously taken with the cutest of the Austrians. My second choice soon moved to the seat beside me after our eyes met several times. Eventually I asked if he spoke English. He didn't, but bought me a drink. The bartender offered his services as interpreter. Yeah, right.

The next thing I knew, the guy who had been trying to get me in his bed all night was talking to the hunk beside me, then saying to me, "His name is Patronas. He likes you. He wants to have sex with you, but he only likes to fuck." What a martyr. I didn't respond to this information except to have the guy translate a few more mundane questions such as where the hunk was from and where he lived. He was from the west of Greece and was stationed at Athens's port city, Piraeus (Piraiévs), which has three gay bars of its own, incidentally. Then I got hit with the clincher. Because he was a soldier, he needed money. Sixty-five dollars, to be exact. I had to spit beer back into my glass to keep from choking on my laughter, then declined to pay sixty-five dollars to be fucked by an attractive Greek soldier. The martyr, my translator, passed on my refusal with satisfaction, then said to me, "He should be paying *you*. The boy's crazy!"

Greece certainly has an amazing armed forces.

Ψ

Which brings me back to my second stop in Athens, my journey's end. Since I would be spending six nights in Athens I was more choosy about a hotel than usual, checking five before taking a room in the Hotel Eva, located at Victoros Hugo 31 in a quiet (for Athens) district near Karaiskaki Square. It was an easy walk to Omonia, from where you could catch buses or the Metro to wherever you were going. I walked most of the time, finding the streets interesting. Besides, the bus system was one of the most difficult to decipher that I've encountered in Europe. The Metro is easy to figure out, for there's only one line. It only costs thirty drachma (twenty cents) to ride, but you must purchase single tickets from a machine and you must have exact change. The tellers at the windows only sell books of tickets and will not give you change, even for a fifty-drachma note. It's ridiculous to have to go to the bank to get change so that you can buy a twenty-cent Metro ticket, but I was forced to do it twice. The tourists in Athens are of a different variety than those on the islands. On the islands you get too much jet set, who think of Athens as polluted and filthy, and give it a wide berth. Athens *is* polluted and filthy, but that's not all it is. If you look hard enough, you can find plenty of relaxing spots. As for art and culture, it doesn't have as much to offer as Rome or Florence, but it still has more than its share. I won't ever spend another six days in Athens, however. Six days can better be spent in Rome.

I slept late every day, sometimes getting strange looks from the Hotel Eva staff when I came down at two p.m., but none of the rudeness I'd experienced on Skyros. They didn't touch my room during my six-night stay, but I didn't care. The four towels in the room were sufficient for six days, and I can make my own bed.

I spent my days doing a bit of shopping and visiting the usual tourist attractions in Athens. The National Garden is an expansive getaway from the hubbub of the city. It's on a scale with Vienna's *Volksgarten* or London's Hyde Park, but not as much fun as Amsterdam's *Vondelpark*. Like Hyde Park, Athens also has its location for men to gather around and pontificate. They do it on one side of Omonia Square.

At the Tomb of the Unknown Warrior, the guards, wearing red caps with two-foot-long black tassels, beige skirts, white body stockings, black knee bands with tassels, and brown shoes with large black pom-poms, do a little march every half hour or so, coming to face each other, touching the soles of their pom-pommed shoes together, holding the position for five or ten seconds, then going back to their corners. If you've got your camera ready, that five or ten seconds when their shoes are touching makes a great photograph. The relief of the Unknown Warrior is very nice, as well. Other photographs I sought out included the statue in front of the Athens Cultural Center of the old man slumped over with his head in his hand, eyes sunk behind bushy eyebrows, lips below bushy moustache. I don't know who it is (the writing was all in Greek and I couldn't unravel it), but I like it. I also took photographs of a few of the shop windows in the chic

Kolonaki district. I especially liked a shop that sold nothing but black and rust-colored clothing, and only long dresses and hooded capes. All of their mannequins looked like Druids, and they had them all in a row, going back into the store, rather than across the window. It looked tough.

The wine festival at Dafni, supposedly modeled after the Bacchanalian festivals of old, was disappointing, but cheap. For only $1.50 you can get in, purchase a glass or vase, and drink wine from all over Greece for hours on end, if you like. There are nine wine stands, each with around twelve barrels of different wines. Some are *retsina* (with resin, the way Greeks prefer it), some aren't. But all were too sweet for my taste. I found the rosé and white wines undrinkable, and the dry red just barely tolerable. The festival also has music, but none of it very good. I didn't stay long. Between Athens and Dafni you pass along the Sacred Way, which no longer seems sacred — it's strewn with litter.

As for the food in Greece, it's definitely an improvement over what you get in Turkey, but no matter how much you pay for it, it isn't as good as you can get at Greek restaurants practically anywhere else in the world. Figure that one out. My best Greek meal was the one my friend Wout treated me to at the Athene restaurant in Delft, Holland.

Spartacus lists twenty-six gay bars in Athens. There is also the gay liberation group (A.K.O.E.), two gay magazines (*Amphi* and *Gay*), a gay cinema, a gay bath house, and a gay beach. The cinema is called the Omonia and is located on Santovriandou Street behind Omonia Square. The bath house, Athens Relax Baths, is also near Omonia, at 8 Xouthou Street. The gay beach is the rocky section of Limanakia Beach, a few minutes from Athens by bus. The cruising areas of Athens are the squares. I've already mentioned my experience at Syntagma, which is so crowded with tourists that it doesn't seem a likely spot. Other squares with reputations include Kaningos, Omonia, Dimachia, Koumoundourou, and Kolonaki. Most are busy day and night, and all could be dangerous — especially Syntagma, Omonia, and Koumoundourou.

The largest concentrations of gay bars are in the Kolonaki district, north of the National Garden, and the area north of Omonia Square and west of the Archaeological Museum. Those in the Kolonaki district are recommended; those north of Omonia are not. Most bars are very discreet, with only a sign on the door. Athens is not Amsterdam.

Of the twenty-six gay bars, four were recommended to me as being the only worthwhile bars in the city. This, of course, is a matter of opinion, but since I didn't have time to visit all twenty-six bars, I thought I would pass that opinion along. One of those four was George's Pub, mentioned previously. The other three — Alexander's (Anagnostopoulou 44), the Gastra Tavern (1 Dimaki Street; it serves food, too), and Aleko's Island (Tsakalof 42) — are all in the Kolonaki district.

You can guess which bar I chose to visit first. In fact, I liked the attractive, somewhat expensive (about four dollars for a beer) gay bar with a name that made it a must, enough that I never got around to visiting the others. Alexander's was a thirty-minute walk from my hotel, but I found it without difficulty. There's an upstairs bar with movie stills and a great, powerful bronze bust that I assume is supposed to be Alexander. It looks more like the busts of Hermes, but I can't say for certain. Whoever it is, it's incredibly seductive, and I spent my first hour in the club giving it more attention than any of the customers.

The club's downstairs contains your basic disco bar. The music wasn't great at either level, but the crowd wasn't bad. I don't think Alexander would have been too displeased.

When I finally got my fill of the bust and went to have a look downstairs, I was immediately pursued by another short-haired, attractive Greek youth whom I suspected to be another hustling soldier. I was wrong. Demetrius was from Lésvos, was twenty-four years old, and had lived in Athens five years. He was all over me in the club and on the street walking to the taxi stop, an unusual experience for me. I had seen other Greek boys walking down the street with arms over each other's shoulders and hands inside shirts, but when I became one of the actors, I was uncomfortable — especially in front of cops and the elite guards in front of the government buildings (I don't know why *I* was uncomfortable — the guards were wearing white *skirts*, for Christ's sake).

At his apartment, Demetrius offered coffee and watermelon — an unusual combination, I thought. I liked Demetrius, and he made it very clear that he liked me. Unfortunately, he acted as if he had never heard of the term "safe sex." I asked if he didn't know there was a deadly epidemic around. He said he did. I told him that he must be more careful, especially with Americans. He asked if I had AIDS. I said I didn't, and wanted to keep it that way. After that, everything was okay for about an hour, but when I was ready to call it a night and get some sleep, he continued to attempt unsafe practices with my body. Finally, I got up and told him I was leaving.

I had no idea where I was, other than the fact that it was on the other side of the Acropolis from my hotel. Wherever I was, it was late enough that there were no people or lights to give me some bearing on which way to look for a cab. I simply started walking and eventually came to a dark traffic circle, where I stood until a taxi did, finally, come along. He already had a couple in the back seat, but motioned me in beside him. I noticed that the meter was off and wondered how much this ride was going to cost me. After he dropped the couple at their destination, however, he started the meter and whisked me across town. I tipped him handsomely.

I returned to Alexander's a few days later to pay more attention to the crowd and less to the bust. Found the attitude thick enough to cut with a knife.

Late at night in my hotel room I was plugging into an Athens radio station playing some of the best music I've ever heard on radio: the Associate's version of Bowie's "Secret Life of Arabia," which sounds like howling queens discovering that T. E. Lawrence of Arabia liked men, Thin White Rope's cover of Vanilla Fudge's "Some Velvet Morning" (*when I'm straight*), the Blues Brothers' hilarious camp remake of the theme song from "Rawhide," and even the Dead Kennedys' "Too Drunk to Fuck."

Sleep was not coming easy, which is one reason I was staying in bed so late in the mornings, trying to catch up. The heat was almost unbearable, and the mosquitoes were a menace. My sheets were stained with the blood of those I had killed.

On the last day of my vacation I sat in a Greek restaurant in a rather poor residential section of Athens, watching the Greeks. There was an older Greek woman in a typical black dress; a younger woman wearing metallic lavender lipstick sitting next to another young woman wearing a t-shirt that read, "Everything a man needs"; Greek men all wearing their shirts unbuttoned to the navel and all smoking cigarettes; an otherwise attractive young man with seven band-aids on his face, and a boy who looked and acted like the best friend of my youngest brother, reminding me of home. They were all sitting and talking, and seemed perfectly in their element. Tomorrow, I thought, I will be in mine.

What did I look forward to going home to? Family, my remaining dog, my car, sleeping in an *air-conditioned* house without the buzz of mosquitoes in my ears, my music collection, receiving mail on a regular basis, my bed and pillows, the *quiet* of rural America, the approaching football and basketball seasons and talking sports with my brothers, hearing news as it happens in my own language, my shower, good food, rain, having an assortment of clothes at my disposal, the wide availability of ice.

Selected Bibliography *

Aristotle, *Politics*

Arrian, *The Campaigns of Alexander*, translated by Aubrey De Selincourt (1971)

Peter Bamm, *Alexander the Great: Power as Destiny* (1968)

Alice Bloom, "On a Greek Holiday" (1983)

John Boswell, *Christianity, Social Tolerance and Homosexuality* (1980)

Rupert Brooke, *Poems 1911; 1914 and Other Poems; Collected Poems* (1918)

Tom Brosnahan, *Turkey: A Travel Survival Kit* (Lonely Planet Guides, Australia)

Lord Byron, *Hebrew Melodies; Childe Harold's Pilgrimage; The Bride of Abydos; The Giaour*

Edward Carpenter, *Ioläus* (1917)

John Crossland and Diana Constance, *Macedonian Greece* (1982)

John Dornberg, *Eastern Europe: A Communist Kaleidoscope* (1980)

Eastern Europe Information Pool, "EEIP Reports" (1982-1989)

Fred Feldkamp, *Not Everybody's Europe* (1976)

Patrick Leigh Fermor, *Roumeli: Travels in Northern Greece* (1966)

M. I. Finley, *The World of Odysseus* (1954)

Ira Friedlander, *The Whirling Dervishes* (1975)

Nicholas Gage, *Hellas: A Portrait of Greece* (1987)

Philip Glazebrook, *Journey to Kars* (1984)

J. R. Hamilton, *Alexander the Great* (1973)

Christopher Hassall, *Rupert Brooke* (1964)

B. W. Henderson, *Life and Principate of Emperor Hadrian* (1923)

Johann Gottfried von Herder, *Ideas on the Philosophy of History*

Homer, *The Iliad*, translated by Richmond Lattimore (1951)

---

*Date of publication not necessarily that of earliest edition.

Ibn'Arabi, *Sufis of Andalusia*, translated by R. W. J. Austin (1971)

Sulamith Ish-Kishor, *Magnificent Hadrian* (1935)

Garabed Kapiklan, *Yeghernabadoum: Story of Genocide* (1978)

Nikos Kazantzakis, *Journey to the Morea* (1965)

Steven Kelman, *Behind the Berlin Wall* (1972)

Harold Lamb, *Alexander of Macedon: The Journey to World's End* (1946)

Royston Lambert, *Beloved and God: The Story of Hadrian and Antinoüs* (1984)

Elizabeth Longford, *Byron's Greece* (1975)

Lucian, *Amores; Concilium Deorum*

Vincent H. Malmström, *Geography of Europe: A Regional Analysis* (1971)

Ovid, *Metamorphoses*, translated by Rolfe Humphries (1955)

The Penguin Book of Homosexual Verse, edited by Stephen Coote (1983)

Plato, *Letters; Phaedo; Republic; Symposium*

Plutarch, *Erotikos; On Bringing Up a Boy; On Fawner and Friend; Life of Pelopidas; Parallel Lives: Alexander and Caesar*, translated by Louise Ropes Loomis (1951).

Mary Renault, *The Nature of Alexander* (1975)

A. L. Rowse, *Homosexuals in History* (1977)

The Rough Guide to Greece

Jalalu'ddin Rumi, *Divani Shamsi Tabriz* (1973); *Mathnawi* (1940); *Rumi, Poet and Mystic* (1964) — all translated by R. A. Nicholson

Second ILGA Pink Book: A Global View of Lesbian and Gay Liberation and Oppression (1988, Utrecht Series on Gay and Lesbian Studies)

Idries Shah, *The Way of the Sufi* (1970)

Vassilis Vassilikos, *Outside the Walls* (1973)

Rebecca West, *Black Lamb and Grey Falcon: A Journey Through Yugoslavia* (1941)

*Alyson Publications publishes a wide
variety of books with gay and lesbian themes.
For a free catalog, or to be placed
on our mailing list, please write to:
Alyson Publications
40 Plympton St.
Boston, MA 02118
Please indicate whether you are interested in
books for gay men, for lesbians, or both.*